The Portable Ethicist
for Mental Health Professionals

Other Books by the Authors

The Portable Lawyer for Mental Health Professions: An A–Z Guide to Protecting Your Clients, Your Practice, and Yourself (1998) John Wiley & Sons, Inc., New York.

and

The Pocket Manual for Mental Health Professionals: A Compendium of Answers to Questions Most Frequently Asked by Professional Counselors, Social Workers, Psychologists, Marriage and Family Therapists, Pastoral Counselors, Addictions Counselors, and Others (2000). A collection of published and unpublished articles, statutes, board rules, and other information helpful to mental health professionals of all disciplines. Available for $28.50 from Thomas L. Hartsell. (Self-Published) Send $28.50 and a *mailing* label to:

Thomas L. Hartsell, Jr.
Attorney at Law
6440 North Central Expressway, Suite 402
University Tower
Dallas, TX 75206

The Portable Ethicist
for Mental Health Professionals

An A–Z Guide
to
Responsible Practice

Barton E. Bernstein
and
Thomas L. Hartsell, Jr.

JOHN WILEY & SONS, INC.

New York • Chichester • Weinheim • Brisbane • Singapore • Toronto

---

Note about Photocopy Rights

The publisher grants purchasers permission to reproduce handouts from this book for professional use with their clients.

Library of Congress Cataloging-in-Publication Data:

Bernstein, Barton E.
    The portable ethicist for mental health professionals: an A–Z guide to responsible practice / Barton E. Bernstein, Thomas L. Hartsell, Jr.
        p. cm.
    ISBN 0-471-38265-5 (pbk. : alk. paper)
    1. Mental health personnel—Professional ethics.   2. Psychiatric ethics.   I. Hartsell, Thomas L. (Thomas Lee), 1955–   II. Title.
    RC455.2.E8 B476 2000
    174′.2—dc21

                                                                        00-036515

Printed in the United States of America.

10 9 8 7 6 5 4 3 2

To my children, Alon Samuel Bernstein, the merchant, and Talya Bernstein, the lawyer.

To my Aunt, my second mother, Anita Springer Bloch. "Teeta" died on August 16, 1999, while this book was being written but before publication. She always listened. And to her daughter, Mallyn Rose Bloch. And to my Aunt, Miriam "Mickey" Springer, who died February 2000; my hostess and mentor during my U.S. Navy days in San Diego, CA.

To my sisters: Rona Mae Solberg, in honor of her retirement after a distinguished career in teaching, and Dr. Berna Gae Haberman, counselor and professor, and my brother-in-law, Dr. Myron "Mike" Solberg, Professor Emeritus, Rutgers University.

And in loving memory of my parents, Suetelle Springer Bernstein and Samuel Bernstein.

With special thanks to my colleague, friend, and distinguished attorney and coauthor Tom Hartsell, who has continued to invigorate and motivate both of us to serve the legal and mental health communities.

B.E.B.

To the hundreds of thousands of mental health professionals who try to get it right and transform lives in the midst of an increasingly risk-filled profession.

To my wife Barbara, who kept me refreshed and focused.

To my sons, Ryan and Jason, who remind me daily why it is necessary for me to work so hard to make their future brighter.

To my parents, Tom and Julie Hartsell, for their never-ending love and support.

To my good friend, mentor, confessor, and colleague, Bart Bernstein, thank you from the bottom of my heart.

T.L.H.

Foreword

Ignorance of the law is no excuse. Ignorance of the ethical canons under which mental health professionals operate is no excuse. Likewise, ignorance of the published guidelines of national, state, and local organizations to which the professional person belongs is no excuse.

And so the question: Why are so many successful, professional, educated, practicing individual providers disciplined on a regular basis for violating ethical rules, codes, regulations, and guidelines? Why do so many envelopes containing the published ethics of the professions languish unopened, unread, and unloved in desk drawers only to be dusted off, opened, and read when a complaint is filed?

Finally, we have a compendium—an easy-to-read collection of the rules and regulations—that informs the practicing provider, the "in-the-trenches" mental health professional, with easily available answers to ethical questions. It covers the kind of questions that arise in the learned life of every practitioner as daily situations become significant and potentially explosive office problems. Before panicking, check this book. There might be an easy, acceptable answer. Certainly, searching for a solution to a problem is better than blundering forward and then finding out an unhappy client has filed a complaint with a licensing body or disciplinary board and an investigation has begun. By understanding what has gone wrong and what can go wrong, the educated, ethical provider can guard against unexpected challenges to the practitioner's art. And, indeed, mental health is an art form. But, of course, every art form has its limits. This work suggests some of the limits.

For the past six years I have served as chair of the Texas State Board of Examiners of Licensed Professional Counselors, which enforces local ethical guidelines and disciplines licensed counselors who violate ethical rules. In that capacity, I have chaired the complaints committee and through that experience have received a liberal education. But let me begin with my own admission of naiveté.

While working for my doctorate, I completed a required course ambiguously entitled, "Legal and Ethical Concepts." At the time, this course seemed to me to be a trivial subject that took the place of a more practical, clinical experience. Some two years after finishing my degree, I found myself working with a couple whose marriage was in great discord and disrepair. To my surprise, the husband in that case (who had recently filed bankruptcy) decided I had breached confidentiality and disclosed his extramarital activities to his wife. So one rainy, Tuesday afternoon, I received my very first certified letter threatening me with a lawsuit. He also filed a complaint with the state licensing board. I can still remember the nauseous, sinking stomach, the anger, the fear, the anxiety, and the desire for revenge. Most disconcerting, I also knew this challenge by an unhappy client could put my professional and personal integrity in question. (Not to mention my career, which had hardly begun.)

What I learned from this personal experience was that even if I did everything right and followed all the rules, I could not predict the insight and motivation of my clients, nor the whimsical response of the Board. It had never occurred to me that a client, angry at a spouse, the legal system, or a lawyer, might strike out at the innocent therapist.

I also had to confront how vulnerable I was, as a professional, as I sat with individuals who often seemed more vulnerable. I have often looked back on this episode, which resolved itself favorably, as one of the most valuable lessons in my training as a therapist. Later, I enrolled in a counselor ethics course and found the old adage that "experience precedes knowledge" to be true. While a graduate student, I could not connect to the lectures nor get excited about reading the text. But as a professional, I deluged the instructor with queries based on daily practice and the professional published guidelines that profoundly affected both myself and my profession.

To work in any of the mental health professions is to find oneself in the most powerfully intimate and conflicted of worlds. The hard work of counseling and therapy often takes the professional into a subterranean cavern with no guaranteed exit. It is the very power that comes from such intense human relationships that gives both joy and anguish to those seeking to be helpers. One does not enter this world without accepting some element of risk. No matter how well trained, how knowledgeable about classical and avant garde theories and techniques a professional may be, those sitting across from the counselor always have the option to challenge this intimate relationship.

Any discussion of ethics goes to the very heart and core of the profession. Perhaps this is one reason for the discomfort in pondering ethical dilemmas among mental health professionals. The complexity of ethical dialogue arises in part because the canons of professional behavior come from many directions: local, state, and national regulations, as well as a multitude of other entities.

Counseling is more art than science, a mixture of intuition and rationality. Where is the independent variable? How will I produce concrete evidence? What is the diagnosis, the appropriate treatment plan, the prognosis? And when, how often, and why should this analysis change? To do counseling, the therapist creates a private space while being prepared to give a public accounting consistent with the ethics of the profession. But, how do we objectify the subjective experience? How do we integrate an evaluative standard into the therapeutic milieu?

We all can think of certain people who seem "special"; we set them apart, and bestow a certain mystique on them. Clergy, medical doctors, teachers, law enforcement all have a unique status that entitles them to intercede in the intimate lives of others. Status, education, and position bring with it power, which is the currency utilized by these special people. Whatever happens in a therapy session, one thing is certain: there is a profound inequity. Others extend deference to the professional, regardless of the credentials hanging on the wall. Since time immemorial, society has granted awesome power to the diviner, sage, confessor, and now, therapist. The authority and the inherent power imbalance require extreme ethical awareness and sensitivity.

What are some of the ethical problems that come out of this power inequity? An obvious list would include confidentiality, clinical labels, establishment of fees, clinical notes, dual relationships, advertising, duty to warn, informed consent, forensic issues, consent to treat, acts of omission and commission, supervisor/supervisee relations, consulting, and business partnerships. To a seasoned professional, these topics and many more are as close to daily practice as any glossary providing diagnostic criteria.

Confidentiality is an ethical necessity between professional and client. The validation of one's existence depends on constructing a meaningful relationship that necessitates intimate sharing. Open and candid communication establishes trust, which ensures further disclosures. Counselors bear a heavy responsibility in protecting the content of treatment sessions. However, it doesn't take the professional much time to discover that contingencies occupy the office along with the client. Certain conditions challenge and modify the very concept of confidentiality. For example, clients who share their suicidal intent, clients who intend to seek revenge, the subpoena that requires disclosure, the adolescent who wants to talk about becoming her own person. But the most insidious threat is potentially the counselor's ignorance. Counselors who are ethically ignorant are a clear and present danger to the public being served as well as themselves. Confusion quickly surfaces, for example, in delineating confidentiality from the legal concept of privileged communication and the myriad exceptions to both.

No problem has caused more pain for professional counselors than the accusation of engaging in a dual relationship. The problem stems from the subtlety of knowing when one has crossed the invisible line between professional services and personal gain and/or exploitation. It seems innocent to barter for services. Who would reject a gift from a sincerely grateful client? And there is always sex. If the inequitable counselor/client relationship is the centerpiece of therapy, built on a foundation of confidentiality, a dual relationship of any type alters the roles and rules of the game. It harms the client, creates ambiguity, and may result in such bitterness that a hurting client may never again trust the necessary shared intimacies of counseling.

Mental health professionals need to spend time reflecting about the nature of being a professional. The granting by society of professional status implies responsibilities as well as privileges. The expense in money and time places a high premium on degrees earned, licensure, and professional responsibility and duty. As a member of the State Board of Examiners, I have been a party to many complaints and disputes that cost therapists large sums of personal money defending themselves, their licenses, and their livelihood. What I have come to understand is that many mental health professionals do not realize that states have administrative and legal authority to grant licenses. Too many therapists trivialize the awesome power of the state regulatory process and state regulatory agencies or naively or narcissistically act with reckless abandon. A mental health professional should not take the regulatory process for granted. *The state grants a license. The state can revoke a license.*

In today's complaint-prone and litigious culture, working with individuals who are already stressed and under emotional discomfort requires continuous vigilance in the practice of the profession. Numerous complaints come to licensing boards regarding the outcome of therapy. These complaints are quickly dismissed. Most therapists do not promise cures and guaranteed remedies. Much more serious are the complaints due to acts of omission and commission. These allegations must be taken seriously and, at this point, the resources of the state come into play. Many state boards have subpoena power, undercover agents, and electronic technology, as well as traditional discovery processes. Therapists need to ask themselves a simple question: In each case, where is my exposure?

Therapy is, by design, a high-risk profession. One does not have to be paranoid, but prudent in the exercise of skills in therapy.

Confidentiality and dual relationships are but two of the numerous ethical issues that Barton E. Bernstein and Thomas L. Hartsell present to the contemporary counselor. It may seem strange, but counselors, too, need expert assistance. The complexities and subtleties of today's ethical dilemmas necessitate the clear and direct answers provided by this book. Therapy is value-laden. Counselors cannot escape their own evaluation by their clients and scrutiny by society, especially as delineated by state board rules and national organizations. The power of the emotional discharge released by counseling weaves itself around the statements that create the therapeutic experience.

Clients and their representatives, family, friends, insurance reviewers, and lawyers all may listen to the replay of clients' encounters with their therapist. The knowledge provided by Bernstein and Hartsell's current book will increase the counselor's confidence in treating such a potentially large audience of consumers.

ANTHONY P. PICCHIONI, PhD
Licensed Professional Counselor

Grapevine, Texas

Preface

About five years ago, the authors were asked to serve on a panel of experts; the topic was "Ethical Problems of Mental Health Professionals." The other two panel members were both providers in the field of mental health; one was a PhD psychologist employed by a fledgling managed care company and the other was a clergyman who, at about age 40, decided to earn a counseling degree and change professions from the ministry to counseling. Armed with his advanced degree, he was pursuing a career as a counselor in a group practice.

When we assembled to prepare for the presentation, both mental health professionals were ready to deal with global questions, such as counseling with children about abortion, dealing with "tough love" parents or children, or the ethical consequences of needed treatment with limited funds. They wanted to discuss the big picture, ethical dilemmas that would make the participants "think." These were problems that would evoke a thought process but would not necessarily provide concrete answers the participants could rely on and carry back to their offices. So the question arose: Did the attendees want to learn how to think or did they seek some practical suggestions about the ethical nuts and bolts of their profession?

When we suggested that ethics, in our opinion, concerned the *published ethical canons or codes of their professions,* we received only a blank stare. The psychologist allowed that she had taken an ethics course in graduate school about 10 years ago but remembered little about it; while the counselor admitted he had never taken a course specifically called "ethics," but he received annual copies of the licensing law which contained the ethical codes. And where were these codes now? Lying unread in the bottom of his desk drawer, available to be studied on a moment's notice should a complaint ever be filed against him with the state licensing board.

We were shocked and disappointed. As advocates and practicing attorneys who have represented mental health professionals before licensing boards, we assumed (incorrectly, apparently) that when the subject of ethics came up, we were referring to canons of ethics promulgated by either licensing boards or national professional organizations. We were aware of the many individuals who had been disciplined by local boards or threatened with expulsion by national organizations. We faithfully read the publications of the various mental health disciplines that lists by name and city the professionals disciplined for all manner of infractions or violations of ethical guidelines and lists those who have been found guilty of misconduct. These individuals needed representation to protect their licenses, livelihood, and reputation. General postulates of ethical rights and wrongs are interesting topics to banter around in a profound conversation, but as attorneys educated in the adversary system, we felt that the target audience of mental health professionals would be more interested in ethical questions such as: How many ways are mental health professionals vulnerable? What does the state require regarding informed consent? Can you get a referral fee for referring clients? What are some obvious and some subtle boundary violations or dual relationships? What kind of records *may* you keep and what kind of records *must* you keep? Guidance for all these problem areas is set forth in the published codes of ethics of the state board (and published in one form or another in the board rules of most sister states).

The argument was long and spirited without resolution. Since we couldn't agree on anything else, each of the four presenters spoke for about 10 minutes followed by a question period. And the questions? Just what we lawyers had anticipated. None of the participants were interested in global issues or clever hypothetical ethical dilemmas that taxed their intellect to find options or solutions. Instead, they wanted to know about records, preservation and documentation, prohibited client relationships, snitch or reporting obligations concerning another therapist who was acting inappropriately, and how to deal with managed care and remain ethical while earning a living.

Most of the participants, licensed people all, were concerned with self-preservation and making a living in peace. They wanted knowledgeable individuals to discuss the important parts of their specific ethical canons so they would recognize any ethical problem on the horizon and could conform their conduct to the requirements of their local board and national organizations. Perhaps they might be inspired to read the codes of conduct, but failing the reading, they would at least, through seminars and workshops, understand the crucial points and most commonly violated rules of their profession. So the lawyers answered specific and general questions like these: How long does the professional have to keep and preserve records? What is therapeutic confidentiality? Is what is told to therapist 100 percent confidential? What happens, ethically, if you know a colleague has had sex with a client or is impaired by drugs or alcohol?

What we discovered in our conversation with the counselor and the psychologist was frightening. Professionals who had graduated from universities only a few years ago might have been exposed to a course in ethics, while those who received their degrees more than 10 years ago viewed professional ethics in summary: "We know the difference between right and wrong, and we don't do what's wrong." Common sense will prevail. They were shocked when we told them that in a conflict between common sense and the licensing law, the licensing law prevails.

From the point of view of a licensing board or the disciplinary committee of a national organization, these mental health professionals were dangerously naive. Many ethical violations are not intentional wrongs, consciously and maliciously performed, but are actions that in years past might have gone unnoticed and unpunished.

There were few complaints to state boards before five or so years ago. Today, litigious clients with a perceived wrong realize they can request a free investigation by a state agency or national organization at no inconvenience and no expense. The only question is whether a rule or regulation has been violated. Heartache, expense, embarrassment, and notoriety await the professional who receives the letter from the licensing entity suggesting that his or her future is on the line. An adverse ruling of the Board can ruin a professional career and deprive a person of a lifetime of positive community recognition.

We realized with our preparation and presentation that practitioners are anxious to know, understand, and honor the rules and regulations of their profession. Once they put these commandments in place, practitioners can relax, proceed with self-assurance, and serve the community with honor and distinction.

The mental health profession is in a constant and often anxiety-producing state of flux. Practices, procedures and rules are changing with lightning speed. Earning a living is complex enough without worrying about a disciplinary committee breathing over your shoulder. And how can you avoid this? By knowing the rules. Like an athlete who knows the rules, a lawyer who knows courtroom procedures, or a musician who knows the score.

Hopefully this book will help avoid a tragedy. And what is that tragedy?

The tragedy is that a person completes undergraduate and perhaps graduate school. Is then armed with advanced degrees and pursues either the advanced designations of his or her professional organization or proceeds to apply and receive a state license. The degree and the license are then framed and proudly mounted on the wall of the clinical office, *and then a complaint is filed.* Some unhappy client writes to the licensing board or the national organization and the investigation begins. Then, if the investigation uncovers an act that is unethical or can be construed to be unethical, the license, loaned to the licensee in the first place, is withdrawn. The licensee can no longer practice the profession for which he or she invested so much study, expense, dedication, and hard work.

This tragedy can be avoided by practicing ethically. And how can one practice ethically? By knowing the ethical canons, codes, and guidelines and practicing within them. But first, one must learn what they are. And that is why this book has been written.

Throughout this book, we have selectively used different codes and code summaries to illustrate problems being discussed. When a real problem occurs, practitioners should consult the most current version of the ethical canons in their jurisdiction, as well as the national standards of their discipline. Ignorance of any of these rules and regulations is not an excuse when a complaint is filed and some disciplinary board is called on to act. Most codes are posted on the Web. Others may be obtained by a telephone call or a letter of inquiry.

BARTON E. BERNSTEIN
THOMAS L. HARTSELL

Dallas, Texas

Acknowledgments

In writing this book, the authors had many friends, acquaintances, and colleagues who provided inspiration, nurturing, and mentoring—all necessary for any work worthy of publication.

We want to thank John Wiley & Sons for realizing the importance of the connection between law and the mental health professions and for understanding the magnitude of the ethical component in any mental health practitioner's practice. We especially want to thank Dorothy Lin, former Associate Editor, for encouraging the project, and Linda Indig, Associate Managing Editor, for managing its initial stages, and providing consistent inspiration. And to Tracey Belmont, Editor, for picking up the baton and racing the book to conclusion. Without her continued inspiration, constant goading, and pleasant assertiveness, the entire proposition would have been delayed. Her stimulus, cooperation, and professional competence were major incentives. And to Kelly Franklin, Publisher, who made the introductory contact, served as overseer, and was always available for consultation. Thank you all.

Encouragement came from many special friends. We want to mention especially Dr. James Callicutt of the Graduate School of Social Work, The University of Texas at Arlington, and Dr. Myron ("Mike") Weiner and Dr. Kenneth Altshuler, Department of Psychiatry, The University of Texas, Southwestern Medical Center at Dallas.

Our personal thanks go to Judy Meagher, M.Ed., who served as devil's advocate and was a sounding board for many concepts in this book, and to longtime personal friends Dr. Martin Davidson and David Shriro, who always wondered what we were going to do next and never let us rest until we did "something."

B.E.B.
T.L.H.

Contents

PART THREE

PRACTICE CONSIDERATIONS

PART FOUR

PROFESSIONAL ISSUES

PART FIVE

SPECIAL THERAPY CONSIDERATIONS

The Portable Ethicist
for Mental Health Professionals

Introduction

Professional ethics can be considered in terms of both a big picture and a little picture. The big picture consists of countless complex philosophical dilemmas that keep graduate students, ethicists, and philosophers in business, endlessly pondering and filling the literature with the "right" and "wrong" answers to unanswerable problems and esoteric, hypothetical, interpersonal ethical situations. The little picture consists of everyday situations that therapists have faced since the dawn of the mental health profession. Such situations, if perceived incorrectly, can cause a professional to be summarily expelled from his or her national organization or subjected to disciplinary action revoking his or her license to practice within the profession. The net effect is that the professional loses the means to earn a living in his or her chosen field.

The *big picture* is heady, deep, penetrating, and profound. However, in this era of credentials, initials, and licenses, the *little picture* is usually more important to the practitioner. These testimonials grant the professional the cloak of governmental authority, representing to the consumer the approval of the state that authorizes the individual to practice a profession. In many jurisdictions, the psychologist, social worker, counselor, therapist, addictions specialist, or mental health provider of any description cannot practice without a license. Therefore, it is important for practicing professionals to protect their credentials from being compromised by charges of an ethical violation.

Definitions

A composite of dictionary definitions of ethics would include:

- The study of standards of conduct and moral judgment.

- The system of morals of a particular person, religion, group, and so on.

- Of or relating to ethics or morality, relating to or dealing with questions of right or wrong.

- Involving or expressing approval or disapproval.

- Being in accord with approved standards of behavior socially or a professional code.

- Conforming to professionally endorsed principles or practices.

- Pertaining to or dealing with morals or the principles of morality: pertaining to right and wrong in conduct.

- In accordance with rules or standards for right conduct or practice, especially the standards of a profession.

Ethics has been defined in dictionaries, philosophical tomes, literary and religious works, countless theoretical treatises, and psychological and psychiatric texts. Definitions such as those listed previously are subject to different interpretations, and making a decision about what is or is not considered ethical is often relative to a particular situation.

Establishing a rule or guideline for individual conduct becomes even more difficult when one considers that each state has its own professional ethical standards, and national and state mental health organizations create, augment, and interpret published public ethical standards differently. In addition, each mental health professional has individual inclinations influenced by theoretical orientation, religious background, training, education, experience, and biology. An individual's total feelings of what is right and wrong affect decisions in any given situation. The result by any objective standard is a somewhat unworkable and amorphous set of guidelines that may offer little specific help to the practitioner who is trying to practice in an ethical manner and maintain a professional license at the same time.

Even the various mental health disciplines differ on fundamental issues. Consider the following questions and their underlying ethical concerns:

- Is it ever acceptable to date a client, and if so, when and under what circumstances?

- How long must records be maintained for adults? For children?

- How much information must be divulged to a parent after a child has requested confidentiality?

- Exactly what must a therapist do when he learns a colleague is seducing a client, has covertly entered a business arrangement, has traded (bought or sold) stocks based on insider information learned from a patient, cheated an insurance company by submitting fraudulent claims or overbilling, or otherwise has violated permissible boundaries and ethical norms?

- If a parent brings a child to the therapist for treatment, who is the client, the parent or the child? If it is the child, can the therapist date the parent? Or can the therapist date the uncle of the child?

Can one depend on a gut reaction or a broad definition of common sense to protect a license? The answer is a resounding "no"! When common sense and published rules conflict, the published rules should control the therapist's conduct. The professional against whom a complaint is filed cannot build a defense on the basis of a purely common sense approach to an ethical problem.

Personal Ethics versus Professional Standards

General ethical principles might serve as a comprehensive guide for social or professional conduct, but if mental health professionals want to remain *members in good standing of a local, state, or national organization*, they must scrupulously adhere to the published standards of that organization. Likewise, mental health professionals who want to *keep and maintain a professional license* must unerringly honor the published rules, regulations, and mandates of the licensing board or whatever state agency publishes, enforces, and disseminates the board's rules. For those states that have no directly published standards, but incorporate by reference national published standards into state board rules, there is a double whammy. If a rule is violated, the individual is disciplined by both the national organization and the state licensing board.

Practice Implications

An awareness of one's personal moral code in relation to knowledge of the professional standards and regulations of one's state and national associations and licensing boards dictates that in the area of mental health ethics, common sense, gut reactions, individual morality training, and personal preference—*even actions which in the opinion of the clinician are in the best interest of the client*—take a back seat to the published guidelines of the profession. As noted, in most jurisdictions a professional license is required to practice. Thus, competence, experience, and compassion are of no value if the practitioner cannot share that expertise with the public (i.e., the consumer) because of a revoked license.

In a simpler age, the mental health professional's personal instincts would usually provide a protective shield, shelter, or umbrella. A dependable feeling guided the conscience and thoughts of what was right and wrong. The pendulum could shift from one side to the other, depending on the individual therapist, the client, and the circumstances. Blatant forms of ethical violations could be avoided by old-fashioned common sense.

In today's litigious society, however, where the "someone has to pay" mentality pervades the minds of consumers, an ethical complaint often follows even when a malpractice case is not pursued. One reason, perhaps, is that filing a complaint and letting the board know of an ostensible inappropriate activity might be good therapy for that individual.

Ethical Flash Points

- Become sensitive, be aware. Learn to recognize potential ethical dilemmas.

- Develop a network of professional colleagues and discuss possible scenarios for ethical violations and how to resolve them. Ensure all scenarios are hypothetical or theoretical, so that the problem can be discussed without anyone feeling uncomfortable.

- Read the ethical guidelines for your professional organizations and licensing boards carefully. When a license or membership is in jeopardy, the enforcement board must prove a published rule or regulation was violated. To avoid violations, practitioners must be aware of the existence, content, and interpretation of the guidelines. Even a letter of reprimand from a licensing authority has serious repercussions when seeking malpractice insurance, applying for hospital privileges or for managed care, seeking employment, and renewing a license.

- When there is a gray area, or if a legitimate question arises concerning whether a particular act or action might be a shade unethical, *don't do it.* If it tweaks your conscience or smells bad, don't do it *ever!*

- If an ethical question arises, talk with a lawyer.

- Even if a particular act may appear to be moral, ethical, appropriate, or in the best interest of the client in the big picture, if it violates a published ethical canon, rule, or regulation in the little picture, the big picture does not count. Violating an ethical rule in the little picture means the license is in peril. And a license is a terrible asset to lose.

Another is that "getting even" for an actual or perceived wrong is as American as apple pie, and what better way than having the alleged offender's state or a national organization fight the battle for the allegedly wounded consumer? The board serves as a free advocate with the whole power of the state or the national organization behind the consumer's complaint process.

So what does this mean for the practitioner? It is simple. Read the rules of the professional organizations and licensing boards. Understand them and don't violate them. Treat each regulation as a commandment or as gospel, and avoid compromising situations.

But what happens when the professional follows all the rules and is still confronted with an ethical dilemma?

This Book

This text covers common ethical problems encountered by providers, educators, supervisors, and consumers of mental health services. The goal is to avoid ethical confrontations and conflicts by recognizing what they are and how they come about; to attain an ethical and profitable practice, one must know the rules and regulations of the profession.

Mental Health Educators, Teachers, and Supervisors

The book is divided into five parts: Client Issues, Ethical Codes and Licensing, Practice Considerations, Professional Issues, and Special Therapy Considerations. Each part is subdivided into chapters, which are alphabetized by topic. Each chapter follows a sequential format: first, a vignette or vignettes illustrate the basic ethical dilemma. Second, a big-picture explanation of the problem indicates how the situation at hand can be used to clarify other similar situations frequently confronting practitioners. Third, selected passages from the various state and national codes or canons of ethics portray the general concept and ethical guidelines that, if violated, can lead to a malpractice suit, loss of license, or removal from membership in a national organization. Finally, the "Ethical Flashpoints" can serve as maxims for the practitioner throughout his or her professional career.

Although ethical codes and standards of professional associations and licensing boards are augmented and amended from time to time, the basic principles generally remain the same. For example, in the past certain ethical codes absolutely prohibited bartering with a client. Cash and cash

only was the rule. Now some codes allow bartering under limited circumstances. Should bartering occur, and should the client complain later, the
burden is on the provider to show that the arrangement was "fair." If the
provider is able to do so, the practice may be considered ethical.

Using the Vignettes

The vignettes can be used as questions for general discussion and clarification or assigned for analysis by individual members of the class. (Supervisors required to instruct their supervisees in ethics could assign the
text and use it in much the same way as an educator or professor.) In
general, the discussion questions might be as follows:

- What ethical problems are involved in the vignette?

- List or itemize the various options available to the therapist. (Note:
  here, as throughout the text, the words therapist, provider, mental
  health professional, counselor, and social worker are used interchangeably. Where ethics are concerned, the general guidelines of the
  so-called talking professions are remarkably similar.)

- Which option would you exercise?

- Why would you choose this particular option and why would you *not*
  choose another option?

- What are the risks involved in exercising this option?

- What are the potential rewards in exercising this option?

In many cases, the problem and the answer change completely by al-
tering the situation slightly; for example:

- If a person is male, change to female.

- If a person is a minor (under 18, unmarried, and unemancipated),
  change the age to 18 or older, married or unmarried.

- If the client and therapist went to a bar, make it a health food juice bar.

- If the client or therapist is married, change the status to single, or
  cohabiting.

- If the therapist is under the influence of medication, increase the
  dosage gradually to the point of intoxication. If the therapist is under
  the influence of alcohol, make it only one drink at first, then two

drinks, a "few" beers. As the consumption increases, notice how the attitude of the class changes.

• If the individuals are heterosexual, make them homosexual, but in the same "significant other" pairing.

Use your imagination and consider how the preceding questions might be discussed differently and answered differently as the situation changes.

When a lawyer first visits with a client, the client normally narrates the facts to the lawyer *conveniently omitting* any admissions that are contrary to the result the client desires. Only after serious, sometimes aggressive cross-examination do all the critical facts emerge. Often the details pulled reluctantly from the client determine the ultimate outcome of the case. In therapy, it is much the same. The therapy will take a different twist if the parties are heterosexual or homosexual, minors or have reached the age of majority, drunk or sober when abuse took place, male or female, "normal" or "disabled" or "retarded," and so forth. Each fact situation can be utilized for numerous discussions and will produce a different result in its ethical emphasis depending on the twist of the verbiage.

Using the Big-Picture Explanation

The big picture serves as the catalyst between the vignette and the various ethical codes. The reader must keep in mind that the actual ethical problem he or she may face will not be *exactly* the same as the scenarios provided in the book. Even slight variations can completely change the ethical risk to the provider and client. The text extrapolates from the facts a general proposition that illustrates an ethical problem. From this general presentation, rules are determined that the professional can apply to other situations. For example, in one class taught by the authors the dilemma of whether or not to date a client was presented. The answer was clear to everyone. Then a shaky hand went up: "How about a second cousin?" Although the codes are clear about direct family and friends, there has not been a second cousin case. Our answer to the student: "It's a bad idea . Do you want to be the first second cousin case to hit the next text in the bookstores?" Such would be a dubious honor.

Using the Ethics Codes

Selected portions of the various national and some state ethical canons are included in the text. Many of these rules are so similar as to be almost identical in verbiage and theory. They are set out in the text for easy reference so readers can go directly to the source when an ethical dilemma comes up. Current codes for each of the national and state professional organizations are also available from the issuing organization and on the Internet. If the answer to a particular ethical question is not answered in the text, readers may find the answer in the codes themselves. A call to the professional association, licensing board, or an Internet search may also produce the answer. Should a reading of the code reveal a conflict in wording or ambiguous interpretation, the organizations involved usually have staff available to answer questions. In addition, all malpractice carriers, ever anxious to avoid litigation, and knowing that ethical canons can be introduced into evidence to indicate minimum standards of conduct, will be happy to be of assistance. Nevertheless, when conferring with any source of advice and interpretation, take copious notes and document the advice offered. These notations can be invaluable if a decision is ever challenged and remember, ethical guidelines are updated on a regular basis. When a "real" problem arises, obtain the latest code available.

The authors have been shocked over the years by the large number of practitioners who have given little attention to their national and state ethics codes since graduate school. Some have updated their knowledge at lectures and seminars, especially in states that require ethics continuing education units to maintain a license. More often than not, however, practitioners receive copies of the ethical canons which remain unread until a complaint is filed.

Ethical codes cannot be advertised as being stimulating reading. There is no plot, no character development, and good does not triumph over evil. Ethical codes are only listings of potential evils with the admonition to avoid committing the "sins" set out in the rules and regulations of each discipline.

In two separate situations, the authors served on a panel of experts concerning ethics in mental health practice. The two other participants were mental health professionals. When preparing for the talk, only the authors had read and digested the local ethical codes. Neither of the other participants had ever read the codes for their profession. Both had practiced for more than 15 years without incident and relied on a common-sense approach that worked. But suppose a presenting problem defied common sense? A knowledge of their individual codes would be essential.

This text offers an introduction to the codes or canons of professional ethics in mental health. This introduction may, as a practical matter, be the only time the novice provider has to discuss and absorb the technical rules and regulations under which he or she operates. Such knowledge is not an academic exercise. It is essential to keeping a license and practicing within a profession.

Using the Ethical Flashpoints

The ethical flashpoints are maxims or sayings for risk-free practice. They are set out in list form for easy reference.

To the educator, they might serve:

- As subjects for discussion and debate.

- As a basis for essay questions that trace the root of the maxim or state the rationale for its existence.

- As a source of argument: Is this rule really necessary and does it serve the best interest of most of the clients most of the time, or some of the clients some of the time?

- As a basis for true-and-false or multiple-choice questions.

- As a test question: The flashpoint is the answer, but where is it found in the profession's code of ethics?

- As a handy reminder of ethical practice.

The provider, supervisor, consumer, and educator can use this book as a general guide to ethical practice. The text, vignettes, published codes, and ethical flashpoints were designed for ease of presentation in the lecture format as well as for class discussion and case review. The flashpoints can also be used as a quick reference in avoiding an ethically questionable situation. It is our hope that long after receiving degrees and entering professions, practitioners will avert ethical problems because they recall these ethical flashpoints and recognize that a path about to be taken with a client is dangerous and that a step backward together with a sensitive review is warranted and appropriate.

Mental Health Services Providers

How can mental health services providers use this book? Each mental health services provider, whether psychologist, psychiatrist, marriage and family therapist, counselor, addictions professional, social worker, or pastoral counselor, faces ethical dilemmas daily. An ethical violation could lead to personal discipline and the end of a professional practice.

Simple solution to potential ethical problems →

Some ethical problems are easily solved, such as rearranging office furniture to prevent prying eyes from peering over a receptionist's desk at a computer screen. Other problems are more difficult in that they involve matters of degree. For example, every ethical code states clearly that a therapist cannot offer treatment to a spouse. Such treatment would defy common sense as there would be no clinical objectivity. But what about a brother-in-law? Or the girlfriend of the brother-in-law? Or the husband of the sister of the brother-in-law? How far removed from the primary relationship must a person be for therapy to be proper and ethical? When you consider stepparents or godparents the issue can become even cloudier. And who wants to take a chance?

Although this book cannot explicitly address all these situations, Chapter 8, "Prohibited Clients," highlights some of the problems involved in working with individuals with whom there is an external relationship and provides guidelines for deciding who is an inappropriate client. Mental health providers need to consider such relationships to avoid ethical complaints, as well as the appearance of committing an ethical violation. In psychotherapy, as in other professions, perception is important, and any act or activity that *appears* to be unethical, will, if supported by media exposure, rumor, gossip, and table conversation, become reality.

The Portable Ethicist for Mental Health Professionals: An A–Z Guide to Responsible Practice tackles dozens of ethical questions in a straightforward manner. It uses the ethical codes of mental health professional associations to respond to these questions and provides guidelines for avoiding ethically questionable behavior. Readers can review the Contents, which lists the topics in each part alphabetically, to find information on a particular area of ethical concern or use the extensive index to find additional references to the topic elsewhere in the book.

Armed with this information, the practitioner can determine how best to avoid an ethical violation or how to best handle the situation if a complaint has been filed. The material in this book may not always provide a definitive answer to the ethical dilemma, but the mental health professional will be in a better position to make an informed decision or judgment about the appropriate action to take. No book can answer all ethical questions with absolute authority. The point to remember is that whatever action is taken, the rationale should be clearly stated and the steps fully documented. The best interest of the client should be the therapist's primary concern.

The best advice may be that if after considering all aspects of the ethical dilemma, you still feel uneasy, don't do it. If you have already done it, call your lawyer first, before saying or doing anything else. Remember that in most cases, an attorney will not be obligated to report a therapist's unethical conduct, but a colleague would be.

Mental Health Services Consumers

How can the consumer of mental health services use this book?

Dorothy is a consumer of mental health services. She is the client of Dr. Silverstone, whom she has been seeing for two years. Occasionally, as small talk at the beginning of a session, they visit and share ideas about music.

~

Sitting in Dorothy's garage is an unused organ that has been in her family for as long as she can remember. Dorothy assigns a value of $2,000 to the organ and offers to trade it to Dr. Silverstone in exchange for 25 sessions. She feels this is a good bargain since Dr. Silverstone's normal charge is $100 per session. He accepts the offer, has the organ removed from her garage, and sends it to a restoration facility. After it is repaired, Dr. Silverstone displays it in his music room where he enjoys its elegance and sound.

~

Meanwhile, Dorothy feels remorse about trading the favorite family organ. She hears through the friend of a friend of Dr. Silverstone that the now mint-condition organ has a beautiful tone, looks like new as a restored valuable antique, and is worth a "fortune." She feels resentful, but is not sure whether the trade was inappropriate or unethical. She ponders the circumstance.

How can Dorothy determine if she has been taken advantage of by this mental health professional?

The Portable Ethicist provides a pathway to the answer in its discussion of bartering. But this text also provides insight to the consumer for a laundry list of other ethical issues. Consider this sampling of situations in which a client might be involved:

• The client responded to an ad in a newspaper, a magazine, or a telephone book that was false or misleading.

- The client consented to therapy but failed to understand the goals, techniques, purposes, or methods of therapy.

- The client was unaware of the limitations on the authorized methods of treatment, the risks of treatment, or alternative treatments available.

- The client found out that her therapist was reimbursing or paying her physician, who made the referral in the first place.

- The therapist suggested that the client attend her church, take a class offered by her at the university, or have coffee with her after a session.

- The therapist made no record of visits or payments and did not maintain clinical notes of treatment.

- The client was gay and the therapist seemed (to the client) uncomfortable around him and uncomfortable when the subject of a gay lifestyle arose.

- The therapist offered treatment by fax and e-mail without ever interviewing the client.

- The client felt that although the therapist never made any overt advances toward her, he seemed to her to be preoccupied with her sexual history over and above what she considered appropriate under the circumstances.

- The client wanted assurances that whatever was said in the clinical setting was *absolutely confidential* and the therapist would not offer such assurances; instead the therapist initiated a dialogue concerning the numerous exceptions to confidentiality.

- The therapist asked the client to sign a consent form that obligated the client to pay the therapist for all time in court on any client-related case, which the client was reluctant to sign.

- The client knew little about client rights and therapist obligations and wanted an in-depth explanation of these rights and obligations.

- The client's repeated requests for copies of his records were ignored and the records were not provided.

In these and many other areas, consumers of mental health services need objective and educational information.

To many clients, especially those who are relatively unsophisticated about the mental health field, therapy of any type is somewhat of a mystery. The consumer/client not only is unschooled in the treatment methods being used but, more to the point, does not know the mental health professional's ethical obligations. This book can be a resource for such information because it uses clear examples, explanations, and ethical flashpoints, along with excerpts from the ethical canons of major mental health professional associations to illustrate both ethical and unethical behavior. The client who feels uneasy with the therapy or the therapist should consult this text to determine if the uneasiness stems from unethical and improper actions of the provider.

Consumer Bill of Rights

1. You have a right to know the therapist's credentials, licensing, educational background, and experience.

2. You have a right to be informed of the nature of the treatment being offered, the fees for treatment, and the amount of copayments expected as well as third-party payments. You should be informed of the provider's "no-show," and cancellation policy and whether the provider is or will be available should you for any reason be involved in litigation.

3. You have a right to know whether what is said in therapy will be confidential and when confidentiality may be legally breached, such as if the therapist is subpoenaed to testify in court. All the exceptions to confidentiality are important, and you should understand them fully before beginning therapy.

4. You have a right to know what to do should the provider prove to be incompetent, dishonest, or unethical in any way, including the right to sue, or to report the provider to the state board, national organization, or district attorney, if appropriate. You may choose not to pursue these options; however, you should be aware of your rights.

5. You have a right to rely on claims made by and about the therapist, and if the claims seem grandiose, to seek verification.

6. You have a right to discuss the treatment plan, the diagnosis, and the prognosis. The more you participate in the treatment process, the greater the opportunity for treatment to succeed.

7. Informed consent includes the right to know the alternative treatments available, the ability to refuse the treatment or any part of the treatment, a full explanation of the risks of treatment (e.g., one risk

risk of marital therapy is that the parties might get a divorce), and the risks of forgoing treatment.

8. You have the right not to be exploited by the therapist, who has a duty to refrain from blurring professional boundaries, to respect professional distances, and to refrain from any act that suggests or implies a dual relationship of any type: social, business, intellectual, personal, sexual, or artistic. Remember, your therapist is your therapist only, not your friend, and any attempt to create any other relationship is unfair, unwise, and unethical. Therapists should not attend a client's family events, religious ceremonies, or parties. Nor should they participate in any other function that might in any way affect clinical objectivity, even remotely. Therapists should not accept gifts, tickets, or invitations. Your therapist should not have personal or business relationships with your family members and friends. The therapist's relationship with you should be limited to the therapeutic treatment.

9. You have a right to a copy of your file, but keep in mind that reading a clinical record is not always a good idea, especially if you do not understand clinical jargon and technical terms and concepts. A freshman course in psychology is typically not adequate preparation when trying to understand a professional file.

10. Honor the rights of teenagers or children if they are seeing a therapist. Once a child realizes a parent or guardian is viewing a clinical record, trust evaporates. Most children want to tell the therapist what they do not tell their parents, and if the therapist is a snitch, frank and honest communication comes to an abrupt halt.

11. If you have time, and if the method of therapy has a label, read some of the literature on the subject. Clinicians often are using a kind of therapy that a layperson can understand in general terms. Read an article or book or watch a movie that illustrates the type of problem you are facing. Sometimes the therapy moves faster if you know the direction and method in advance. Therapists like to deal with educated clients.

12. You have a right to limited confidentiality in one-on-one therapy. In a group, you can count on the facilitator to respect what is said, but signed statements of confidentiality, oral pledges, and announcements that "what is said here, remains here" are no guarantee that another group participant will not gossip. Group therapy can be

[margin note: No dual relationships betw practitioner & client]

economical and helpful. However, there is a downside risk of breached confidentiality.

13. You have a right not to be discriminated against because of race, color, creed, religion, nationality, or disability. However, if the therapist is unable to understand parts of your ethnic or cultural background, a referral may be made or a consultant engaged. Therapists are aware that some cultural diversities are difficult to understand and even more difficult to treat. No therapist is knowledgeable in all religions, ethnic varieties, and national customs to the extent that he or she can understand the impact of that background and put it into perspective. If you feel the therapist does not understand your background, explain as best you can and then discuss the problem with the therapist. An agreeable solution can usually be reached. The same is helpful if a clinician does not fully comprehend the full physical or emotional impact of a disability.

14. You have the right to terminate therapy, unless it is court ordered, at any time. Your therapist has a duty to terminate therapy when progress is not being achieved or all goals have been reached. If further mental health care is necessary you have a right to be advised of the kind of care needed and provided with referral sources for such care.

15. You have the right to be better informed about the ethical standards of the mental health profession by reading the rest of this book.

If a mental health consumer decides that the therapist has acted unethically, he or she may take the following actions:

- Call a lawyer and discuss the problem.

- Confront the therapist, explain the ethical perception, and resolve the matter between the two parties.

- Call the therapist's licensing board for an opinion.

- File a complaint with the licensing board. (Note: Once a complaint is filed with a licensing board, there is no turning back. The complaint is a serious matter and is taken seriously. The complainant must realize that filing a complaint means getting involved in an administrative process that concerns a governmental agency, a licensing board and board members, perhaps a state attorney and investigators, and a permanent state record. Filing a complaint is not something to do lightly or in haste.)

• Terminate the therapy and ask the therapist to make a referral.

Mental health consumers should carefully consider all the options before taking any action.

There are times when a violated client whose mental health provider has acted unethically should take immediate affirmative action to redress the wrong, seeking the maximum punishment available from a disciplinary body. There are also times when a violated client's personal mental health would benefit from talking the violation through with a compassionate professional and letting it drop, perhaps with a telephone call or a note. It is appropriate for each client to make the final decision about how to handle such situations . . . as long as the decision is informed.

PART ONE

CLIENT ISSUES

1

Alternative Treatment Methods

In the past, clients arrived for their appointments, took off their shoes, relaxed on the clinical couch, and in a soft and unemotional voice discussed the day's problems. The therapist, meanwhile, sat in a comfortable chair jotting down occasional phrases, intermittently making a suggestion or two to keep the conversation focused. At the end of 50 minutes of practically uninterrupted monologue, the parties shook hands, the client paid cash, and left. The therapist closed the client's file and picked up the one for the next client. "Thank you, Dr. Freud," the client thought.

⁓

Today, Dr. Freud Jr. has a busy schedule and is happy to talk to clients over the phone in an emergency. He makes his fees clear in his intake form, which states that 6-minute (.1 hour) phone calls are free, but calls over 6 minutes are charged at his usual hourly rate computed in 10-minute segments. He has a timer on his telephone, and each call is coded and transferred electronically to the client file. One day, Dr. Freud receives an emergency call from a prospective client. The potential client was properly referred to Dr. Freud, but they had not yet met. Should he offer emergency treatment over the phone without seeing the client first, or should he, ethically, refuse to offer any consultation without first insisting on an office interview? If he chooses the latter, may he continue telephone therapy after the initial consultation using his electronic billing method? Is telephone therapy an accepted method of treatment? Would it make a difference if each phone had a picture monitor so the client could be seen on the tube? How much of therapy is voice transmission and how much is body language, facial expression, or other visual hints of a person's attitude, demeanor, and meaning?

⁓

Dr. Freud III was tired of practicing the same old "talk therapy" he'd been using for years. True, his dad and granddad listened and made history by listening to clients' problems, recording their findings, and publishing the results, but he was a therapist of the electronic age and sought modern treatment methods. One day a thought flashed in his mind: He would create a Web page; advertise his credentials, experience, and interests; and offer (with a certain amount of built-in name recognition) e-mail therapy. He searched his profession's ethics codes. The codes did not contain an absolute ethical prohibition for e-mail therapy. He would insist that prospective clients use a credit card to open an account with him before beginning therapy, and then he would respond to their e-mail inquiries and bill their credit card for his time. He would no longer suffer through face-to-face confrontations with clients who started talking and then, thinking themselves on a roll, refused to leave. Could this be the dawn of a new era—treating clients without ever seeing them?

A Plethora of Treatment Options

Years ago—and not so long ago—most therapy followed the model in the first example. Today on the other hand, there is much to do before therapy can even begin! First clients must sign a carefully worded consent to treatment form, which is often drafted and almost always reviewed by a lawyer. Next, clients complete an intake form, listing all the mental health details of their lives so the therapist can never be accused of failing to discover some important detail about a client's past life that might be critical to continuing therapy. No stone is left unturned before treatment begins. Ethics guidelines dictate what therapists must explain to clients prior to beginning therapy, including the concept of "informed consent." And while "talk therapy" was the most favored treatment in the past, therapists now use a plethora of techniques to effect change in their clients.

Distance Therapy

Many ethics guidelines provide that primary therapy should be offered in person and imply that other communication methods such as e-mail, telephone, fax, or other electronic transmission should be selectively used on an emergency basis or, perhaps, only as a supplement to face-to-face therapy.

Is it ethical to offer "distance" therapy? Many ethics guidelines provide that primary therapy should be offered in person and imply that other communication methods such as e-mail, telephone, fax, or other electronic transmission should be selectively used on an emergency basis or, perhaps, only as a supplement to face-to-face therapy. Currently, ethics codes are sketchy when it comes to supporting or discouraging so-called distance therapy. It will likely take a court proceeding to set a precedent regarding these new treatment options. Thus, once the court or a licensing board disciplines a practitioner for committing an ethical infraction when inappropriately practicing therapy using the telephone or some other electronic method, we will have some idea how to caution therapists about practicing distance therapy.

E-Mail

Today, many therapists offer e-mail counseling either as a primary form of therapy or an adjunct to regular therapy sessions. E-mail therapy began as a matter of convenience for many practitioners: a way to schedule appointments or answer a quick question between sessions. Others strategically added computer-based education, counseling, or therapy sessions to build a varied menu of private pay services. Many licensed clinicians now offer therapy services ranging from a single interaction, to ongoing sessions, to hypnotherapy by electronic mail (see *Practice Strategies, A Business Guide for Behavioral Healthcare Providers*, March 1999, p. 1, American Association of Marriage and Family Therapists).

There are several problems with this approach. For example, therapists cannot observe a client's physical disability using only electronic communication. Likewise, if clients do not complete a mental health intake form or complete it untruthfully, therapists may be unaware of existing conditions (e.g., the client may be pedophile with a criminal record). They may also be unaware of existing sources of support (e.g., a client who asks about "moderate" drinking may be a member of AA). Using electronic communication, therapists usually are unable to see their clients' physical appearance, which often gives clues to their mental health state. Might a face-to-face therapeutic interface yield different results from on-line therapy, where the only contact is words floating across a screen?

Other difficulties also exist with on-line therapy. First, fees for different types of e-mail therapy may vary, and collecting fees for e-mail services is difficult. Second, it is difficult to positively identify clients because the therapist is not meeting them face-to-face. Is the e-mail client a sincere client or someone having a good time at the therapist's expense? Third, how confidential can e-mail therapy be? How can a therapist ensure that an e-mail client will complete and sign an informed consent form and complete the intake form, which includes information required by state licensing laws? Fourth, if e-mail communication crosses state lines, does the provider need to be licensed to practice in the recipient's state? Can the provider ethically process third-party payments in another state?

One way to avoid ethical problems is to call any e-mail or on-line communication between therapist and client educational rather than therapeutic. If therapists take this route, the rules change. For example, if the advice is considered "education" rather than "therapy," informed

One way to avoid ethical problems is to call any e-mail or on-line communication between therapist and client educational rather than therapeutic.

consent is not necessary, nor is a detailed intake form. The therapist is not entirely free of responsibility, however, by using this option. Even if the therapist has stated numerous times that the communication is only educational, there can be a problem if on-line clients interpret the advice as therapy. In such cases, there is a good chance that a court or licensing board will side with the complaining or damaged client.

Eventually, advanced telecommunications will catch up with the therapeutic community. Until licensing boards publish definitive rulings or legal cases determine the limits to be placed on the practice, however, mental health professionals who augment their practice with on-line education or therapy could be vulnerable to sanctions. For now, therapists should exercise caution when exploring their options to practice over the Internet.

Agreed on therapy in an office is clearly therapy. The boundaries begin to blur when clinicians use e-mail or answer therapeutic questions in "ask Dr. _____" columns in the newspaper, on TV, or on the radio. Self-help books and newspaper and magazine articles purport to offer educational information but often provide therapeutic instructions. To date, few consumers have complained about the errors in self-help books or "feel good" articles. However, the electronic age, coupled with the enthusiastic enforcement of licensing and disciplinary boards throughout the country, opens a new avenue of ethical concerns. The best option is to consult the ethics codes, the licensing boards, and the malpractice carrier before beginning any on-line communications with clients. Find out if the malpractice policy covers new or novel treatment approaches before being sued or brought before the licensing board for an ethical complaint.

The best option is to consult the ethics codes, the licensing boards, and the malpractice carrier before beginning any on-line communications with clients.

National Guidelines for Electronic Communication

NASW Code of Ethics

4.01 Competence.

(b) Social Workers should strive to become and remain proficient in professional practice and the performance of professional functions. Social workers should critically examine and *keep current with emerging knowledge relevant to social work*. Social Workers should routinely *review the professional literature* and participate in continuing education relevant to social work practice and social work ethics. (italics added)

New and Novel Treatment Approaches

The Texas state licensing statute for professional counselors lists authorized counseling methods and practices, including individual counseling, group counseling, marriage counseling, family counseling, chemical dependency counseling, rehabilitation counseling, education counseling, career development counseling, sexual issues counseling, referral counseling, psychotherapy, play therapy, hypnotherapy, expressive therapies, biofeedback, assessing and appraising, and consulting. In all these fields, there is a constantly emerging body of literature with which the professional is ethically obligated to be up to date and informed. Moreover, many subspecialties have published ethical guidelines that bind their members.

Obligations for Ethical Practice

- Professionals must keep current with the literature in their field.

- Professionals must be knowledgeable in all areas in which they claim special training (e.g., couples therapy, school counseling).

- As various mental health disciplines develop new counseling or therapeutic theories, providers in those disciplines must become familiar with these developments.

- New, novel, electronic, and computer-oriented methods are being used and developed every day. Mental health professionals have a responsibility to offer these options to their clients, who have a right to receive the latest proven treatment available.

- Nevertheless, when practitioners make use of these new or novel approaches, they must be thoroughly knowledgeable about the new approach, and *ensure the new approach is applicable to the particular client in treatment.*

- Using new and novel approaches can be an ethical risk for providers because they often are not supported by a substantiated body of empirical or historic literature. Thus, providers must provide excellent documentation to support all new therapeutic approaches to therapy, especially if they deviate from commonly accepted norms.

- Every ethical treatment modality must be generally accepted by a majority of practitioners or a learned minority. When challenged, the provider has the burden of proving the modality used was appropriate to *this* client.

Ethical Flash Points

- Modern electronic communications such as e-mail do not have a long and professionally accepted history.

- Read all the published literature concerning electronic treatment before incorporating it into your practice.

- When using electronic communications, faxes, e-mail, chat rooms, or Web sites, remember that the recipient may not be the person you envision. The provider is responsible for providing ethical treatment to specific, identifiable clients, from the time therapy begins to the time it ends and records are no longer preserved. All communications become part of the clinical record if they influence the diagnosis, treatment plan or prognosis (see Chapters 11 and 17, "Terminating Therapy" and "Closing a Practice").

- Once a person is charged for an electronic consultation, he or she is a client and subject to the same rights as any other clients.

- Licenses apply to the state of issuance only, leading to ethical questions if the electronic client resides in another jurisdiction. Does therapy originate from the provider's workstation or the client's computer? Who has jurisdiction over the therapeutic consultation?

- Each state and each discipline as well as subspecialties within each discipline may have its own directive concerning electronic communications. Each must be consulted.

- Don't take unnecessary risks in implementing modern technology in therapy, but don't ignore such methods either.

Summary

Ethics codes have not yet incorporated guidelines for using modern communication methods in therapy, but practitioners should consider what the canons do say before embarking on a new treatment plan or using a diagnostic tool that depends in whole or in part on electronic methods. Being ahead of the pack is wonderful as long as one does not place a professional reputation at risk.

Technological developments are occurring so rapidly that any comments made today might be totally obsolete tomorrow, as emerging technology changes the rationale behind the ethical guidelines. An old legal maxim states, "When the reason for the rule fails, the rule itself should fail." In the area of technology, today's rationale can be tomorrow's failing. Thus practitioners should consider new technological treatment options but use caution in employing them. Contact your board, national association, malpractice carrier, and lawyer before plunging headlong into a new therapeutic theory or using a new technology.

2

Boundary Violations

At a recent therapy session, Mrs. Jones laments how her son cannot line up enough lawns to mow for the summer. Her therapist, Dr. Good, usually hires high school students about the same age as Mrs. Jones's child to mow her lawn. Can Dr. Good employ Mrs. Jones's son to mow, edge, and trim the lawn?

~

One day at the beauty shop, Dr. Good talks with her beautician. As soon as the beautician realizes Dr. Good is a therapist, she starts talking about her son, a poor student, who has taken up with a bad crowd and who, she thinks, has a drinking problem. Dr. Good handles just this sort of problem in her therapeutic practice and thinks she could help this child. After her appointment, the beautician asks if she can talk to Dr. Good in private. She admits her son does have a proven alcohol problem and wants help, but she is low on funds. She suggests a trade, in which Dr. Good would treat her son in exchange for beauty services. She already has a similar arrangement with her lawyer, dentist, and physician. On its face, the offer seems like a win, win, win (Dr. Good, child, mother) situation. Should Dr. Good accept her offer?

~

Dr. Moore consults with a team of professionals to keep his practice going. He retains a lawyer, a stock broker, and a financial planner, as well as an accountant, a banker, and an insurance agent. At church, he is friends with the minister, the choir director, the janitor, and the church secretary. All of them (along with his family members) know that Dr. Moore is a therapist and often share their problems on a "by the way" basis when they see him. Should Dr. Moore offer to treat any of these individuals as in-office clients or accept them for treatment if they approach him first? Is there a potential danger if Dr. Moore engages in a conversation that he considers small talk but the other person considers an insightful exchange of therapeutic perceptiveness, that is, a sort of informal treatment session?

~

One of Dr. Megabucks's therapy clients is a venture capitalist—stock broker. The client shares a hot tip with her that could make her an instant millionaire once the stock comes on the market. Is it ethical for Dr. Megabucks to subscribe to this new issue by opening an account with her client? What if she chose a different broker? Would therapeutic objectivity be compromised if the stock she purchased decreased in value or if it were later discovered that the new issue was the result of hype and fraud?

Identifying Boundary Violations

Boundary violations sometimes sneak up on the mental health professional when least expected. In the case of sexual or very close social or intimate contacts, the inappropriateness of the encounter is obvious. Chapter 10, "Sexual Misconduct," carefully sets out how a sexual need, activity, or satisfaction can bring disastrous consequences for the helping professional. When we discuss personal needs and activities in this chapter, we are referring to a less obvious type of relationship that would be innocent, customary, and acceptable for most professionals, but when applied to mental health providers is unethical or has the appearance of unethical conduct. Encounters with more or less subtle overtones might seem harmless at first glance but nonetheless represent an ethical violation that can haunt the mental health service provider.

Encounters with more or less subtle overtones might seem harmless at first glance but nonetheless represent an ethical violation that can haunt the mental health service provider.

Most ethics codes have both general and specific statements concerning therapists meeting personal needs and promoting personal activities at their clients' expense. In fact, such activities need not be at a client's expense to be considered unethical. These activities would also be inappropriate if engaging in them would compromise the therapist's objectivity toward the client or even have a tendency to compromise it.

National Guidelines for Identifying Potential Boundary Violations

APA Ethical Principles for Psychologists and Code of Conduct

1.   General Standards . . .

1.17   Multiple Relationships

(a)   In many communities and situations, it may not be feasible or reasonable for psychologists to avoid social or other nonprofessional contacts with persons such as patients, clients, students, supervisees, or research participants. Psychologists must always be sensitive to the potential harmful effects of other contacts on their work and on those persons with whom they deal. A psychologist refrains from entering into or promising another personal, scientific, professional, financial, or other relationship with such persons if it appears likely that such a relationship reasonably might impair the psychologist's objectivity or otherwise interfere with the psychologist's effectively performing his or her functions as a psychologist, or might harm or exploit the other party.

ACA Code of Ethics and Standards of Practice

Section A   The Counseling Relationship, A.1 Client Welfare

A.6   Dual Relationships

a. *Avoid When Possible.*

Counselors are aware of their influential positions with respect to clients, and they avoid exploiting the trust and dependency of clients. Counselors make every effort to avoid dual relationships with clients that could impair professional judgment or increase the risk of harm to clients. (Examples of such relationships include, but are not limited to, familial, social, financial, business, or close personal relationships with clients.) When a dual relationship cannot be avoided, counselors take appropriate professional precautions, such as informed consent, consultation, supervision, and documentation, to ensure that judgment is not impaired and no exploitation occurs. (See F.1.b.)

Anticipating Potential Boundary Violations

There is no way to predict all the circumstances under which a client or prospective client might approach a therapist. It is clear that therapists do not treat family, friends, business associates, or individuals with whom they have an existing relationship that might impair their objectivity or affect their clinical judgment. The following 12 situations describe some not-so-obvious conflicting relationships:

1. After several sessions, a therapist discovers that two separate clients in therapy for help in choosing a mate are actually talking about each other. To avoid any possible conflict, therapists should terminate

treatment when they discover a previously unrecognized relationship between two clients.

2. Therapists cannot control whom a relative marries. If a client marries into the family, the therapist should refer that person to another provider.

3. Resist the temptation to offer informal therapeutic services to friends and family. Most will respect the boundaries a therapist firmly establishes. Remember, therapists cannot control whether an individual will consider their comments to be casual conversation or therapeutic advice.

4. Avoid cocktail chatter that has therapeutic or counseling overtones. It is unusual to meet a mental health professional who has never been tapped for free consultations at a social gathering. Not only is such talk unethical, but it compromises the whole concept of obtaining informed consent and taking a mental health history. Therapy should be conducted in the proper forum after all preliminary steps have been completed, including an informed consent to treatment agreement and a clinical history.

Therapy should be conducted in the proper forum after all preliminary steps have been completed, including an informed consent to treatment agreement and a clinical history.

5. A shift in boundaries is usually gradual, not abrupt. A lawyer drafts a therapist's will and then casually asks about omitting his rebellious daughter from his own will. An insurance salesperson, after reviewing a therapist's policy, wants to talk about his feelings concerning the allocation of his own insurance proceeds between the children of his first marriage and his current wife. A therapist's banker, always a supportive father, feels guilty when he does not want to endorse and guarantee his son's note so his son can go into business. All mental health professionals have to be sensitive to the gradual shifts that blur boundaries and compromise objectivity. Therapists can engage a lawyer, a banker, or an insurance professional but cannot then offer professional consultations to any of them. Helping professionals want to help. But there can be no dual relationships.

6. Avoid accepting proffered tickets to sporting events, cultural performances, or to exotic places using clients' frequent flyer miles. Do not buy from or sell anything to a client, nor accept any service from them.

Do not buy from or sell anything to a client, nor accept any service from them.

7. In a small city or town where contact is inevitable, make sure that clients recognize the limits and guidelines imposed by the therapeutic

relationship and insert a carefully drawn clause into your intake form that sets out the nature of unavoidable contacts and the manner in which such contacts are being handled in your community.

8. Your client has a mint condition 1957 Chevrolet that you would love. It cannot be traded for a lifetime of therapy.

9. You treat a client who is a locally recognized painter, selling paintings with a fair market value of $200 each. Can you take a painting and credit $200 to the account? Suppose the painting increases in value to $20,000 and the client feels you took advantage of her?

10. Painters, plumbers, mechanics, and roofers may have personal problems or problem children. But you should not trade or barter for their services. Would your clinical objectivity be compromised if you traded services with your hairdresser and a day after having your hair treated it turned green?

11. Do not invite a client to sing tenor in your barbershop quartet or participate in other groups to which you belong.

12. Your lawyer calls you at night in a panic. He claims an emergency with his child and only you can help. Should you offer assistance? Probably yes, but document the nature of the emergency, the reason for seeing the lawyer's child in this particular emergency, and then make a referral as soon as is practicable.

Ethical Flash Points

- There is no absolute guide concerning boundary violations that indicate a provider is meeting personal needs or promoting personal activities at a client's expense. Rather therapists must be aware that the wall of professionalism between the therapist and the client is high. A therapist who feels any hint of compromising an ethical boundary, should immediately raise and reinforce that wall.

- Therapists, like other workers, need to make a living. This concept of "need" (as in meeting personal needs) only comes into question when clients use something other than dollars to pay for treatment. Only dollars have a fixed, recognized value that cannot be questioned later.

- For the dedicated mental health professional, saying "no" to a client is not easy, but saying "no" is easier than defending a claim for unethical conduct.

Summary

Before embarking on a questionable relationship, call your lawyer for suggestions concerning worst case scenarios.

In each situation described in this chapter, what started out as an innocent supportive venture or gesture could, should the client or a colleague become unhappy, turn into an ethical nightmare. Before embarking on a questionable relationship, call your lawyer for suggestions concerning worst case scenarios. Think through all the "what if" possibilities and then check those scenarios against your professional association's published guidelines. A lawyer with extensive education, training, and experience in dealing with the risks faced by mental health professionals usually can create a worst case situation. If there is none, and the therapist feels comfortable with the evolving situation, it is probably ethical and within the appropriate professional boundaries.

3

Confidentiality

Anita was a patient in the local hospital when she was seen by the hospital social worker. Her adult daughter was also present and asked the social worker many questions about her mother's health care. The social worker on rounds grew impatient but answered the questions and finally left the room in what might be called a controlled "huff." About an hour later when the daughter was meandering through the halls taking a break from sitting with her mother, she overheard the social worker in the nursing station talking with the nurses about the "hysterical daughter in 504 who asks silly and irrelevant questions." The target of the invective could be identified since 504 was a room on the floor and the daughter was the only person, in addition to the patient, who was in the room. Is this a breach of the patient's right of privacy? Is this an example of unethical behavior or simply unprofessional behavior?

~

Dr. Knight counsels clients with sexual dysfunction. One day, a client entered the office for his weekly therapy session and told Dr. Knight about his remarkable recovery from impotence after using Viagra. Dr. Knight dutifully recorded the information and then altered his treatment plan to indicate that the client's sexual functions had improved with the use of this specific medication and that future treatment would shift to handling the client's other interpersonal problems. Later, while sitting in a booth at the office building cafeteria, he shared with another therapist the information that the client who came in at 10:00 A.M. was helped by Viagra and now is facing the world with renewed potency. Both twitter a little, as men sometimes do, as they discuss this subject. Unknown to either therapist, the client's "significant other" is sitting in the next booth. She overhears the entire conversation. No names were ever used; however, she knows exactly whom they are talking about and their amusement is extremely distressing to her.

~

Dr. Green is active on the lecture circuit in addition to her busy clinical practice. She uses many case illustrations to illustrate the points she wants to emphasize in her seminars but always changes the names, the location, and any descriptive data. If possible, she does not use an example in a city where the situation might have gained some notoriety. In one complex case study, she has made what she thinks is a complete deidentifying transition. Nothing is the same and no stranger, or perhaps even a friend, could identify the client. Unbeknownst to her, the client to whom she is referring in the case study has become a licensed therapist during the past three years and is sitting in the audience. Although all names and personal information have been changed, Dr. Green's former client is clearly able to identify herself as the source for the case study. As a result, she feels that the entire mental health community (or at least all those in the audience) now know her problems. As with many individuals in therapy, she has shared her problems with some of her friends, many of them classmates in the counseling curriculum, and knows that, if they think about it, they could gather the evidence, compare their conversations with her to Dr. Green's example, and conclude correctly that she is the client being described. The example used was not an assemblage of different cases and clients but an accurate description of her personal, intimate, and former therapeutic situation, including her diagnosis, treatment plan, and the outcome of her therapy. Has the woman's confidentiality been breached?

~

Dr. Strange, a professor of clinical psychology, has retired after 30 years with the university. During all those years, he maintained a log of bizarre cases and, in retirement, intends to disguise all the cases and write a book about the clinical practice he maintained while he was teaching. Word has leaked out around the campus about Dr. Strange's book, although it is only rumor and gossip. One of Dr. Strange's former clients is now involved in litigation in which the client's mental health is an issue. The attorney for the defendant (the person the client/plaintiff is suing) hears about the future manuscript and the "bizarre cases" file and, on a whim, issues a subpoena to compel Dr. Strange to bring the record to a deposition where it will be examined. Then Dr. Strange will be asked questions about it. Is Dr. Strange's case file considered a clinical record? Must Dr. Strange bring this record, which refers to actual cases, but which is not really a part of a particular client's clinical file, to the deposition? And how about the other cases that are not connected with the defendant or the plaintiff? Should Dr. Strange be required to surrender these files as well?

~

When Dr. Pepper retired, she took all her files home and stored them in a locked room constructed in the corner of her garage. Finally, after 10 years, at age 75, she needed the space, so she disposed of them by carting off one cardboard box at a time, once each week, and putting it in a dumpster behind the Dairy Queen. Imagine her surprise when a group of children, playing in the dumpster found a box, opened it up, and took out selected files . . . the ones that concerned the preacher, school teachers, and neighbors. Surprise was only the beginning of her troubles.

~

Dr. Smiley started practicing as a clinician in the "old days" about 15 years ago, when therapy began with a handshake and a one-sentence consent form. She has preserved all her clinical files in locked cabinets, even though the new licensing law only requires her to keep and maintain them for 7 years. Jackie, a client treated by Dr. Smiley 14 years ago, becomes involved in litigation concerning custody of a teenage daughter. The angry husband/plaintiff issues a subpoena to Dr. Smiley to appear in court with the 14-year-old record. Jackie is furious. She was never informed that her old clinical files could be subpoenaed and further tells Dr. Smiley that she would never have been so honest, revealing, and loquacious if she knew her words would come back to haunt her. There is nothing in the file to indicate an understanding of this particular exception to confidentiality. Indeed, 15 years ago, few therapists were concerned about the technical exceptions. What can Dr. Smiley do now?

Confidentiality and Therapy

The words *confidentiality* and *trust* are inextricably tied together in the lexicon of therapy. Few clients would consent to therapy if they thought that what they said in a therapy session would become part of the public domain or community gossip. Clients have a right to expect confidentiality. That is why under normal circumstances what is said in therapy is absolutely confidential and will *never ever* be repeated. That is only a general rule, however, and is subject to many exceptions, especially when the client or the therapist is involved in the court or legal system.

The rules of confidentiality state that what is said to the therapist in therapy is confidential and cannot be voluntarily repeated, but under the direction of a judge or other magistrate, or when directed under other rules of law, the therapist may be compelled to testify concerning the client, the client's records, or the client's history as contained in the therapist's notes and intake data.

In litigation, the rules of evidence in that jurisdiction prevail, and the question of confidentiality becomes one of privilege. Privilege issues are decided by judicial authority; the judge determines what is or is not subject to revelation in court. In such cases, the rules of confidentiality state that what is said to the therapist in therapy is confidential and cannot be *voluntarily* repeated, but under the direction of a judge or other magistrate, or when directed under other rules of law, the therapist may be compelled to testify concerning the client, the client's records, or the client's history as contained in the therapist's notes and intake data.

The questions we must answer are: What are examples of "confidentiality" and "privilege" and how do they differ?

Masking Identity of Clients and Cases in Conversation

Some elements of confidentiality are clear, especially when reduced to simple terms and in simple situations. Therapists do not gossip about identifiable clients. *Identifiable* does not just mean using a name but also providing enough information so that anyone knowing the person and the facts could make the connection. In conversation, the names, circumstances, places, ages, number of children, and professions must be eliminated, along with other details that might lead to self-identification or allow one individual to identify another. Using composite examples is helpful, but even then all principal facts must be so distorted that identification is impossible.

Identifiable does not just mean using a name but also providing enough information so that anyone knowing the person and the facts could make the connection.

Informed Consent

A client can waive confidentiality in writing, as in a "Consent to Disclosure of Client Records," "Consent for Release of Information," or "Consent for Release of Confidential Information" form (see Bernstein & Hartsell, *Portable Lawyer*, 1998), and in that case information about the client can be shared freely. However, providers must be careful when dealing with a client's waiver of confidentiality or consent to release confidential information if the information is to be made public or semipublic. The **"rule of unintended consequences"** confines client consent to the waiver of confidentiality regarding predictable consequences. If the consequences prove to be terribly harmful to the client in an unintended, unpredictable, or unanticipated manner, the client could complain that the waiver was overreaching and that the release of information was not appropriately consented to by the client. Put another way, the client may consent to the release of information, but it must be an informed consent. "Informed" would *require being informed of all the foreseeable consequences of the release*.

The client may consent to the release of information, but it must be an informed consent.

Confidentiality versus Privilege

Confidentiality is both an ethical precept and a traditional rule when offering therapy. Privilege, on the other hand, is a rule of law. Without a statute, there is no privilege. Bernstein and Hartsell (1998) in *The Portable Lawyer* indicated:

> Privilege . . . belongs to the client. If the client directs the therapist to disclose confidential information, then the therapist must do so. The client's request should be written, signed, and dated. In some states, it may have to be notarized. If a therapist feels, as a matter of professional judgment, that the file should not be made public, he or she may file a motion with the appropriate court to restrict publication of the file. This motion will lead to a hearing and a judicial determination. The therapist does not possess the right to refuse to disclose the file if the client and court determine it should be made public. The burden of proof is on the therapist. The court must be shown that revealing the file to the client or anyone else would be harmful to the client, and that the best interest of the client would be served by keeping the file confidential, even from the client. (pp. 6–7)

Privilege is granted by statute, applies to the judicial or court system only, and must be claimed by the client. If, in the context of litigation, a third party requests client information or records and the client does not consent to the release of information or the therapist believes therapeutically that a disclosure would harm the client, the therapist must file a motion for a protective order or motion to quash and assert privilege. Privilege, if granted, allows that certain information, although possessed by a therapist, is protected by law from disclosure in a court proceeding. Some examples of privilege include the priest-penitent, lawyer-client, husband-wife relationships, among others.

Privilege is granted by statute, applies to the judicial or court system only, and must be claimed by the client.

Although some statutes grant a privilege for mental health information, many of them are so diluted by the statutory exceptions that they have little effect. If a privilege is to be claimed, the client and the therapist must consult a lawyer and then assert the appropriate specific privilege in court by motion before a judge. The judge will rule if the privilege applies and will either grant the privilege and block testimony or overrule it and compel testimony or disclosure of records, in which case the therapist as a witness must either testify or risk being held in contempt for failure to testify and possibly be fined or incarcerated.

There are many exceptions to privilege. When the question arises in any jurisdiction, the therapist should consult an attorney in that jurisdiction to determine the verbiage of the local privilege statute, the limits indicated by case law, the exceptions, and the client-related public relations aspects. Sometimes it is better for the therapist to raise the privilege question loudly and clearly before the court just so the client understands that the therapist has made every effort to protect a file if ordered to testify or reveal a record. On the other hand, the therapist does not have to object so enthusiastically that the judge holds the therapist in contempt and orders the therapist to be incarcerated. When ordered by the court, the therapist must be sworn in by the bailiff, take the witness stand, answer questions, and give testimony in the traditional manner.

National Guidelines for Protecting Confidentiality

APA Ethical Principles of Psychologists and Code of Conduct

5.   Privacy and Confidentiality

5.01   Discussing the Limits of Confidentiality.

(a) Psychologists discuss with persons and organizations with whom they establish a scientific or professional relationship (including, to the extent feasible, minors and their legal representatives) (1) the relevant limitations on confidentiality, including limitations where applicable in group, marital, and family therapy or in organizational consulting, and (2) the foreseeable uses of the information generated through their services.

(b) Unless it is not feasible or is contraindicated, the discussion of confidentiality occurs at the outset of the relationship and thereafter as new circumstances may warrant.

(c) Permission for electronic recording of interviews is secured from clients and patients.

5.02   Maintaining Confidentiality . . .

AAMFT Code of Ethics

2. Confidentiality

Marriage and family therapists have unique confidentiality concerns because the client in a therapeutic relationship may be more than one person. Therapists respect and guard confidences of each individual.

2.1 Marriage and family therapists may not disclose client confidences except: (a) as mandated by law; (b) to prevent a clear and immediate danger to a person or persons; (c) where the therapist is a defendant in a civil, criminal, or disciplinary action arising from the therapy (in which case client confidences may be disclosed only in the course of that action); or (d) if there is a waiver previously obtained in writing, and then such information may be revealed only in accordance with the terms of the waiver. In circumstances where more than one person in a family receives therapy, each such family member who is legally competent to execute a waiver must agree to the waiver required by subparagraph (d). Without such a waiver from each family member legally competent to execute a waiver, a therapist cannot disclose information received from any family member.

2.2 Marriage and family therapists use client and/or clinical materials in teaching, writing, and public presentations only if a written waiver has been obtained in accordance with Subprinciple 2.1 (d), or when appropriate steps have been taken to protect client identity and confidentiality.

2.3 Marriage and family therapists store or dispose of client records in ways that maintain confidentiality.

ACA *Code of Ethics and Standards of Practice*

Section B: Confidentiality

B.1.   Right to Privacy

a. Respect for Privacy.

Counselors respect their clients' right to privacy and avoid illegal and unwarranted disclosures of confidential information. (See A.3.a and B.6.a.)

b. Client Waiver.

The right to privacy may be waived by the client or their legally recognized representative.

c. Exceptions.

The general requirement that counselors keep information confidential does not apply when disclosure is required* to prevent clear and imminent danger to the client or others or when legal requirements demand that confidential information be revealed. Counselors consult with other professionals when in doubt as to the validity of an exception.

d. Contagious, Fatal Diseases.

A counselor who receives information confirming that a client has a disease commonly known to be both communicable and fatal is justified in disclosing information to an identifiable third party, who by his or her relationship with the client is at a high risk of contracting the disease. Prior to making a disclosure the counselor should ascertain that the client has not already informed the third party about his or her disease and that the client is not intending to inform the third party in the immediate future. (See B.1.c and B.1.f.)

e. Court Ordered Disclosure . . .

f. Minimal Disclosure . . .

g. Explanation of Limitations . . .

h. Subordinates.

*Such disclosure, called the "duty to warn" concept, is controlled by statute in some jurisdictions and by case law in others. When the problem arises, contact the state board for your profession, your malpractice insurance carrier, your lawyer, and your national organization. This is an evolving area in law. No statement made today would necessarily be valid tomorrow (see Chapter 22).

Counselors make every effort to ensure that privacy and confidentiality of clients are maintained by subordinates including employees, supervisees, clerical assistants, and volunteers. (See B.1.a.)

i. Treatment Teams.

If client treatment will involve a continued review by a treatment team, the client will be informed of the team's existence and composition.

NASW Code of Ethics

1.07 Privacy and Confidentiality

(a) Social workers should respect clients' right to privacy. Social workers should not solicit private information from clients unless it is essential to providing services or conducting social work evaluation or research. Once private information is shared, standards of confidentiality apply . . .

(f) When social workers provide counseling services to families, couples, or groups, social workers should seek agreement among the parties involved concerning each individual's right to confidentiality and obligation to preserve the confidentiality of information shared by others. Social workers should inform participants in family, couple, or group counseling that social workers cannot guarantee that all participants will honor such agreements . . .

(k) Social workers should protect the confidentiality of clients when responding to requests from members of the media . . .

(o) Social workers should take reasonable precautions to protect client confidentiality in the event of the social workers termination of practice, incapacitation, or death . . .

(r) Social workers should protect the confidentiality of deceased clients consistent with the preceding standards.

Common Threads among Ethics Codes

- Clients are entitled to confidentiality as that word is commonly understood by laypersons.
- Therapists have to resist the temptation to gossip, tell "war stories," or use thinly disguised examples of clients in social conversations. A client should never be identified.

A client should never be identified.

- Clients have the right to be informed concerning the exceptions to confidentiality, such as child abuse; elder abuse; duty to warn, where it applies; exceptions when there is involvement in the judicial system; custody cases; and other situations that, when they become part of litigation, are not protected by confidentiality.

- The limits to absolute confidentiality should be stated on the informed consent form and clearly discussed before therapy begins.

- Records have to be both maintained and preserved according to professional guidelines or state statute.

- Clients have a right to waive confidentiality in writing.

Client confidentiality continues after the death of the therapist or the client.

- Client confidentiality continues after the death of the therapist or the client.

- Preparations have to be made to accommodate the death of the client or the therapist.

- The final word has not been established concerning contagious diseases, especially AIDS. Therapists would be helped if national legislation issued a blanket policy with protective language concerning sexually transmitted diseases setting out exactly what a therapist can do and how to do it. There is some confusion between the various disciplines and the law itself at local, state, and federal levels.

- Where confidences have to be disclosed, the least information possible or necessary should be disclosed.

- Confidentiality binds employees, subordinates, agents, and servants, as well as temporary help. All have to be educated and trained concerning the applicability of confidentiality rules that apply to the therapist and understand that these rules apply to them. Each person in the office should sign or initial a confidentiality memorandum.

- Clients being treated by a treatment team have a right to know who is on the team and why.

- Information received and shared should be on a "need to know" basis.

- Families, couples, and groups need special sensitivity. Each person in the system has individual rights.

Beware of the media.

- Beware of the media. Clever reporters can put words in a therapist's mouth that may be embarrassing, misleading, and downright dangerous to the therapist and the client, especially when taken out of context.

Ethical Flash Points

- Punishment for violating confidentiality can be meted out by licensing boards and national organizations. Punishment can also lead to a malpractice suit.

- The client must be informed, prior to the commencement of therapy, of all the limits to confidentiality. This includes the special situations that can arise if there is involvement in the judicial system. The clinician should talk with the client about the possibility of litigation during the initial interview and explain the therapeutic pitfalls. Often litigation and the threat of litigation create their own mental health problems.

- Confidentiality continues to be an issue after the death of either the client or the therapist. A protocol has to be established by every mental health provider or agency to take care of the client, the file, and the continuation of therapy if needed. The intake and consent form is the place to provide for disposition of the file on the death of either.

- Check the local legal rules when a client threatens to commit suicide or threatens to injure or kill another readily identifiable person. The instinct is to warn the potential victim. It *may not* be ethical. Check your state law. Check it now. The therapist may not have time when the actual event occurs, especially if the threat occurs at night or over a weekend.

- Store records so as to protect them from curious eyes. They should be locked and safe from fire and natural disasters.

- If using case examples in lectures or otherwise, explain that the case represents a composite problem, not a real person, and then deidentify the case as much as possible. *No one should be able to discern the identity of any case illustration.*

- With proper information, a client can always waive confidentiality.

- The therapist, with motion and order before the proper court, can object to waiving confidentiality if the therapist feels it would be a danger to the client or others. This would include letting the client see his or her own file.

- Protecting confidentiality includes training agents, employees, servants, receptionists, transcription services, answering services, and others who learn about therapists' files, to recognize that from their point of view **everything is confidential.** The provider alone issues the order to share information.

- Train all temporary help and new employees on issues of confidentiality.

- When information is shared, it should be the minimum necessary to do the job (i.e., the least necessary amount of information to convey what needs to be known by the other person).

- Where there are multiple members of a group, keep a separate file for each member, including children. This will lead to more paperwork, but less confusion if an individual file must be examined.

- When in doubt, call your lawyer and your malpractice insurance carrier.

Summary

*Communications
between a
provider and
client and a
client's records,
however created
or stored, are
confidential.*

All ethics canons or codes of the mental health professions and most of
its subgroups provide that communications between a provider and
client and a client's records, however created or stored, are confidential.
Further, the codes charge that the therapist shall not disclose any communication, record, or identity of a client except when required under
rules of law or statute. Improper breaches of confidentiality are unethical
and can lead to licensing board disciplinary actions and malpractice
suits. Thus, although records are mandated under the mental health
codes, these records are represented to the client as being confidential
and not available to the curious eyes of meddling others. They are, in a
sense, sacrosanct. But there are exceptions to confidentiality and under
the ethics canons, the client has a right to be informed concerning the
exceptions to confidentiality.

One concept is clear: although reporting statutes provide for reporting such offenses as child abuse, the therapist is vulnerable if he or she
recklessly disregards the confidentiality of the clients who have placed
their trust in a professional relationship. There is zero tolerance for the
gossipy provider, the chatty clinician, or the talkative therapist who reveals too much confidential information to the wrong person or people.
The exceptions often apply to the judicial system. They do not ever give
license to the clinician to reveal confidences in an inappropriate context
or setting. Such is grounds for disciplinary action.

The professional cannot gossip, identify a client in a verbal conversation, or use an identifiable client in a talk as an illustration of a point, or
in a written work or electronic presentation When mandated, the wall
surrounding confidentiality seems to crumble, however. Confidentiality
may be compromised in cases of child abuse or elder abuse, in response to
a lawfully issued subpoena, when mental health is a concern in litigation,
when the client sues a therapist, when a judge orders a therapist to testify
under penalty of contempt of court, or when a therapist sues a client (ill-
advised) for an unpaid bill. Confidentiality may also be compromised
when a therapist is called to determine credibility of a witness in court.

Although state and federal rules differ, a therapist cannot represent to
a client that the record is absolutely sacred and the contents of a record or
the therapeutic session that created the record or that produced the
record, will never be disclosed. Ethically, then, what is confidentiality and
what are the limitations? The broad concepts are set out in the various
guidelines. The exceptions usually arise when the therapist is involved in a

judicial system that is seeking the truth. This quest sometimes affects the therapist's ability to protect the client from disclosure.

A review of the ethical standards of the mental health organizations indicates that each organization seeks to protect clients from the disclosure of their personal remarks, thoughts, histories, and inner feelings as well as the records made of all these therapeutic moments. The codes differ in verbiage but are nearly identical in their philosophy of client protection. Some are more comprehensive than others, but all are remarkably consistent.

4

Discrimination

Katherine is a "right to life" supporter, both politically and religiously. She belongs to a church that regularly pickets abortion clinics and has regularly participated in such protests. She does not condone violence against physicians or abortion clinic employees, but she does support her right to exercise free speech. Her views did not change when she attended graduate school nor when she received her graduate degree in social work. She is now employed at an agency that offers general counseling to any woman who walks in the door. All women are entitled to a reduced fee scale in what is considered to be a clinically objective atmosphere. One day a woman (who is 4 weeks pregnant) comes in for abortion counseling. Her mind is not made up. She wants to consider the ramifications of all her options rather than feel pressured to select a particular alternative. Katherine is not married. The client is not married. Can Katherine have a definite point of view and still be clinically objective?

Katherine and the woman like each other and enjoy the therapy session. All the options are presented. A few days later the woman seeks additional counseling at the local abortion clinic. Katherine is outside with a picket sign. They exchange glances, but do not speak. After seeing Katherine picketing at the abortion clinic, will her client ever feel the abortion options were presented objectively?

~

Dr. Stevens is a heterosexual therapist in private practice. Her practice has been limited to couples contemplating divorce, and she has a fine community reputation for reconciling couples in troubled marriages. On the third visit, John, a married client, asks whether he can bring in a friend. Dr. Stevens reluctantly says "yes" and John appears for the next session with Billy Bob, his significant other. Dr. Stevens has had no experience with gay clients and is very uncomfortable as the two men sit in her office holding hands. However, she is convinced John needs therapy to help with his marriage and with a plethora of newly discovered other problems. As the session continues, her discomfort grows. What should Dr. Stevens do next?

⌒

Martha works for an agency where she deals with adults and teens. A change of administration indicates she must now handle preadolescent children. She is a single woman, does not like being around young children, and underwent sterilization to void the risk of ever having a child. At first, she makes deals with other therapists to handle her "child" case load. Finally she faces the facts. Much to her chagrin her new job description mandates that she must work with children. Considering her attitude toward children, can she handle her growing case load of 5- to 10-year-olds? Will she discriminate without intending to be prejudicial?

⌒

Judy is a card-carrying New York Republican of the young George Bush variety. Her client is an enthusiastic Democrat, but that does not seem to make any difference to either of them. The therapy is effective and competent. Her client, Bill, knows Judy's political leanings by seeing her picture in the news, but he brushes it off. One day, after a session, Judy sees Bill walk slowly by her car and stop for a moment when he goes by the front and the rear. She thinks little of it until she heads to the parking lot at the end of the day. There, on both bumpers appears a huge political sticker: "HILLARY RODHAM CLINTON FOR SENATOR, THE PEOPLE'S CHOICE." How should Judy react during the next session? Or, should she react at all? Can Judy continue to treat this client without regard to the fact that he is a Democrat?

⌒

Melissa comes from a dysfunctional family where her father and mother were alcoholics. She hates liquor and married a man who never touches alcohol. The thought, sight, or smell of any liquor makes her ill. When she enrolled in graduate school, she resolved to take any other type case, but not addictions of any classification, including drugs, smoking, or drinking. Recently, her husband, an engineer, was transferred to a new community. The only therapy position available is treating the high-risk alcoholic population. She and her husband need a second income. Should Melissa apply for the job?

Overt versus Subtle Discrimination

Whether a client is old or young, in robust health or infirm, the client is entitled to competent therapy. Whether a client is a man or woman, gay

Age, race, gender, color, national origin, religion, disability, sexual orientation, or political affiliation should never influence the availability or quality of therapy.

or straight, the client is entitled to competent therapy. Color, race, nationality, or country of origin should not in any way affect the availability of competent therapy. Physically and emotionally challenged individuals are also entitled to mental health counseling and treatment. Democrats, republicans, communists, socialists, Buddhists, Hindus, and all types of affiliated and unaffiliated individuals are entitled to treatment regardless of the label they carry. Age, race, gender, color, national origin, religion, disability, sexual orientation, or political affiliation should never influence the availability or quality of therapy. The right to such treatment is codified in the canons of ethics, and practitioners are subject to disciplinary action if they ignore their profession's ethical canons and exhibit discrimination in any form.

Discrimination in any form is unethical.

The guidelines are clear. Discrimination in any form is unethical. Yet calling someone a "racist" seems to be common when a disagreement rises to the surface. Discrimination is a subtle problem, for *although discrimination exists in the mind of the person who feels discriminated against, it does not necessarily exist in the mind of the person accused.* Therapists must strive for objectivity and fairness with all clients and be particularly sensitive to issues of discrimination to avoid problems.

National Guidelines Regarding Discrimination

Ethical Standards for School Counselors: ASCA

E2.   Multicultural Skills

The professional school counselor:

> understands the diverse cultural backgrounds of the counselees with whom he/she works. This includes, but is not limited to, learning how the school counselor's own cultural/ethnic/racial identity impacts his/her values and beliefs about the counseling process.

NASW Code of Ethics

4.02 Discrimination

Social workers should not practice, condone, facilitate, or collaborate with any form of discrimination on the basis of race, ethnicity, national origin, color, sex, sexual orientation, age, marital status, political belief, religion, or mental or physical disability.

4.03 Private Conduct

Social workers should not permit their private conduct to interfere with their ability to fulfill their professional responsibilities.

ACA *Code of Ethics and Standards of Practice*

C.5. Public Responsibility

a. Nondiscrimination.

Counselors do not discriminate against clients, students, or supervisees in a manner that has a negative impact based on their age, color, culture, disability, ethnic group, gender, race, religion, sexual orientation, or socioeconomic status, or for any other reason. (See A.2.a.)

b. Sexual Harassment.

Counselors do not engage in sexual harassment. Sexual harassment is defined as sexual solicitation, physical advances, or verbal or nonverbal conduct that is sexual in nature, that occurs in connection with professional activities or roles, and that either (1) is unwelcome, is offensive, or creates a hostile workplace environment, and counselors know or are told this; or (2) is sufficiently severe or intense to be perceived as harassment to a reasonable person in the context. Sexual harassment can consist of a single intense or severe act or multiple persistent or pervasive acts.

APA *Ethical Principles of Psychologists and Code of Conduct*

1.10 Nondiscrimination.

In their work related activities, psychologists do not engage in unfair discrimination based on age, gender, race, ethnicity, national origin, religion, sexual orientation, disability, socioeconomic status, or any basis proscribed by law.

AAMFT *Code of Ethics*

1.1 Marriage and Family therapists do not discriminate against or refuse professional service to anyone on the basis of race, gender, religion, national origin or sexual orientation.

General Guidelines for Avoiding Discrimination

All the mental health professions have clear guidelines. People who seek help from clinicians are entitled to assistance regardless of their background, and they are entitled to competent treatment free from prejudice. The consuming public must obtain the services needed with clinical objectivity free from discrimination. The public is also sensitive to discrimination—more sensitive, perhaps, than the provider—for in many cases the recipient has lived with discrimination for years and has an antenna that picks up on bigotry, intolerance, or narrow-mindedness of any type. The client is a reactive victim. Therapists therefore must be sensitive to their own feelings as well as their clients' feelings. A chance remark, mildly inappropriate under other circumstances, can produce a tornado of reaction among sensitive clients. Whenever a hint of discrimination appears, overt or subtle, internal or external, it is to be eliminated at once. The therapist might require therapy or sensitivity training. If a bias is acted on, and if it interferes with any part of the therapy, it violates the ethical codes of the state licensing regulations as well as the antidiscrimination clauses of national organizations. Therapeutic objectivity as well as common sense precludes discrimination of any type.

Therapeutic objectivity as well as common sense precludes discrimination of any type.

When Discrimination Interferes with Responsible Practice

Sometimes providers are concerned about treating clients from a religious or cultural orientation completely foreign to them. The professional might believe that the client may misunderstand or misinterpret aspects of treatment, or the professional might feel incapable of understanding the client's background or point of view adequately enough to provide helpful therapy. Should the therapist provide therapy anyway or make a referral to another provider? Suppose the provider's political or religious orientation cannot be reconciled with the client's position on abortion, birth control, homosexuality, alcoholic beverages, or political leanings. The list of possible biases and prejudices is too numerous to mention. Can the provider offer therapeutically appropriate services? Each provider, within his or her own frame of reference, must make this decision and document the rationale for the determination.

There is a delicate balancing of forces between discrimination and exceeding one's level of competence and objectivity. The friction must be recognized, considered, pondered, and then handled in an ethical manner. Treating a client from a background completely unknown to the therapist is difficult. If the therapist is unable to understand the client's particular orientation, it would not be discriminatory to make a referral to a provider who can. Nevertheless, it is important to document all aspects of the decision to refer the client elsewhere. Recognizing one's limitations concerning objectivity is not unethical but it must be handled appropriately within the guidelines of the profession.

If the therapist is unable to understand the client's particular orientation, it would not be discriminatory to make a referral to a provider who can.

Ethical Flash Points

- Discrimination of any type is a violation of all ethical canons and codes.
- Discrimination comes in many forms. The clinician must be sensitive to his or her own feelings and instincts and work to eliminate any feelings that are negative to any specific person or class.
- Equal services are to be provided to all consumers of mental health services.
- If there is ever a hint, an accusation, or an intimation of discrimination, the problem is to be handled at once.
- Discrimination complaints have a habit of becoming media events, political footballs, and public affairs. When the suggestion appears, the situation must immediately be sensitively handled.
- A mental health professional assigned to a geographic area, or to an agency that deals with the public at large, cannot insist on serving only a limited population in that area because of bias or prejudice.
- Sometimes, we all have to look in the emotional mirror and see where our feelings take root. Then we have to control those that in any way hinder an open mind or clinical abilities.
- Do not *ever* disregard or minimize a discrimination complaint. It can be the professional's undoing.

Summary

A mental health services provider shall not refuse to perform any act or service for which the person is licensed or qualified solely on the basis of a client's age, gender, race, color, religion, national origin, ethnicity, disability, sexual orientation, or political affiliation. To refuse to provide effective treatment or services to any of these, or perhaps other, identifiable groups is unethical. And remember, each of the group members in these identifiable groups is sensitive and aware of their right to treatment and to the various laws, codes, rules and regulations which protect them. If they are not aware today, they become aware quickly when a problem arises. Lawyers, other clinicians, the boards, the literature, and other friends within a common interest group will educate unhappy clients quickly.

A complication arises when the client has a religious or national orientation which is completely foreign or unknown to the provider, and the professional feels that if services are granted the client or the provider will be misunderstood. Or, suppose the historic and powerful religious orientation of the provider has irreconcilable differences with the client in the area of abortion, birth control, homosexuality, liquor or alcoholic beverages of any type or even anticommunism, and so on. The list of possible biases and prejudices is too numerous to mention here. Can the provider offer therapeutically appropriate services? Each provider, within his or her own frame of reference, must make this decision. And document the rationale for the determination.

There is a delicate balancing of forces between exceeding one's level of competence and objectivity and discrimination. The friction must be recognized, considered, pondered, and then handled in an ethical manner. Treating a client whose orientation is so esoteric as to be misunderstood is difficult. Some backgrounds are hard to clinically fathom and are beyond the capacity of the therapist to understand. Making a referral in a case such as this would not be discrimination. It would be good sense if properly documented.

Caveat

Discrimination is unethical.

Recognizing one's limitations concerning objectivity is not unethical. However it must be handled appropriately within the guidelines of the profession.

5

False and Misleading Statements

Sam's first love was engineering, and he pursued and received a Ph.D. at the Colorado School of Mines. After 20 years in the field, he was downsized and later obtained a master's degree in counseling. He is now in private practice. His counseling business card and other office promotional material do not indicate his Ph.D., as he knows that would be conspicuously misleading and prohibited, but one evening while being introduced at a church forum to talk about "blended families," he was praised as "Dr. Sam Johnson, the eminent local counselor," with a profound expertise regarding second marriages. Is Sam obligated to explain that the degree that entitles him to be called "Dr." was in engineering?

~

One day, while walking down the street with a friend and colleague, Susan, a social worker, was approached by an effusive former client. This client enthusiastically blurted out with hardly a pause how, following therapy with Susan, her life had changed, her health had improved, and how Susan was the most marvelous therapist in the world. Susan sought some moderation in the monologue, but the praise continued until the former client rushed away to an appointment. Does Susan have an obligation to "set the record straight" with her friend and colleague, and can she do so without revealing confidential information about the client?

~

On his resume, used for introductions at lectures, Dr. Smith indicates he teaches at the state university. That is true. He teaches one course each year (3 hours) for one semester. At a recent seminar, the person introducing him refers to him as a practitioner in private practice and as a "professor at the state university." Does such an introduction mandate clarification? Would this be a false and misleading statement? Is it misleading without being unethical? Suppose an adjunct professor is introduced as "professor," or an assistant professor is introduced as "professor." At what point does a harmless error or an exaggeration become an ethical disaster? Remember that any jealous colleague sitting in the audience can file a complaint, and some boards accept anonymous complaints.

Responding to Exaggerated Claims

There is always a tendency for the satisfied client to speak well of the therapist, and such endorsements are appropriate and professional.

Therapists should not make any false, misleading, fraudulent, or exaggerated claims or statements and should discourage clients from holding overstated or inaccurate ideas about professional services. There is always a tendency for the satisfied client to speak well of the therapist, and such endorsements are appropriate and professional. In fact, private practices depend on the good words of satisfied clients.

Occasionally the practitioner will hear through the grapevine or from a new client that a former client has made statements about the competence, credentials, experience, or even success of the therapist that the therapist knows to be untrue or so exaggerated as to be misleading. In such cases, the therapist is obligated to correct the record. That is, the therapist is obligated to review what was said and put it in a correct perspective.

The therapist is obligated to review what was said and put it in a correct perspective.

Three social workers, two professional counselors, and three psychologists formed a group to market and practice together because they realized the benefits of size: that praising another was easier than self-praise and that sharing experience, expertise, and expenses would be valuable. They also realized the importance of hiring a professional marketer. A week later when the marketer presented the preliminary plan, they found it completely unacceptable. Each of the eight professionals had forgotten the same thing. They had neglected to give the marketer all the applicable advertising and promotional rules and regulations relating to each profession, with the admonition that any plan advanced would have to comply with every applicable state and national guideline and standard of the discipline of each and every participant. Once the guidelines were assembled, a workable marketing plan was easily generated.

~

A therapist took a lawyer to lunch and casually asked the lawyer to look over her most recent promotional literature from the advertising agency. It contained the following phrases: "guaranteed results . . ." and "if you visit me, we will establish a relationship, and I will always be here for you if needed." The lawyer was appalled. No therapist can guarantee results, and should not claim to be able to do so in promotional literature. Likewise, no therapist can represent to a client that she will "always" be there for the client. Consider what would happen if the therapist had to relocate when her husband's promotion took him to a new city.

Advertising

In general, providers may advertise so long as they "accurately represent their competence, education, training, and experience relevant to their practice . . ." Also, they must assure that advertisements and publications in any media (such as directories, announcements, business cards, newspapers, radio, television, and facsimiles) convey information that is necessary for the public to make an appropriate selection of professional services.

In this competitive era, the mental health professional may seek professional help when preparing a logo, letterhead, brochures and other advertising materials. The advertising agency may be familiar with the products the provider desires, but may not be aware of the ethical issues surrounding responsible advertising of mental health services. For example, an ad agency may be tempted to market the provider as a product, using inappropriate adjectives, solicited testimonials, or success stories that may be perfectly acceptable when selling cars, boats, or breakfast cereals but unacceptable when marketing mental health services. Keep in mind that the person punished for false advertising is the professional, not the advertising executive.

When hiring an outside agency for advertising or public relations services, mental health agencies should provide:

The advertising agency may be familiar with the products the provider desires, but may not be aware of the ethical issues surrounding responsible advertising of mental health services.

- A copy of the state standards or board rules concerning advertising.

- A copy of the standards concerning advertising of every state and national organization to which the provider belongs.

- An understanding that the provider may face serious consequences if advertising and promotional enthusiasm exceed acceptable standards.

Selecting a Name

There are limits when using a business name that could mislead the public. Advertising may not include a statement or claim that is false, fraudulent, misleading, or deceptive. In addition, therapists must "correct, wherever possible, false, misleading, or inaccurate information and representations made by others concerning the therapist's qualifications, services, or products" (AAMFT Code of Ethics, Sec. 8.5). The mental health professions must all conform to their recognized and accepted standards for accurate representation of their practice and credentials.

Advertising may not include a statement or claim that is false, fraudulent, misleading, or deceptive.

National Guidelines Regarding Advertising

The ACA (C.3.a. Accurate Advertising) and AAMFT (AAMFT Code of Ethics, Sec. 8) have published excellent guidelines concerning advertising that includes information about accurate advertising, testimonials, statements by others, recruitment through employment, products and training advertisements, promoting to those served, and professional association involvement.

The state of Texas Licensing Act for professional counselors publishes helpful guidelines concerning advertising and announcements to guide the ethical professional in developing sound promotional material. The highlights include:

- Can't be false, inaccurate, misleading, incomplete, out of context, deceptive, or not readily verifiable.

- Can't create unjustified expectations about the results of a health-care service or procedure.

- Can't cause confusion or misunderstanding as to the credentials, education, or licensure of a health-care professional.

- Must be careful about the waiving of insurance deductibles.

- Can't make a representation that is designed to take advantage of the fears or emotions of a particularly susceptible patient.

- Can't confuse titles.

- A licensee who retains or hires others to advertise or promote the licensee's practice remains responsible for the statements and representations made.

Dr. Smiley, a clinical psychologist, was between patients when a call came in from a local newsperson. The reporter asked him about his time in practice, credentials, education, and publications and then asked a seemingly innocent question about the "mess" (the reporter's word) in the housing of mental health patients. Taken off guard but somewhat flattered by press attention, Dr. Smiley uttered a few innocuous (in his opinion) remarks and in a short time ended the interview. A few days later, his entire biography was published in an interview that implied that Dr. Smiley agreed there was a "mess" in the housing of mental health patients. Indirectly, the published interview implied that Dr. Smiley used the word "mess."

The Media

As long as the information concerning biographical information given to the reporter is factual and not misleading, there is no inherent problem in dealing with reporters or the press in general. Mental health professionals who are contacted by the media need to keep in mind that the reason for the interview is to get information to sell newspapers or magazines. Once information is shared with the press, control over its use is in the hands of the reporter and the editor. Mental health professionals are permitted and even encouraged to speak with the press. But an interview can be cast in a context that is misleading and, in some cases, downright false.

Before granting an interview, seek and obtain information concerning its purpose. Then speak gingerly. Being quoted out of context may cause irreparable harm. If the reporter writes a flowery, but exaggerated and possibly misleading, description of you and your services, at the minimum call and inform the reporter of the facts and make a note of the call in case some person reading the article accuses you of inappropriate self-promotion.

Before granting an interview, seek and obtain information concerning its purpose. Then speak gingerly.

Ethical Flash Points

- One can have a legitimate credential, but if it cannot be applied to the practice of mental health, it cannot be used.

- Therapists have an affirmative duty to correct false and misleading statements made about them.

- When determining guidelines for advertising and promotion, the practitioner is bound by the licensing law (more than one if there is more than one license) and the advertising ethical canons of every organization to which the professional belongs.

- If using a professional marketer, furnish the marketer with all applicable guidelines.

- Be careful that resumes are accurate.

- When creating an assumed name for business purposes, make sure it is not false or deceptive.

- Guidelines are constantly changing; keep your information up to date.

- When two or more professionals of different disciplines join in a professional venture, the codes of all must be respected.

- Remember—the buck stops with the professional.

Summary

It is the obligation of the professional whether the situation concerns advertising, a simple introduction, or a public announcement to guarantee that the announcement is true and correct, not false and misleading.

The canons of ethics control advertisements, introductions, what we say, and what is said about us. It is the obligation of the professional whether the situation concerns advertising, a simple introduction, or a public announcement to guarantee that the announcement is true and correct, not false and misleading. When we hire another person to promote us, we face the same obligation. The professional has the ultimate obligation to see that the final promotional product conforms to *all* ethical standards. Begin with the standards in this book, then continue with your personal affiliations and determine the allowable, permissible, and prohibited. Use only ethically approved promotional materials.

6

Informed Consent

Dr. Kindheart, a licensed professional counselor, greets a potential new client, Harold, in his office late Friday afternoon at the end of a very slow week. Harold, in the midst of an affair, is concerned about confidentiality. When he asks Dr. Kindheart if their therapy sessions will be kept confidential, Dr. Kindheart responds, "Absolutely." Three months later, Harold is walking out of Dr. Kindheart's office when he is served with divorce papers. At the same time, Dr. Kindheart is served with a subpoena to appear at a temporary hearing to testify and produce Harold's records. Does Harold have anything to be concerned about? How about Dr. Kindheart? Is confidentiality ever absolute?

~

Carol, under the influence of alcohol and amphetamines, comes in for therapy at a local counseling center. A nonlicensed staff worker conducts the intake session and has Carol sign the center's standard consent for therapy form. She then ushers Carol into the office of one of the center's five therapists. After talking with the therapist for 2 hours, Carol leaves the center without paying for services. On receiving a bill from the counseling center, Carol tells them she is not going to pay. Can the counseling center confidently pursue collection action for payment? What happens when Carol argues that she was too upset and did not have the capacity to consent at the time she presented herself at the counseling center?

~

A concerned, noncustodial father, during an extended visitation period, takes his daughter to see a psychologist experienced in sexual abuse cases after the girl complains about her stepfather giving her baths when her mother is not at home. He completes the psychologist's intake forms and gives consent for evaluation and treatment if necessary. When the girl's mother finds out that her daughter is seeing a therapist, she angrily contacts the psychologist and faxes a copy of the relevant pages from the divorce decree giving her the exclusive right to consent to mental health care and treatment for the child absent an emergency. An emergency is defined as a serious and immediate threat to the health, safety, or welfare of the child. She asserts that the psychologist wrongfully provided mental health services and threatens to file an ethical complaint with the state licensing board and to sue for malpractice if her daughter is emotionally harmed by the sessions with the psychologist. In this case, what is considered appropriate informed consent? Can the noncustodial parent legally consent to treatment of a minor child during visitation periods?

Why "Informed" Is Important

Informed consent is a prerequisite to the commencement of the therapeutic relationship.

Informed consent is a prerequisite to the commencement of the therapeutic relationship. Virtually every mental health profession's ethics code contains provisions requiring therapists to secure potential clients' informed consent before providing any mental health services. Licensing boards are particularly interested in making sure that clients are thoroughly informed on important matters before consenting to therapy. This is understandable when one realizes that consumer protection is one of the primary reasons behind the establishment and continued existence of state licensing boards. Society and the mental health professions desire educated consumers who knowingly and voluntarily consent to mental health care and treatment.

National Guidelines for Informed Consent

NASW Code of Ethics

Section 1.03   Informed Consent

(a) Social workers should provide services to clients only in the context of a professional relationship based, when appropriate, on valid informed consent. Social workers should use clear and understandable language to inform clients of the purpose of the services, risks related to the services, limits to services because of the requirements of a third-party payer, relevant costs, reasonable alternatives, clients' right to refuse or withdraw consent, and the time frame covered by the consent. Social workers should provide clients with an opportunity to ask questions.

APA *Ethical Principles of Psychologists and Code of Conduct*

Section 4.02   Informed Consent to Therapy.

(a) Psychologists obtain appropriate informed consent to therapy or related procedures, using language that is reasonably understandable to participants. The content of informed consent will vary depending on many circumstances; however, informed consent generally implies that the person (1) has the capacity to consent, (2) has been informed of significant information concerning the procedure, (3) has freely and without undue influence expressed consent, and (4) consent has been documented.

ACA *Code of Ethics and Standards of Practice*

Section A.3   Client Rights

a. *Disclosure to Clients.*

When counseling is initiated, and throughout the counseling process as necessary, counselors inform clients of the purposes, goals, techniques, procedures, limitations, potential risks, and benefits of services to be performed, and other pertinent information. Counselors take steps to ensure that clients understand the implications of diagnosis, the intended use of tests and reports, fees, and billing arrangement. Clients have the right to expect confidentiality and to be provided with an explanation of its limitations, including supervision and/or treatment team professionals; to obtain clear information about their case records, to participate in the ongoing counseling plans; and to refuse any recommended services and to be advised of the consequences of such refusal.

What Constitutes Informed Consent?

The meaningful question is not whether informed consent should be obtained but rather what constitutes informed consent. A client has the right to information about many things in order to properly give consent for treatment. The more information the client receives, the less likely there can be an allegation of improper consent. The ramifications of failing to secure informed consent are varied and serious. It is an ethical requirement to secure informed consent as the previously cited provisions indicate, and the therapist who fails to do so is vulnerable (see Chapter 24). Moreover, without informed consent, the client can argue

*The best way to
document
informed consent
is with a detailed
intake and
consent form that
provides in clear
and easily
understood
language the
information
needed to turn a
potential client
into an informed
consumer*

that he or she is not required to keep the client's end of the bargain (i.e.,
pay for services rendered).

The best way to document informed consent is with a detailed intake
and consent form that provides in clear and easily understood language
the information needed to turn a potential client into an informed consumer who can knowingly and intelligently enter into a therapeutic relationship. A signed, detailed intake and consent form, of which the client
is given a copy, ensures there will be little controversy regarding the information provided to the client and the client's consent to treatment.
This form constitutes written evidence of the client's consent to services
and becomes part of the client's permanent file. The client will have a
difficult time convincing a judge, jury, or licensing board that he or she
was not adequately informed before consenting to therapy when confronted with his or her signed, detailed intake and consent form.

*Note. The Portable Lawyer (Bernstein & Hartsell, Wiley 1998) contains
useful forms for the mental health professional including client forms
(pp. 23 & 42); consent forms (pp. 11, 13, 75, 76, & 212); waiver forms
(pp. 46 & 57); and miscellaneous forms (pp. 67, 174, & 215).*

Constructing an Informed Consent Form

Ethics codes provide direction for creating an intake and consent form
that properly documents informed consent. The form should include at a
minimum the following information:

- Information regarding the therapist and other professional or staff
  members who will be involved in the client's care and treatment, including their educational backgrounds, licensing, training, and experience. If a professional under supervision or on probation by a
  licensing board will participate in the delivery of services, this should
  be disclosed. Any relationship to an entity (i.e., independent contractor, provider to ABC Managed Care Company, employee of XYZ
  Counseling Center) should be set out. A client has a right to know
  and to choose the provider of his or her mental health services.

- Fees for services, including session rates, copays, charges for phone contacts, missed appointments, cancellations, responding to subpoenas and
  request for records, testing, report writing, and late payment fees should
  be specifically stated. A client should be advised that although third-
  party payers may be expected to make payment, the client is ultimately

responsible in the event payment is refused by a third party. (*Note. A managed care provider contract may prohibit the charging of any fee to the client except a copay so careful reading of all provider contracts and the tailoring of intake and consent form provisions is critical.*)

- Confidentiality and its limitations should be outlined. The client must be informed of exceptions that limit the client's right to confidentiality and the therapist's duty to warn. The legal exceptions to confidentiality should be listed including child abuse, elder abuse, abuse of the physically or mentally disabled, child custody cases, any case in which the mental or emotional health of a party is in issue, sexual exploitation by a mental health professional, criminal cases, fee disputes, malpractice actions, licensing board cases, and imminent physical or emotional danger of the client or a third party (see Chapter 22, for specific information). Disclosure of client information is not required by law in other instances but is necessary in connection with the client's care and treatment (i.e., submitting information to third-party payers, providing services when the therapist is under supervision, staff meetings and consultations with other professionals). Specific consent for disclosure under these circumstance should be obtained in the intake and consent form or in a subsequent consent form.

  Confidentiality and its limitations should be outlined.

- Clients should be advised of when and how the therapist or the therapist's office might contact them and consent to being contacted in a specified manner and at specific locations and phone numbers, fax numbers, or e-mail.

- The client has the right to be a knowledgeable participant in his or her therapy. The initial goals, purposes, and techniques of therapy should be listed. Any subsequent changes should be documented and signed by the client.

  The client has the right to be a knowledgeable participant in his or her therapy.

- All available alternative treatments should be disclosed along with information on the relative risks, benefits, and costs, together with the risk of refusing treatment.

- Confidentiality survives the death or incompetence of the therapist as well as the client. A therapist is under an obligation to provide for these contingencies in advance of therapy. For example, the APA Ethical Principles of Psychologists and Code of Conduct states:

Section 4.08 Interruption of Services

(a) Psychologists make reasonable efforts to plan for facilitating care in the event that psychological services are interrupted by factors such as the psychologist's illness, death, unavailability, or relocation or by the client's relocation or financial limitation.

- It is unethical for a therapist to become involved in a dual relationship with the client, but the client can violate boundaries with impunity. The client should be advised that boundary violations by either the therapist or the client must be avoided or the therapeutic relationship will be jeopardized. The client should be warned that gift giving, social interaction, and personal or business relationships cannot occur. The form should further state that should the client attempt to draw the therapist into a dual relationship or boundary violation, termination of the therapy and referral to another provider will be the probable result.

- The client should be informed about all testing—the nature and purpose of each test, as well as the identities and credentials of each person involved in the testing process. Consent to the testing and the involvement of all participants in the testing process should be procured.

- Special circumstances require special disclosure, information, and consent. For example, often a therapist will wish to video- or audiotape a session with a client for self-protection such as with a flirtatious client or one prone to ignoring competent advice. The AAMFT Code of Ethics states,

  Section 1.8 Marriage and family therapists obtain written informed consent from clients before videotaping, audio taping, or permitting third party observation.

- Therapy involves risks. Legal disclosure of confidential information in a client's file is just one. Clients may learn about facts or feelings, or come to realize traits about themselves that they didn't want to admit or face. Clients should be advised of the risk. Nontraditional therapies such as animal therapy involve special and unique risks that the client should be warned about as part of informed consent. There are also risks when services are provided via electronic media (i.e., computer and telephone) that should be discussed and disclosed.

The client can never receive too much information where informed consent is concerned.

This is by no means an exhaustive attempt to list all matters that should be discussed and disclosed to potential clients to ensure that informed consent is secured prior to beginning the therapeutic relationship. Nevertheless, it is representative of the minimal information required by the various ethics codes. The client can never receive too much information where informed consent is concerned. The greater the amount of information disseminated to a potential client, the less chance that the client will be able to establish lack of informed consent in the future.

Who Provides Informed Consent?

Consent is useless if it is not obtained from a person with the capacity to consent or the authority to consent for another individual. A person under the influence of alcohol or drugs or a person with diminished mental capacity regardless of cause does not have the mental capacity to give informed consent to treatment. If a person presents himself or herself for therapy while under the influence of alcohol or drugs, informed consent should not be attempted until such time as the person is clearly sober.

If informed consent is not possible because of a person's diminished mental capacity, a therapist should determine if the individual has a legal guardian or someone acting under a lawful power of attorney who can provide informed consent. If there is no legal guardian, the therapist should decline to provide mental care or treatment until one is appointed.

It is not enough to accept the word of the court-appointed guardian. A careful approach requires the therapist to request a copy of the guardian's letter of authority from the court or a copy of the court order appointing the guardian. On receipt, the document should be reviewed to be sure there are no limitations to the guardian's authority to consent for mental health care or treatment. If there is any doubt, a lawyer should be consulted and therapy postponed until such time as the therapist is convinced of the guardian's legal authority to offer consent. Even when clients suffer from diminished mental capacity, mental health professionals should inform them as fully as possible, taking into account the clients' ability to comprehend.

If informed consent is not possible because of a person's diminished mental capacity, a therapist should determine if the individual has a legal guardian or someone acting under a lawful power of attorney who can provide informed consent.

National Guidelines for Obtaining Informed Consent

APA Ethical Principles of Psychologists and Code of Conduct

Section 4.02   Informed Consent to Therapy.

(b) When persons are legally incapable of giving informed consent, psychologists obtain informed permission from a legally authorized person, if such substitute consent is permitted by law.

NASW Code of Ethics

Section 1.03   Informed Consent

(c) In instances when clients lack the capacity to provide informed consent, social workers should protect clients' interests by seeking permission from an appropriate third party, informing clients consistent with the client's level of understanding. In such instances social workers should seek to ensure that the third party acts in a manner consistent with the client's wishes and interests. Social workers should take reasonable steps to enhance such client's ability to give informed consent.

Obtaining Informed Consent in Cases of Joint Custody

In today's environment where parents enjoy joint custody of their children, it is increasingly difficult for mental health professionals to determine which parent, or whether each parent, has the right to consent to mental health care or treatment for a minor child. Usually a minor child is defined as a child under 18 and unmarried. In some states, children are considered adults for purposes of consenting to mental health treatment when they marry or when they are emancipated or have their disabilities of minority removed.

Consent in writing given by the wrong person or by a person without legal authority, is no consent at all.

As with adult mentally incompetent clients, therapists should insist on reviewing a copy of the most recent custody order if the parents are not married to each other and living together before consenting to treat a child. Therapists should keep a copy of the relevant provisions of the custody decree in the child's file. Again, if there is uncertainty, providers should consult their lawyer before providing services. *Consent in writing given by the wrong person or by a person without legal authority, is no consent at all. Consent for treatment of a minor or an incompetent must be authorized by a legally appointed person.*

Obtaining Informed Consent from Minors

In most states, minors can consent to mental health care or treatment in limited circumstances such as suicide prevention, chemical dependency, and abuse. Therapists working with minors should familiarize themselves with the statutes in their state to be sure they can rely on the informed consent of the minor. When obtaining the minor's informed consent, special care must be given to explaining all the information in terms that the minor can understand.

Summary

In summary, informed consent is an ethical precondition to the provision of mental health services. The failure to procure informed consent subjects the practitioner to ethics complaints and malpractice actions. Without it, the client's obligation to pay for services is impacted. Informed consent must be obtained from the client or a person legally authorized to consent for the client.

When obtaining the minor's informed consent, special care must be given to explaining all the information in terms that the minor can understand.

Ethical Flash Points

- Ethics statutes require mental health professionals to secure informed consent from each client before providing services.

- Ethics codes provide the minimum amount of information that must be disclosed and discussed with a client in order to establish informed consent.

- Unique treatment methods involve special risks that must be adequately and specifically disclosed. Such methods must be supported by a majority of clinicians or by a learned minority. Before embarking on cutting-edge therapy, assemble a research file to support the methodology.

- Informed consent must be documented. The best way to document informed consent is with a detailed intake and consent form signed by the client.

- Copies of letters of authority, guardianship orders, general and limited power of attorney, and custody orders should be obtained and reviewed with legal consultation if necessary. Only then can you rely on the informed consent of a third party. A legal document file must be maintained for each client where applicable.

7

Interviewing

Dr. Sweet has practiced for 10 years using traditional "talk" therapy methods. After filling out a mental health history form and a detailed, lawyer-drafted, consent to treatment form, clients enter his office and therapy begins. His office is on the outskirts of town near a freeway with relatively easy parking and is convenient to most individuals who seek his services. One day, a new client announces, at her first interview, that coming to Dr. Sweet's office is not cost-effective for her. In fact, she implies that one-on-one therapy is a relic of the dark ages. It is a pain and a nuisance. In her firm, almost all communication is electronic and she wonders why therapy should be different. She is the CEO of a major company and to visit Dr. Sweet for an hour really means an afternoon out of the office when she factors in travel time and waiting at Dr. Sweet's office for her appointment. If she sees Dr. Sweet one hour (50 minutes) each week, she is actually losing two days of productivity every month, since every visit takes one-half day of productive time. She tells Dr. Sweet that her time is worth more than he charges, and time out of the office is money lost and never regained. She proposes five alternatives:

1. *Now that they have met, they could correspond by e-mail when problems arise. She can ask her questions and make her comments at her leisure and convenience and Dr. Sweet can respond at his convenience.*

2. *They could continue therapy with regularly scheduled e-mail conferences. At the appointed time, each would log on and carry on a conversation and exchange reactions via instant message and the keyboard.*

3. *Each could install a device that permits telephone type communication with a picture on the computer screen. The result would be like a personal interview only the words would be transmitted electronically while her picture appears on the screen.*

4. *They could communicate by fax. She will write out the thoughts she has and he will fill in the blanks and respond. They can fax to each other through a secure line that guarantees the confidentiality of the exchange.*

5. *They could continue therapy by telephone. Since both have cell phones, the therapy can continue while he is home with his children and she is in her automobile, boat, or backyard relaxing by the pool.*

~

Lucille has been confined to a wheelchair since birth. This challenging situation has not impeded her scholarship and this spring she will receive her master's degree. Lucille is seeking on-line therapy since she finds mobility difficult. Finally she locates a therapist who is willing to treat her using e-mail. The therapist sends Lucille a complete history form and a detailed intake and consent to treatment form that Lucille dutifully completes and returns. The therapy begins, with both Lucille and her therapist corresponding on their AOL accounts. This is a major convenience to them both. Billing is monthly. How might therapy have been different if the therapist could observe the emotion of the moment in addition to the words of the moment? Might the therapeutic modality be different if Lucille participated in one-on-one treatment in addition to e-mail?

We live in an electronic age. In the past, most therapists probably couldn't conceive any acceptable therapy except a personal face-to-face interview. Most would find a telephone session or two acceptable once the therapist–client relationship was established, and such calls would typically be brief and without charge. Certainly the idea of treating clients without meeting them first was not within their comprehension.

Today, however, the mental health professions are trying to determine how and in what manner modern technology is adaptable to fresh, unique, and innovative therapeutic methods using the whole panoply of equipment available.

Traditional Therapy

Traditional mental health services using either "talking therapy" or medication was based on a personal relationship between therapist and client. Sigmund Freud's "statement that his development of the analytic method began with his pioneering analysis of himself" (*Time,* November 29, 1993, p. 49) highlights the personal connection between the therapist and the client. One cannot imagine Freud sending himself a fax, an e-mail, or using some other electronic method when offering therapy to

One cannot imagine Freud sending himself a fax, an e-mail, or using some other electronic method when offering therapy to either himself or a client.

either himself or a client. Nor can one get a mental picture of Freud typing on a laptop while recording notes or providing answers to questions, which are then fed into a computer. Rather we think of patients lounging on a couch chatting away while Freud, pencil in hand, is taking notes and responding.

Advantages of the Face-to-Face Interview

The clinician who interviews the client in person can observe all manner of physical appearances including any disability, nervous habits, body language, and facial and body gestures. Voice changes of volume, pitch, and resonance can also tell the therapist a great deal about the client that can impact the dialogue. In addition, some problems are brought into clearer focus if the therapist knows what the client looks like and how the client reacts to a given question, statement, or inquiry.

Some problems are brought into clearer focus if the therapist knows what the client looks like and how the client reacts to a given question, statement, or inquiry.

Informed consent mandates a certain dialogue between the provider and the client during which, in addition to explaining the intake and consent form, the therapist answers questions concerning fees, goals, and techniques of treatment, limits to confidentiality, whether the therapist will willingly appear in court if needed, and when and how records are available to a client. The interview is important to make certain that the client had ample opportunity to review the forms signed, seek clarification if necessary, and consent personally to the consultation.

National Guidelines Regarding Use of Technology in Therapy

ACA Code of Ethics and Standards of Practice

A.12. Computer Technology

a. Use of Computers.

When computer applications are used in counseling services, counselors ensure that (1) the client is intellectually, emotionally, and physically capable of using the computer application; (2) the computer application is appropriate for the needs of the client; (3) the client understands the purpose and operation of the computer applications; and (4) a follow-up of use of a computer application is provided to correct possible misconceptions, discover inappropriate use, and assess subsequent needs.

b. Explanations of Limitations.

Counselors ensure that clients are provided information as a part of the counseling relationship that adequately explains the limitations of computer technology.

c. Access to Computer Applications.

Counselors provide for equal access to computer applications in counseling services. (See A.2.a.)

APA Ethical Principles of Psychologists and Code of Conduct

4.01   Structuring the Relationship

(a) Psychologists discuss with clients or patients as early as is feasible in the therapeutic relationship appropriate issues, such as the nature and anticipated course of therapy, fees, and confidentiality . . .

(d) Psychologists make reasonable efforts to answer patients' questions and to avoid apparent misunderstandings about therapy . . .

Ethical Standards for School Counselors: ASCA

A10.   Computer Technology

b. Counselors who communicate with counselees via Internet should follow the NBCC Standards for WebCounseling.

Texas State Board of Examiners of Professional Counselors

681.32   General Ethical Requirements

(s) A licensee shall not evaluate any individual's mental, emotional, or behavioral condition unless the licensee has personally interviewed the individual or the licensee discloses with the evaluation that the licensee has NOT personally interviewed the individual.

Risks and Rewards of Technology-Driven Therapy

A blessing of computer-generated therapy is that the client does not have to leave work or comfortable surroundings, drive through traffic-filled streets, and then wait at the therapist's office for the session to begin. Another advantage is that the client can seek advice at the time it is needed or at least when the problem occurs. True, the counseling or therapy may not be available at all convenient times, but neither is that the case for one-on-one therapy. No therapy implies a coordination between crisis events and crisis intervention.

A benefit to both therapist and client is that electronic messages can be printed and a hard copy of each question and answer preserved. This is a two-faced coin. On the one hand, all therapy may be reduced to writing; on the other, some words take on different meanings when placed on the printed page. If humor is utilized in therapy, it may look flat, rude, or inappropriate on paper. Also, voice inflections, timing, hesitations, volume, pitch, and speed of transmission are all lost or compromised when sent by fax or e-mail. For example, a scowl, which might be important for a therapist to observe, would be lost in a fax transmission.

In one-on-one therapy, the therapist can control confidentiality and the security of what is said and discussed. The therapist can also control what is recorded in the clinical record. The restrictions of the law govern what might be required in court, and other rules might govern what happens if a therapist learns of the unethical conduct of another therapist, but in general the therapist has some control over the dissemination and recording of information received in a therapy session. Most cell phones are not secure. Telephone therapy is similar, although the dangers are not so great. Generally either person to a telephone conversation can easily record the call and keep the recording or reduce it to writing. Fax transmission is as secure as a local telephone call, but if the wrong digit is pressed, the unintended recipient is under no legal duty to inform the sender that he or she has received confidential information. In truth, the receiver of a wrongly transmitted letter may tell the world, if there is any feeling that the world is interested.

Emerging Technology and Ethics

The ethical canons do not prohibit the use of computers as such in therapy. Certainly there is no direct general code reference that indicates one-on-one, face-to-face, individual therapy is the only way to offer treatment to a client. However, there are limitations. The therapist must ensure that the client understands the computer application, what it is used for, and its possible effects. Also, if the computer makes an error, the final ethical and professional responsibility is with the provider, who must establish ethical safeguards to see to the reliability and accuracy of the computer technology.

The provider must also accept responsibility for explaining all the ramifications, good and bad, of computer therapy to the client and structure the relationship so that the computer is an acceptable adjunct to interpersonal therapy. The provider has the responsibility to explain to the client all information that clarifies the place, security, and importance of computer use in the therapy. Finally, the provider needs to caution the client that the very nature of therapy implies that treatment will be less effective unless the therapist and client meet in person at some point in the therapeutic relationship. An exception to this is in crisis intervention (e.g., a crisis hot line), but in therapy designed to produce long-term results, a personal visit would be warranted.

The provider has the responsibility to explain to the client all information that clarifies the place, security, and importance of computer use in the therapy.

The Personal Interview in Forensic Consultations

A question also arises about the use of technology and the absence of a personal interview in forensic consultations. The general rule implied in the ethical guidelines is that a therapist shall not testify concerning a person's ability to function, parent, or cope, nor shall a provider evaluate any individual's mental, emotional, or behavioral condition unless the provider has personally interviewed the individual or the provider discloses with the evaluation that the provider has not personally interviewed the individual (for more information, see Chapter 26).

Occasionally, there is a temptation to form opinions based on the input of others such as newspaper reports, magazine articles, information from former spouses or business associates or the children of a marriage without contacting the individual involved and seeking and obtaining a personal interview using commonly accepted therapeutic standards. Nevertheless, professional evaluation, assessment, and appraisal, as well as treatment, diagnosis, and establishing a prognosis require at least one face-to-face interview unless there is a clear documented mental health emergency.

Professional evaluation, assessment, and appraisal, as well as treatment, diagnosis, and establishing a prognosis require at least one face-to-face interview.

Danger lurks around the corner for a therapist who interviews only a former husband (father), stepmother, and child and then testifies that the biological mother is a less suitable parent and the best interest of the child would be served by father and stepmother rearing the child. Even if this is a correct assessment, failing to interview the natural or birth mother is an ethical violation, especially if she is available, ready, willing, and able to be interviewed. To comment on an individual, that person must be personally interviewed. Despite reviewing any of a number of psychological tests,

===== *Ethical Flash Points* =====

- Don't worry. Mental health professionals will not be replaced by computers.
- Computers are like any other therapy tool or technique. They must be explained to the client and their use, function, reliability, and position in the scheme of therapy clearly understood.
- Informed consent includes consenting to the use of computers and other types of electronic communications.
- Don't assume the client understands computer use and application. Insert in your intake and consent form some protective language that indicates the client understands the use and function of computers in the therapeutic framework.
- Computer disks, records, printouts, and, perhaps, even hard drives can be subpoenaed into court.
- "Delete" on a computer, does not always mean "delete." The words are in computer heaven somewhere and a clever hacker can locate and retrieve them.
- Therapy has a long history in which conversation was the prime focus. When using computers, tests, or test results, or having the client answer questions on a computer screen, make sure the technique is fitting for this particular client at this time. Make sure you have assembled the literature so that either a majority of practitioners or a learned minority supports the technique used. If the technological process is challenged as being too novel, the therapist is the person who must defend its use.
- Therapists who use modern technology to increase their cash flow or bottom line are cautioned to ensure that the technology being used is appropriate for the type of treatment.
- Check licensing laws when the client resides or receives information in another jurisdiction. Is your license to practice valid in the recipient's locale, or are you practicing in another state without a license? *Get legal and ethical clearance before crossing state lines.*
- Therapists are required to keep current with the latest treatment techniques. If an approach is known, available, and *unused,* the therapist is involved in an unethical practice.
- In many cases, the provider is disciplined for failing to do something that might have been done (an act of omission) rather than for doing something that was wrong (i.e., an act of commission).
- Any therapist who testifies concerning a client who has not been personally interviewed is skating on very thin ethical ice.
- Complaints will be filed for unethical conduct if an individual loses a court case based on computer-generated opinions stated in court and sworn to from the witness stand. The party who lost the case will file the complaint.
- Mental, emotional, and behavioral conditions have to be observed. They cannot be detected solely by computer printouts or electronic correspondence. This argues for at least some face-to-face communication in therapy.
- Secondary evidence that might find itself in a report, such as magazines, newspapers, and interviews with third persons are sometimes helpful, but ultimately clinical objectivity militates that the interview with the client is the definitive factor in determining a diagnosis, prognosis, and treatment plan.
- Technology is evolving at breakneck speed. Its relevance to therapy is gradually improving and will continue to grow and change in the twenty-first century.

and, indeed submitting an electronic test or having an e-mail instant conversation, an opinion should not be expressed in the absence of some face-to-face evaluation.

Summary

There is a lure to substitute electronics and the time-saving investigative genius of the telecommunication age to accumulate information and make assessments. One should resist this temptation and adhere to the personal interview in all cases where an opinion is sought. When the electronic age is joined with modern developments and a personal interview, the therapist needs documentation to identify the relative weight of all the information gathered. Any opinion formed must include sensible interviewing techniques as well as the benefits gathered from emerging technology. Together, they offer the information needed to reach a defensible assessment, diagnosis, treatment plan, and prognosis.

Any opinion formed must include sensible interviewing techniques as well as the benefits gathered from emerging technology.

8

Prohibited Clients

Dr. Clean has earned the reputation of a scholar-oriented professor who is always available to students when they have a problem requiring therapeutic assistance. Usually the encounters are brief and do not take a lot of professorial time. Certainly, Dr. Clean does not consider them "therapy." One day, a student approaches him and indicates that her problem requires more than a brief conversation. Instead, she wants in-depth consultation. Dr. Clean, a licensed professional, is reluctant at first, but later relents and visits with the student. He performs this service without charge. Would the rules change if Dr. Clean charged a fee for his services? Would the rules change further if the student were in a program requiring supervision and Dr. Clean was the supervising therapist?

∼

Bob, a master's-level licensed professional counselor, is active in Toastmasters. He offers presentations often to polish his public speaking skills. One day, he is scheduled to deliver his "Ice Breaker," a talk where the novice speaker offers a biographical sketch of his life to date, his field of interest, and his reason for developing speaking skills. Just as he is about to begin, a guest is introduced to the group. To Bob's horror, the guest is a very troubled woman client. Bob is well aware of the usual therapeutic prohibition against inappropriate self-disclosure. He also knows that an Ice Breaker is full of personal self-disclosure, intimate insights, individual and family experiences, and family history. Information will be shared that a client should not hear. Can Bob proceed? Suppose Bob did not notice that the client was in the room, and she heard it all? And then assume that the client is thrilled because her therapist is also a Toastmaster, and she insists on joining the group. After joining, she maneuvers to sit next to him at every meeting.

∼

Ms. Sweet is the president of the symphony board and also a marriage and family therapist. One of her clients has an interest in this cultural activity and, after a few years apprenticeship, gradually climbs the ladder to officialdom. She is running for vice president and solicits the support of Ms. Sweet.

As usual, there is always a certain amount of small town politicking going on and the Ms. Sweet's endorsement would be important. Can Ms. Sweet have anything to do with her client's cultural ambitions? Must she terminate the therapist–client relationship? If therapy is terminated, can Ms. Sweet then promote her client to her friends?

Mrs. O'Reilly is very proud her daughter has finally graduated from the university with an advanced degree in counseling and is authorized and licensed by the state board to enter into a private practice. As she did with her son, a lawyer, she prepares an announcement list of all her friends, family, acquaintances, and business associates. The proud mother intends to offer her daughter's services and recommend that the individuals and businesses on the list consider her daughter when seeking counseling and therapy. In fact, the list contains the names and addresses of just about everyone Mrs. O'Reilly has ever come into contact with socially or casually. When her daughter discovers that her mother is about to undertake the unabashed wholesale solicitation of clients, should she (a) destroy the list, (b) send out announcements to everyone on the list indicating she is in private practice and soliciting business, (c) send out a bland announcement but nothing else, (d) hire a publicity manager to create literature encouraging new prospective clients to call her, or (e) other?

Identifying Prohibited Clients

The maxim often quoted by lawyers is that the "large print *giveth* and the small print *taketh* away." In the case of mental health services, the large print maintains that therapists in a free society may offer services to any person who requests help. The small print, however, places necessary restrictions on therapists against treating certain individuals. A cursory search shows that national ethics codes list several categories of potential clients who cannot be served, and state guidelines and the professional literature offer others.

Mental health professionals must treat individuals in a context where therapeutic objectivity is not compromised (i.e., the only connection between client and therapist is the therapeutic relationship). The therapist cannot achieve this objectivity with current or previous family members, personal friends or business associates, or any of the other relationships to be mentioned. Certainly, it is impossible to maintain objectivity with past or current sexual partners or individuals with whom the therapist would like to be intimate.

Mental health professionals must treat individuals in a context where therapeutic objectivity is not compromised.

Mental health professionals cannot treat persons currently receiving treatment from another counselor without the other provider's knowledge and consent.

In addition, mental health professionals cannot treat persons currently receiving treatment from another counselor without the other provider's knowledge and consent, because they must coordinate treatment plans and use a unified approach. Also many agencies have, by contract with agents, servants, and employees, as well as independent contractors, rules and internal prohibitions against private practitioners building their practice by diverting clients away from the agencies and into the practice of the private or moonlighting provider. These standards are appropriate and must be honored.

Then there are the fuzzy questions: What happens when a long-term client marries into the family and suddenly becomes an in-law? Or when a business associate with no therapeutic connection sells a business interest to a present or former client, or after weeks or months or even years of effective treatment, the client approaches the therapist with a "by the way, I have been seeing 'X,' another therapist, for a second opinion and I had actually seen her before I came to see you"? When do formerly acceptable and suitable clients fall within unacceptable ranges or degrees of relationships to the extent that therapeutic objectivity is or can be, lost? When this happens, what is the best way to avoid an actual, possible, or perceived ethical infraction?

The Intake Interview

A careful intake interview can prevent many problems with a potential prohibited client. Insightful questioning during the first conference will often uncover current and possibly past and future relationships. When a thread of a conflict appears, fully develop the line of questioning and do not undertake treatment until fully satisfied that the client is ethically eligible. Refusing to begin the client-therapist relationship is easier than terminating it at a later date because of newly discovered information that should have been uncovered in the first session.

National Guidelines for Prohibited Clients

APA Ethical Principles of Psychologists and Code of Conduct

1.15 Misuse of Psychologists' Influence
Because psychologists' scientific and professional judgments and actions may affect the lives of others, they are alert to and guard against personal,

financial, social, organizational, or political factors that might lead to misuse of their influence . . .

1.17 Multiple Relationships

(a) . . . avoid social or other nonprofessional contacts with persons such as patients, clients, students, supervisees, or research participants . . . might impair the psychologist's objectivity . . . or otherwise interfere . . .

1.19 Exploitative Relationships

. . . do not exploit persons over whom they have supervisory, evaluative, or other authority such as students, supervisees, employees, research participants, and clients or patients.

4.07 Sexual Intimacies with Former Therapy Patients

". . . do not . . ." (any more is really redundant)

Ethical Standards for School Counselors: ASCA

A.4. Dual Relationships

The professional school counselor:

avoids dual relationships, which might impair his/her objectivity and increase the risk of harm to the client (e.g., counseling one's family members, close friends or associates). If a dual relationship is unavoidable, the counselor is responsible for taking action to eliminate or reduce the potential for harm. Such safeguards might include informed consent, consultation, supervision and documentation . . .

F.1. Professionalism

f. Does not use his/her professional position to recruit or gain clients, consultees for his/her private practice, seek and receive unjustified personal gains, unfair advantage, sexual favors, or unearned goods or services.

AAMFT Code of Ethics

1.12   . . . avoid dual relationships . . . Examples of such dual relationships include, but are not limited to, business or close personal relationships with clients. Sexual intimacy with clients is prohibited. Sexual intimacy with former clients for two years following the termination of therapy is prohibited . . .

3.5   Marriage and family therapists do not engage in sexual or other harassment or exploitation of clients, students, trainees, supervisees, employees, colleagues, research subjects, or actual or potential witnesses or complainants in investigations and ethical proceedings . . .

4.1   . . . Examples of such dual relationships include, but are not limited to, business or close personal relationships with students, employees, or supervisees. Provision of therapy to students, employees, or supervisees is prohibited. Sexual intimacy with students or supervisees is prohibited . . .

5.3   . . . make every effort to avoid dual relationships with research participants that could impair professional judgment or increase the risk of exploitation.

NASW Code of Ethics

1.06 Conflicts of Interest

(c) . . . should not engage in dual or multiple relationships with clients or former clients in which there is a risk of exploitation or potential harm to the client . . . (Dual or multiple relationships occur when social workers relate to clients in more than one relationship, whether professional, social, or business. Dual or multiple relationships can occur simultaneously or consecutively.)

ACA Code of Ethics and Standards of Practice

A.6   Dual Relationships

a.   Avoid When Possible.

. . . avoid dual relationships . . . (Examples of such relationships include, but are not limited to, familial, social, financial, business, or close personal relationships with clients.) . . .

b.   Superior/Subordinate Relationships.
Counselors do not accept as clients superiors or subordinates with whom they have administrative, supervisory, or evaluative relationships.

d.   Recruiting Through Employment.
Counselors do not use their places of employment or institutional affiliation to recruit or gain clients, supervisees, or consultees for their private practices. (See C.5.e.)

Texas State Board of Professional Counselors

(681.32)   General Ethical Requirements

(k) A licensee shall not provide counseling treatment intervention to the licensee's current or previous family members, personal friends, or business associates.

Individuals to Avoid Engaging in Therapy

The ethical canons contain guidelines for accepting clients that affect mental health professionals as they practice their profession. Besides those cited previously, the complete guidelines can be found in the appendixes. Based on these guidelines, however, the list of potential clients whom therapists must refer elsewhere include:

The ethical canons contain guidelines for accepting clients that affect mental health professionals as they practice their profession.

- Personal friends.
- Financial associates.
- Social or organizational acquaintances.
- Political associates or cronies.
- Clients of an agency with whom you do business if that agency prohibits you from offering private therapy to them.
- Students.
- Supervisees.
- Research participants.
- Any individual with whom you customarily barter.
- Anyone with whom you have an evaluative relationship.
- Employees.
- Former and current sexual partners.
- Future contemplated sexual partners.
- Family members.

Deciding Who Qualifies as "Family"

There is no clear definition of who constitutes a family member in the ethics codes. The fluidity of family structure and varying degrees of kinship make definite rules hard to evaluate. There are cousins one never sees, and "kissing cousins" who are not related by blood but always participate in family activities. When contemplating offering therapy to a close family friend, a family member, or to an individual who may later join the family (e.g., a brother's girlfriend), the conventional wisdom is to make a referral.

Tough Calls

Individuals with whom the therapist's relationship is in a gray area of the ethical guidelines are better referred to another therapist.

It is better to lose a potential client than a license!

If the presenting client is not specifically mentioned in the previous list but might be *construed* by some to be a member of a prohibited category, it is better not to take a chance. Individuals with whom the therapist's relationship is in a gray area of the ethical guidelines are better referred to another therapist. Remember that questions of impropriety only present themselves when a complaint is filed. At that time, the general feeling is that consumerism would lean toward the complaining member of the public. In this case, it would be the provider's responsibility to prove that the client was not within a prohibited class of clients. It is better to lose a potential client than a license!

Occasional Clients

Relationships of any type are by their nature fluid. Therapists cannot control who signs up for a course offered at the university, nor can research participants always be limited. Indeed, therapists who are active in the community will often bump into present and former clients in the form of students, supervisees selected by a school or agency, or the salesperson who sold the therapist an automobile. In most cases, the ethical concern is easily handled by a referral or an explanation to the client together with documentation of the event and the agreed on solution. There are few documented cases of ethical violations when therapists used common sense to accept or decline to treat someone. However, this should not minimize the potential problem.

When relationships change to bring the client within prohibited boundaries, proceed with caution. No clinician wants to be the first test case of a possible prohibited client boundary violation (see also Chapter 2).

========= *Ethical Flash Points* =========

- Do not treat a client who falls within the degree of kinship or relationship as outlined in this chapter.

- If there is a question concerning whether a client or potential client falls within a prohibited category, consult the canons of ethics first to see if the relationship is specifically prohibited. If concern continues, contact your lawyer, licensing board, malpractice carrier, and a learned colleague. Get clarification and permission in all questionable cases.

- If a current client marries into the family, tread gingerly and make sure you have obtained and documented informed consent. At least acknowledge that the client was informed and understood the professional guidelines. If at all possible without injuring the client, make a referral and document the rationale for the referral. If appropriate, give the client a copy of the guidelines to help clarify the reason for the referral and offer to cooperate with any future therapist.

- When in doubt, do not accept the client into treatment.

- Call your professional association or licensing board before proceeding and record their response in the clinical file. Include the presenting problem, the date, the person to whom you spoke, the advice received, and how you complied with it. Be prepared to show a good faith effort to comply with the published canons of ethics.

- Do not be intimidated by third-party payers. Remember, *your* license is on the line, not theirs.

Summary

Generally, the mental health professional treats individuals in a context where therapeutic objectivity is not compromised, for example, the transaction is arm's length and the only connection between client and therapist is therapeutic. This cannot be realized where current or previous family members, personal friends, or business associates or any of the other relationships listed above are involved. And certainly, do not treat any past or current sexual partners, nor any you intend to "visit" in the future.

In addition, the professional cannot treat an individual currently receiving treatment from another counselor without the other providers knowledge and consent, as treatment plans must be coordinated and a unified approach used. Also, many agencies have, by contract with agents, servants, and employees, as well as independent contractors, rules and internal prohibitions against private practitioners building their practice by diverting clients away from the agencies and into the practice of the private or moonlighting provider. These standards are appropriate and must be honored.

Then there are the fuzzy questions: What happens when a long-term client marries into the family and suddenly becomes an in-law. Or a business associate with no therapeutic connection sells a business interest to a present or former client, or, after weeks or months or even years of effective treatment, the client approaches the therapist with a "by the way . . ." I have been seeing "X," another therapist, for a second opinion and I had actually seen her before I came to see you.

When does an acceptable and suitable client fall within unacceptable ranges or degrees of relationships to the extent that therapeutic objectivity is or can be, lost.

And then, what is the best way to avoid an actual, possible, or the appearance of an ethical infraction. This chapter suggests some of the options.

Note. Many of the "Prohibited Client" problems can be avoided by a careful intake interview. Insightful questioning during the first conference will often uncover current and possible past and future relationships. When a thread of a prohibition appears, fully develop the line of questioning and do not undertake treatment until fully satisfied that the client is ethically eligible. Refusing to begin the client–therapist relationship is easier than terminating it at a later date because of newly discovered information which should have been uncovered in the first place.

9

Repressed and Recovered Memory

A mature woman visits with a therapist. Under hypnosis or, perhaps after probing questions, she vaguely remembers being touched inappropriately by her uncle when she was very young. As the therapy visits continue, the "touching" comes more clearly into focus. Finally, she cuts off all contact with her uncle and his family and extended family. The family system is chaotic and what was once a loving family is now totally estranged. Three years after the therapy terminates, she concludes (correctly or incorrectly) that the therapist implanted the idea of the touching in her mind. She recants. But by now the family damage is complete. Love can never be restored. She complains to the licensing board about the therapist and indicates she was led to inappropriate, incorrect, and damaging conclusions. Or, her uncle, having been cleared of any wrongdoing, feels cheated out of years of uncle-niece love and affection. He files a complaint with the licensing board. Fast forward to the trial. The mature woman is now in court. A parade of expert witnesses testify, with ponderous tomes to back them up that repressed and recovered memory are in fact valid theories and capable of being discovered, diagnosed, and treated. At the same time another group of expert witnesses testify (after affirming or swearing on a Bible) that repressed and recovered memories, no matter how they come to the surface, are not reliable. Who decides which theory is correct? In a trial, it is the judge, usually a lawyer, or a jury of laypeople chosen from the community. The factfinder or decision maker is not a mental health professional, but a lay individual. In a complaint to the licensing board, the factfinders are usually coprofessionals with a mental health background who understand the concept of repressed and recovered memory, together with the method of diagnosis and treatment. However, this is not to imply that professional boards are without prejudices. A casual survey would indicate that there are militant advocates and contrary opinions. Therefore, exercise caution when diagnosing a recovered or repressed memory. The reputation you save may be your own.

Professional Liability Today

"Periodically, therapists get an urgent wake-up call about specific dangers concerning particular professional liability issues. In the 1970s the *Tarasoff* case pointed out risks when therapists fail to warn potential victims about patients' threats to identifiable intended victims. In the '80s, multimillion dollar awards in sexual misconduct cases forced providers to rethink their conduct—and pay higher insurance premiums. Now, a tide of repressed memory lawsuits are roiling the liability waters." (*Psychotherapy Finances*, V. 24, N. 2, Issue 286, February, 1998).

On September 3, 1999, the Wausau *Daily Herald* reported that a jury awarded $825,000.00 to the wife of a former mayor in a suit she filed against her psychiatrist. The psychiatrist allegedly implanted memories of childhood sexual abuse and satanic rituals in her mind. The article quoted Dr. Sionag Black, a three-year member of the American Psychological Association's Ethics Committee as saying, "It's (treating a patient for multiple personality disorder) been pretty clear that's a very dangerous thing to do. It opens therapists up to exactly what happened to this man." In referring to relaxation and discipline over bad habits, Dr. Black stated, "Hypnosis can be a very valuable tool in other areas. But to use as a form of, 'Let's use it to see what your past is,' is a very risky thing to do. This is another scary case that shows us that." The article further reported that in 1997 an Appleton resident settled out of court for $2.4 million in a similar suit against a Montana psychiatrist. (This information can be accessed through the Wausau *Daily Herald*'s Web site: http://vh30084.vh3.infi .net/headlines/hessletters.html)

As mental health and legal scholars debate whether repressed memory is a valid scientific theory, juries are making it clear that they don't like it and are assessing large damage awards.

As mental health and legal scholars debate whether repressed memory is a valid scientific theory, juries are making it clear that they don't like it and are assessing large damage awards; insurance companies are demonstrating they are afraid of it, settling cases for substantial sums. In *Shazade v Gregory*, 923 F. Supp. 286 (D. Mass. 1996), Judge Edward F. Harrington wrestled with the admissibility of evidence and testimony regarding repressed memory. The judge reviewed prior case decisions that disallowed repressed memory evidence and testimony on the basis that the theory was not widely accepted in the field of psychology. Citing that the *Diagnostic and Statistical Manual of Mental Disorders* (*DSM-IV*, 1994) recognizes the concept of repressed memories, and psychological studies, Judge Harrington made the following findings:

1. The theory has been the subject of various tests.

2. The theory has been subject to peer review publication.

3. Repressed memory, as is true with ordinary memories, cannot be tested empirically; and may not always be accurate, however, the theory itself has been established to be valid through various studies.

4. The theory has attained general acceptance within the relevant scientific community of clinical psychiatrists.

Judge Harrington ruled in favor of allowing evidence and testimony based on the recovered memories of the victim. Other courts have declined to allow the evidence and testimony on the basis that repressed and recovered memories have not been shown to be scientifically reliable. When that happens, it is not hard to understand how courts and juries can find against a therapist who considers the repressed memory concept and diagnosis scientifically reliable and embarks on a course of treatment consistent with that belief.

As the acceptance of repressed memory theory has grown, there has not been equal acceptance or agreement on treatment methodology. Until mental health professionals achieve a consensus on how best to treat patients with repressed and recovered memories, there will continue to be an abundance of claims and lawsuits.

The Role of Informed Consent in Repressed Memory Cases

Failing to secure informed consent has been a theory of negligence for which juries have consistently found therapists liable in malpractice cases, including repressed memory cases. *Psychotherapy Finance* reported that in a recent Texas case, lack of informed consent helped convince a jury to award a patient $5.8 million after the patient spent five years in therapy with little improvement (*Psychotherapy Finances*, V. 24, N. 2, Issue 286, February, 1998).

Informed consent provisions can be found in most ethical codes. (i.e., Section 1.03 of the NASW Code of Ethics and Section A.3,

Mental health professionals should learn from repressed memory lawsuits that informed consent requires disclosure and consent on the type of treatment given, the risks and benefits of the type of treatment presented and, just as important, the alternative treatment methods available.

Client Rights, of the ACA Code of Ethics and Standards of Practice (see Chapter 6).

Many therapists think that as long as they discuss confidentiality and fees with a client they have satisfied their informed consent obligation. Mental health professionals should learn from repressed memory lawsuits that informed consent requires disclosure and consent on the type of treatment given, the risks and benefits of the type of treatment presented and, just as important, the alternative treatment methods available. It is critical to document informed consent. Failure to provide this information is an ethical violation and can result (and has) in a substantial jury award. Written information that the client signs or acknowledges receipt of in writing can go a long way when defending against an allegation of a lack of informed consent.

Informed Consent and Experimental Therapies

New or experimental therapies have often been attacked in lawsuits by former clients and patients and their attorneys (e.g., aggressive reparenting where adults crawl around on the floor drinking from baby bottles; psychic surgery; past life regression, entity releasement; life regression; and hitting with foam bats). Securing informed consent when using new and cutting-edge therapy may be difficult to establish for the typical juror who is predisposed to view mental health care with skepticism. Without published studies and research to document the effectiveness of a type of therapy, it may be impossible to advise clients on the risks and benefits, thereby precluding the informed consent ethical codes require.

Without published studies and research to document the effectiveness of a type of therapy, it may be impossible to advise clients on the risks and benefits, thereby precluding the informed consent ethical codes require.

Whenever using a treatment that is "generally accepted" but not "universally accepted," such as therapy to uncover repressed and recovered memory, the therapist should draft an appropriate consent form in which the client consents, in writing, to the treatment and send it to a lawyer knowledgeable in mental health law for review. If one reviews the consent forms hospitals and some physicians and dentists require their patients to sign, the advantage of a provider serving form becomes obvious. Therapists can never be protected from all risks in our litigious society, but consent forms that inform the client generally and specifically of the risks involved in therapy can afford some protection from litigation and complaints to licensing boards. Gone are the days of the one-sentence or one-paragraph consent form. When the lawyer approves the form, the therapist should ask the client to sign and date it, and give the client a copy. Written consent serves as a bulwark against a client's later claim that "I was not informed of the nature of the treatment, the consequences, nor the techniques." It is all spelled out in clear and lay language for the client to read, question, and discuss. A thorough, lawyer/therapist-drafted informed consent form is the first line of defense in any claim for either an ethics violation or a malpractice suit.

The Role of Therapist Competence in Repressed Memory Cases

The question of the mental health professional's competence often plays a large role in a repressed memory lawsuit. These suits frequently involve a dissociative identity disorder diagnosis. Lack of adequate professional training and experience in this area can certainly doom a lawsuit to a poor and possibly tragic result for a therapist. Ethically, mental health professionals are strictly admonished to provide services only within the scope of their competency.

Do not exceed your level of competence. It sounds so simple but mental health professionals who are sincerely motivated by their desire to help clients often let their hearts cloud their judgment. A professional mental health license or a university degree does not make a therapist competent to handle clients with difficult problems such as those presented by repressed memory and dissociative identity disorder. Know your limits. When the client or the client's problems exceed the level of competence, a mental health professional is ethically obligated to terminate and refer the client to another provider better able to treat the client.

Because professional's dispute the validity of repressed memories and uncertainty exists regarding what treatment techniques should be used, only the most careful, educated, trained, and experienced therapists should attempt to treat clients in this area. Unless the therapist fits this description, referral is the only ethical option.

Every professional has personal standards of formal and informal sources of continuing education, with workshops, seminars, classes, and personal readings providing important information that increases the provider's individual competence. Therapists should document every course, seminar, workshop, and individual study and reading they undertake. Thus if challenged in court or by a disciplinary committee, the therapist would be able instantly to show evidence of learning, training, and experience (i.e., competence) by demonstrated background on the subject at hand.

Do not exceed your level of competence.

Because professional's dispute the validity of repressed memories and uncertainty exists regarding what treatment techniques should be used, only the most careful, educated, trained, and experienced therapists should attempt to treat clients in this area.

Consider the following scenario: Suppose a therapist, through hypnosis, or in the course of numerous visits uncovers a repressed memory that affects the client in a serious and negative manner. Then the therapist elects to make a referral (realizing a level of competence has been exceeded) and there is no one in the community who will accept this kind of referral because of the risks involved. Then what? Abandonment?

National Guidelines for Therapist Competency

NASW Code of Ethics

1.04 Competence

(a) Social workers should provide services and represent themselves as competent only within the boundaries of their education, training, license, certification, consultation received, supervised experience, or other relevant professional experience.

(b) Social workers should provide services in substantive areas or use intervention techniques or approaches that are new to them only after engaging in appropriate study, training, consultation, and supervision from people who are competent in those interventions or techniques.

ACA Code of Ethics and Standards of Practice

STANDARD OF PRACTICE EIGHT (SP-8) INABILITY TO ASSIST CLIENTS. Counselors must avoid entering or immediately terminate a counseling relationship if it is determined that they are unable to be of professional assistance to a client . . .

Section A.11. Termination and Referral

b. . . . Counselors are knowledgeable about referral sources and suggest appropriate alternatives . . .

Hypnosis and Relaxation Techniques

Hypnosis and its functional equivalent, relaxation and visualization techniques, have come under attack in repressed memory and other types of damage suits. In *Borawick v Shay* (842 F. Supp. 1501 (D. Conn. 1994); aff'd 68 F.3d 597 (2d Cir. 1995), the federal court ruled that a victim could not testify because her recollection had been rendered unreliable by the past use of hypnosis for therapeutic purposes. A noted side effect of hypnosis is the creation of memories that may not be accurate: the phenomenon of false and implanted memories. Failing to advise the client of this side effect and the failure of the therapist to recognize that a "recovered memory" of abuse may not be true and to seek corroboration has resulted in a finding of negligence. If mental health professionals are going to use hypnosis, it is critical that they be thoroughly trained and experienced and closely follow the guidelines of the American Society for Clinical Hypnosis.

A noted side effect of hypnosis is the creation of memories that may not be accurate: the phenomenon of false and implanted memories.

Ethical Flash Points

- Beware the client who reveals "repressed memories."
- Repressed memory cases have resulted in substantial jury awards and settlements.
- The lack of universal acceptance of the validity of repressed memory as a scientific theory with appropriate treatment techniques makes this an attractive and fertile area for malpractice suits as well as ethical complaints.
- Failing to adequately secure informed consent is an ethical violation and a common allegation in repressed memory lawsuits.
- Informed consent includes advising clients of alternative forms of treatment not just the benefits and risks of the type of treatment used.
- Therapist competence is critical in treating repressed memory clients or when employing hypnosis and other less proven types of therapy.
- A wise therapist maintains a lifelong log of all training received as well as personal readings and studies.
- Always attempt to corroborate recovered memories and never accept them as accurate without corroboration.
- Failure to terminate and refer when a therapist lacks the education, training, license, and experience to treat a client's problem is an ethical violation and a basis for establishing professional negligence.
- Hypnosis can cause false memories and the client should be advised of this fact as part of informed consent to this type of treatment.
- New or unconventional types of therapy may be so unproved that they defy informed consent.

Summary

Even though a therapist may secure the education, license, training, and experience that would allow other mental health professionals to view him as competent with respect to certain types of therapy it does not insure that the complaints committee of a disciplinary board or a jury will look upon his competence and his treatment and services as favorably. Debated and unproved theories and types of treatment make the kind of informed consent required by ethics codes difficult to obtain.

Repressed memory and repressed memory treatment fall into this category and should cause every mental health professional to seriously reflect on whether they wish to become professionally involved with a repressed memory client. When a client reveals a repressed memory a therapist should be wary not only about the accuracy of the memory but also about the therapists ability to treat the client. A referral may be a better course of action.

A theoretical scenario: what if the therapist, through hypnosis, or in the process of numerous visits uncovers a repressed memory which affects the client in a serious and negative manner. Then the therapist elects to make a referral (realizing a level of competence has been exceeded) and there is no one in the community who will accept this kind of referral because of the risks involved. Then What! Abandonment?

10

Sexual Misconduct

Mickey, a tall, attractive woman, checked herself in to the charity hospital emergency room. The psychiatric intern on call, Randy, was compassionate, understanding, and single. As soon as Mickey saw him, her spirits soared. She insisted he treat her personally and later came to his office in the medical school wearing a miniskirt, spiked heels, and flattering makeup. She captivated Randy, and after a few months of outpatient treatment, they met for coffee in the medical school cafeteria. Later they met for a movie, then a few drinks, and finally they began an affair. This was heaven to Mickey as long as she received all of Randy's attention but, as any professional can imagine, her underlying problems did not go away. Finally the intern called Mickey to terminate both their social and professional relationship. Mickey was mortified. She felt this was another male rejection made by the man she trusted most. Devastated, she took an overdose of sleeping pills and found herself back in the emergency room where she related her relationship with Randy to another intern. It all became part of the medical school-psychiatric clinical file. Still angry, Mickey called a lawyer. Randy lost his medical license and Mickey gained a substantial settlement. Why would educated, intelligent people allow themselves to be seduced in a situation so clearly dangerous, destined to fail, and unethical?

(Note. Some literature and case law suggests that if an affair occurred between the patient/client and another medical staff member, but not the actual treating physician, it would still constitute an ethical infraction and liability. No one on the professional staff who meets Mickey as a result of her seeking therapeutic help should change the relationship from therapeutic to social. The boundary wall surrounds Mickey and protects her from everyone in the hospital whom she encounters as a result of her quest for professional treatment.)

~

Thelma, a social worker, led a lesbian therapy group. One woman attended the first session and then dropped out. Later, she called Thelma for lunch. Soon after, they started dating and ultimately moved in together. Another group member observed the one-time visit in group therapy and later saw the two women together in an apparently affectionate situation. Jealous, she investigated and determined that the relationship was unethical and forwarded her findings (a summary of community gossip) to the licensing board. The facts were admitted and the board took disciplinary action. There was no way to justify the relationship between Thelma and any person whose introduction occurred in a therapeutic framework and who was listed on the group roster as a person receiving or participating in a group therapy session she facilitated.

~

John, a therapist, and Susan, his client, met in Massachusetts while he was pursuing his doctorate in counseling psychology. He treated her under the supervision of a clinical professor when she sought help from the counseling center where he was enrolled in a practicum. After graduation, he remained in the same city where he occasionally saw Susan in church, but nothing ever happened between them except a friendly "hello" and a nod. Later John relocated to California, and five years later by complete coincidence Susan moved to the same town and joined his church and Sunday School class. This time they began dating, but he later broke things off with her. Susan was furious and filed a complaint. She said she had fantasized about John for the past five years, that he knew about her fantasies, and in dating her took advantage of their former intern-client relationship. In her complaint, she indicated that she was so emotionally damaged by the social relationship that she would never recover. John was subject to disciplinary action by his licensing board. The board concluded that he should have resisted becoming involved with Susan because their relationship had a tendency to be exploitative. John, as a mental health professional, was the responsible party.

Prevalence of Sexual Misconduct

Engaging in sexual misconduct with clients is more prevalent among mental health professionals than we might imagine. In the state of Texas for example, two consecutive issues of the Texas State Board of Examiners of Professional Counselors newsletters listed a total of eleven professional counselors who lost their licenses due to sexual misconduct.

The authors have lectured throughout the country urging mental health professionals to maintain a clinical distance between themselves and their clients. The danger legally and ethically of dual relationships and boundary violations, particularly those involving sexual misconduct, causes much grief, anxiety, and concern for mental health professionals and the boards who enforce the rules. Nevertheless, somewhere in the nation at any given time therapists are busily engaging in such activities, whether they pursue a client sexually or intimately, or a client pursues them and they cannot resist the temptation. Either way, it is the mental health professional who ultimately loses. If caught, providers may be dismissed from their national organizations, found guilty of a felony in some states, and certainly risk having their licenses revoked for committing an unethical act. Considering most professional organizations and licensing boards have a zero tolerance level for sexual intimacies with a client, why does it happen?

There is no therapeutic modality or school for training mental health providers that permits sex with a client and no accepted literature that in any way condones such a relationship. Indeed, schools, the literature, the pundits in the field, and every speaker the authors have ever heard condemned the practice. Yet sex with a client continues to disturb therapeutic relationships and causes physical, psychological, and emotional damage. There is nothing right about having sex with a client. Sexual misconduct with a client is ethically, legally, and criminally wrong.

Sexual misconduct with a client is ethically, legally, and criminally wrong.

Consider the big picture. When one mental health provider is caught having sex with a client, he or she destroys the reputation of helping professionals in general. Most cases of sexual exploitation lead to media exposure that fans the flames of public cynicism against the mental health field and destroys or at least minimizes the excellent work that the vast majority of helping professionals offer to the community in general and individuals and families in particular.

Rarely does sex with a client happen quickly. Usually, an honest clinical relationship first develops between the therapist and the client. The therapist knows that to cross clinical boundaries is wrong and resists any other relationship at first. Gradually, however, the barriers break down, and one activity leads to another. If the relationship sours, the client may feel hurt, humiliated, or taken advantage of, and may go so far as to file a licensing board complaint or malpractice suit.

Of course, some therapist-client relationships do last. There are numerous cases where the parties have married, but this does not make the

Marriage is not a cure or panacea for unethical conduct.

therapist's conduct ethical. Marriage is not a cure or panacea for unethical conduct. If either the therapist or the client is married or in a significant relationship when the affair began, the client's or therapist's significant other or both are sure to at least consider reporting the unethical liaison. Jilted spouses do not take kindly to therapist-client sexual relationships that break up marriages. The natural inclination is to file a report and let the professional boards do the investigating and take appropriate action.

The ethics codes of mental health disciplines are remarkably similar relating to sex with clients, sexual intimacies, or any social/sexual relationship. Nearly every code contains some restrictive language that prohibits sex with a client, a former client, or anyone who might consider him- or herself to be a client.

National Guidelines for Sexual Misconduct

AAMFT Code of Ethics

1.2 . . . make every effort to avoid dual relationships with clients that could impair professional judgment or increase the risk of exploitation. . . . Examples of such dual relationships include, but are not limited to, business or close personal relationships with clients. Sexual intimacy with clients is prohibited. Sexual intimacy with former clients for two years following the termination of therapy is prohibited.

NASW Code of Ethics

1.09 Sexual Relationships

(a) Social workers should under no circumstances engage in sexual activities or sexual contact with current clients, whether such contact is consensual or forced.

(b) Social workers should not engage in sexual activities or sexual contact with clients' relatives or other individuals with whom clients maintain a close personal relationship when there is a risk of exploitation or potential harm to the client. Sexual activity or sexual contact with clients' relatives or other individuals with whom clients maintain a personal relationship has the potential to be harmful to the client and may make it difficult for the social worker and client to maintain appropriate professional boundaries. Social workers—not their clients, their clients' relatives, or other individuals with whom the client maintains a personal relationship—assume the full burden for setting clear, appropriate, and culturally sensitive boundaries.

(c) Social workers should not engage in sexual activities or sexual contact with former clients because of the potential for harm to the client. If social workers engage in conduct contrary to this prohibition or claim that an exception to this prohibition is warranted because of extraordinary circumstances, it is social workers—not their clients— who assume the full burden of demonstrating that the former client has not been exploited, coerced, or manipulated, intentionally or unintentionally.

(d) Social workers should not provide clinical services to individuals with whom they have had a prior sexual relationship. Providing clinical services to a former sexual partner has the potential to be harmful to the individual and is likely to make it difficult for the social worker and individual to maintain appropriate professional boundaries.

1.10 Physical Contact

Social workers should not engage in physical contact with clients when there is a possibility of psychological harm to the client as a result of the contact (such as cradling or caressing clients). Social workers who engage in appropriate physical contact with clients are responsible for setting clear, appropriate, and culturally sensitive boundaries that govern such physical contact.

ACA *Code of Ethics and Standards of Practice*

A. Current Clients

Counselors do not have any type of sexual intimacies with clients and do not counsel persons with whom they have had a sexual relationship.

B. Former Clients

Counselors do not engage in sexual intimacies with former clients within a minimum of two years after terminating the counseling relationship. Counselors who engage in such relationship *after* two years following termination have the responsibility to thoroughly examine and document that such relations did not have an exploitative nature, based on factors, such as duration of counseling, amount of time since counseling, termination circumstances, client's personal history and mental status, adverse impact on the client and actions by the counselor suggesting a plan to initiate a sexual relationship with the client after termination.

Is Sex with Clients Ever Okay?

To tell mental health professionals of any discipline that sex with a client is prohibited seems redundant. Every practitioner in the field knows that exploitative behavior is not tolerated in the profession, and dual relationships, boundary violations, and sex with clients are clearly unethical. Yet a reminder is necessary because therapists continue to disregard this prohibition.

Mental health professionals should not engage in sexual contact with an intern the professional supervises, a student at an educational institution at which the professional provides professional or educational services, or close friends or relations of clients or former clients.

Ethics codes generally prohibit sexual contact with any client or former client. Some codes provide that sexual contact with a client is prohibited during the clinical relationship and for two years thereafter. After two years of zero contact, some codes allow a social/sexual relationship between therapists and clients as long as the client is no longer emotionally dependent on the therapist. Nevertheless, to be safe, the authors advocate that *mental health providers should never engage in anything other than a clinical relationship with clients or former clients.*

Furthermore, mental health professionals should not engage in sexual contact with an intern the professional supervises, a student at an educational institution at which the professional provides professional or educational services, or close friends or relations of clients or former clients. It is not an adequate defense to say the sexual contact, sexual exploitation, or therapeutic deception with the person occurred with the person's consent, outside the person's professional counseling sessions, or off the premises regularly used by the provider for the professional counseling sessions. Besides sexual intimacy, other prohibited acts include sexual harassment, creating a hostile environment, making improper comments or gestures, requesting sexual details beyond those needed for the client's therapy, requesting a date, and so forth. Some codes mention with particularity all the parts of the client's body professionals should not touch.

========= *Ethical Flash Points* =========

- Every mental health discipline prohibits sexual intimacy with clients.

- *Intimacy* means anything that a client could interpret to be either sexual or intimate. The authors have had a client who wanted to file a complaint because the therapist exhaled too hard and the client thought he was panting with excitement over the client!

- Sexual intimacies are a common problem in the mental health field judging by the number of complaints filed in this area. Malpractice insurance policies generally limit coverage in this area because of the number of reported incidents. Most policies contain specific monetary limits for sexual misconduct cases. Read your policy.

- Malpractice coverage for representation before a disciplinary board is even more limited. Therapists are responsible for all fees incurred beyond their deductible paid—usually no more than $5,000. Read your policy.

- The "two years after termination" permissive language in some ethics codes is usually drafted to shift the responsibility to the therapist to ensure that no harm befalls the client.

- Some guidelines require that therapists who discover or receive knowledge of another therapist's inappropriate sexual contact with a client are ethically bound to report it or their own license is in danger.

- Most disciplinary boards usually ignore convoluted explanations (sometimes called fairy tales) to justify unethical sexual misconduct.

- Sex with clients drifts between the top two or three major ethical infractions committed by therapists of all disciplines.

- When sex between a therapist and client takes place, the therapist has no defense.

- In a "he said" versus "she said" swearing match, the therapist is usually discounted and the consumer of mental health services is believed unless there are very unusual circumstances (e.g., the encounter could not have taken place the way the consumer/client narrated the story; the consumer/client has repeated the story several times, and each time there are significant differences and sufficient inconsistencies to make the tale unbelievable).

- Sex = exploitation.

Summary

The good news is that all mental health professionals know on some level that sex with a client is bad. The bad news is that sexual exploitation continues to be a constant source of client complaints and irritation to licensing boards and national organizations, not to mention damage to the exploited client. When the therapist feels, clinically, that a client has

Handle clients who appear to be interested sexually as a clinical problem of transference.

more than a professional interest, the problem has to be brought to the surface, discussed, and handled. The client must be made to understand the professional's ethical guidelines and told that such activities are prohibited (providing a copy of the guidelines if needed). The method of diffusing a possible explosive situation must be documented. Remember, the client may feel rejected, and some anger may result. Handle clients who appear to be interested sexually as a clinical problem of transference. But the end result must always be to just say NO!

11

Terminating Therapy

Susan had been in therapy with Dr. Smith for about five months and was feeling better about herself, her family, and her environment. In fact, Dr. Smith told Susan the time had come to end therapy. The next visit would be an "exit" interview, where they would recapitulate the treatment plan, review how it had been successful, and terminate their professional relationship. Of course Susan could contact Dr. Smith again should another problem occur, but for now she no longer required regular visits with him. Susan was a private pay client and did not claim managed care benefits nor did she process an insurance claim. Although Dr. Smith indicated that further therapy was unnecessary at this time, Susan said she was willing to continue to pay Dr. Smith weekly for the opportunity to visit and talk to him, as he was the only person who would listen to her without interruption. Should a therapist continue to see a client who just wishes to chat? Could it be considered abandonment to refuse to see a client who wants to continue the client-therapist relationship after the therapist has indicated the client is able to function normally without further treatment?

~

Jack had been in therapy for about a year without measurable improvement. He did not feel better, nor did he feel worse. The therapist tried various treatment techniques, none of which seemed to bring about any positive change in the presenting problem. The therapist wondered if the therapy itself was not working or if there was a problem with the therapist–client relationship, some unknown circumstance, or possibly some client-centered but undiagnosed problem. The therapist asked herself if ethically, the client's situation must always improve with therapy for it to be considered successful, or if therapeutic success might be claimed also when a client's condition doesn't deteriorate further? In either case, should the therapist continue the therapy even though the client's condition is not measurably improved?

~

Joan had been in therapy for about a year with excellent results. After discussing terminating treatment with the client, the therapist and client agreed to conclude therapy. The client left the office feeling happy with the therapy, happy with the therapist, and happy with herself. The first day of the rest of her life was going to be a glorious reawakening of new opportunities. But how does the therapist close the file? Is it automatically closed because no appointments are scheduled and the client does not, at this point, intend to return? What does the client have in writing—only a canceled check marked "paid in full"? Is that adequate?

～

John had been in therapy off and on for several years. When he needed a consultation, he called Susan, his social worker, made an appointment or appointments as needed, and then waited until the next stress period to call again. On one of these occasions, after a mutually satisfactory three-session series, John mentioned that he was being transferred and would be leaving town in about a month to accept a promotion 1,000 miles away at company headquarters. Susan said "congratulations," and John left. That brief dialogue served as the termination interview. Susan later heard through the grapevine that John had become overwhelmed in his new position and was subsequently dismissed. He was now unemployed, very distressed, and unsuccessfully seeking gainful employment. Does ethical follow-up mandate that therapists who casually hear a rumor of unhappiness contact a former client and suggest continuing therapy?

～

Earnest was hostile and angry. At the end of his last session, he made malicious but indirect threats, suggesting dangers to himself and others, before storming out of the therapist's office. He did, however, make another appointment for the next week before leaving. His next appointment came and went, but Earnest did not appear. His therapist could not locate him by phone, and letters to his last known address were returned unopened. In a sense, Earnest had himself, unilaterally, terminated the therapeutic relationship. Does such an act serve to terminate the therapeutic relationship or is there an ethical responsibility binding therapist to client until there is a formalized termination? Does a "no show" and a "can't locate" signal an official termination? And, ethically, what happens next?

～

Sam had been a client on and off for five years when he and his therapist mutually agreed to terminate his treatment. Over the next few years, Sam's life *turned downward. He had family and domestic problems, the upward trend of his career leveled out and was less rewarding spiritually and financially, and, in general, he thought his life was in decline. On reflection, he feels the therapist "should have" and "could have" done more for him. In a fit of pique, he calls his former therapist.*

The Therapeutic Relationship

Therapy begins with an express or implied contract between clients and therapists, in which therapists represent that they will provide competent treatment to their clients; and clients, advised of the various ramifications of therapy, give informed consent to the treatment offered. With that offer and acceptance, the therapy begins.

Therapy ends when the treatment is terminated. Final or temporary termination can happen for different reasons. For example, treatment can end when the client simply stops keeping appointments and disappears into oblivion despite the therapist's best efforts to make contact. It can also end by mutual agreement or because the third-party payer declines further payment and the client is unable to afford additional sessions without such reimbursement. At such times, therapists usually inform clients of available community resources and wish them well. Therapy may also be terminated when clients are transferred or when the therapist retires, becomes ill, moves, or terminates with the current association or agency and another therapist is assigned to the file. Therapy can end when it clearly is no longer benefiting the client, or when the client or therapist, for whatever reason, is no longer comfortable with the treatment plan. Often therapy terminates when the client and therapist mutually agree that the treatment goals have been realized and further treatment is no longer appropriate.

When to Terminate Therapy

The therapist–client relationship should be terminated when:

- The future services needed are not within the provider's professional competency.
- The provider is or becomes impaired due to physical or mental ill health or the use of medication, drugs, or alcohol.

- Continued service is not in the client's best interest.

- Professional ethical canons are violated because of relationships within or outside the provider's control.

- In the professional's opinion, the client is not benefiting from those services offered, but *when services to the client are still indicated, the provider should take reasonable steps to facilitate the transfer to an appropriate source of care.*

- A person who needs a license to practice has the license revoked, suspended, or otherwise limited or canceled.

- A client joins the same church and sits next to you in the choir, marries your sister, threatens to sue you, threatens to harm you, or otherwise expresses forceful displeasure with you, your treatment, or your profession.

National Guidelines for Terminating Therapy

Every mental health discipline has published ethical guidelines concerning appropriate termination. State or national licensing boards have disciplined many mental health professionals because they did not strictly follow their published guidelines, did not properly document that the guidelines were followed, or both. Chapter 13 indicates that ethical guidelines, when not followed, may be introduced as evidence in a malpractice suit to indicate minimum standards of practice. Termination with less than minimum standards might indicate civil negligence.

ACA Code of Ethics and Standards of Practice

A.11. Termination and Referral

a.   Abandonment Prohibited

Counselors do not abandon or neglect clients in counseling. Counselors assist in making appropriate arrangements for the continuation of treatment, when necessary, during interruptions, such as vacations, and following termination.

b.   Inability to Assist Clients

If counselors determine an inability to be of professional assistance to clients, they avoid entering or immediately terminate a counseling relationship. Counselors are knowledgeable about referral resources and suggest appropriate alternatives. If clients decline the suggested referral, counselors should discontinue the relationship.

c. Appropriate Termination

Counselors terminate a counseling relationship, securing client agreement when possible, when it is reasonably clear that the client is no longer benefiting, when services are no longer required, when counseling no longer serves the client's needs or interests, when clients do not pay fees charged, or when agency or institution limits do not allow provision of further counseling services. (See A.10b and C.2.g.)

Standard of Practice Seven (SP-7) Termination

Counselors must assist in making appropriate arrangements for the continuation of treatment of clients, when necessary, following termination of counseling relationships. (See A.10. a–d. and A.11.c.)

The Termination Process

In a sense, the termination process begins with a complete intake form. At this time, be sure to obtain one or two addresses and phone numbers, and—most important—explicit written consent to contact the client at the phone numbers and addresses furnished. (The fact that the client has given the therapist an address and phone number does not specifically indicate that the client has given permission to be called, contacted by mail, or otherwise communicated with at that address or number.) Since termination has ramifications both ethically and as a malpractice risk, the therapist should take certain additional precautions whenever terminating a client-therapist relationship.

First, be sure to document the rationale for termination: why it is taking place, and how it is in the client's best interest. Therapists are usually held liable for something they failed to do, not something they did. Thus, it is a good idea to have a termination process and procedure in place in which therapists inform clients of all further treatment they might need, and the means they might utilize to obtain further treatment. The following checklist is for use at termination. All the items are essential to protect the provider from an ethical infraction. Some procedures will be more rigorous than ones you may be currently using, but that is the point. Malpractice suits and ethical complaints to the licensing boards are America's new national pastime.

First, be sure to document the rationale for termination: why it is taking place, and how it is in the client's best interest.

Termination is always a potential problem—even when the decision at the time is mutual and friendly. If the proper steps are not followed, the termination can come back to haunt you—even years later. Relationships are fickle. At one time, most clients were satisfied clients.

Checklist for Terminating Therapy

• Schedule an exit session or termination interview to make sure clients understand: (1) what is taking place, (2) the reasons behind it, and (3) any recommendations you have.

• Prepare a termination letter (see Figure 11.1) ahead of that session. Review it with the client, then have the client sign it and take a copy.

• If you feel further treatment is advisable or necessary, make that explicit both in your interview and in the letter. Psychiatrists need to tell patients who are on medication to continue their medication subject to medical controls. Patients must understand that a psychiatrist has to review the medications periodically to determine if they are still appropriate or if they should be discontinued. Limitations must be placed on prescriptions.

• If the client is moving to a place where no mental health professional is available, contact the client periodically to make sure the client is doing well. Clients should agree in writing that if a problem arises, they will contact a professional, or call an emergency number before hurting themselves or others.

• Be persistent in trying to reach a client, especially one who simply fails to show up or make another appointment. If a face-to-face termination interview isn't possible—because the client refuses, or for any other reason—a phone conference should be attempted. A copy of the termination letter should be sent to an authorized mailing address (i.e., an address where the client has said the therapist may send correspondence), especially if you believe the person needs further treatment. Be sure to explain in detail the need for continuing mental health treatment. Recommend at least three other therapists or referral sources in the letter. If the client can't be reached, two copies of the termination letter, including a self-addressed, stamped envelope, should be sent: one by standard, first-class mail, and one by certified mail with return receipt requested. Ask the client to sign both copies and return one to you.

Anthony Kindheart, LPC

6894 Forest Park Drive
Suite 268
Dallas, Texas 75206
July 17, 20____

Mr. Kevin Jones
1425 Centenary
Dallas, Texas 75210

Re: Termination of Treatment

Dear Mr. Kevin Jones:

It has become necessary, for the reasons stated below, to terminate our professional and therapeutic relationship. I will maintain your records for the period required by law and will make copies of your records available to you upon written request. You may be charged a reasonable fee for the cost of duplicating the records.

Our work together began on July 1, 1996, and ended on this date. During this time, we worked on improving your occupational and social functioning and alleviating your depression by addressing factors that may have caused, contributed to, or aggravated your depression.

In the exercise of my professional judgment, I have concluded that you have not made satisfactory progress in improving your social and occupational functioning and with your depression. I believe you are in need of additional mental health services for treatment of your depression and possible chemical dependency. These services can be best provided to you by one of the following:

Richard Lewins, MD, (214) 489-3624, 1900 Main Street, Suite 120, Dallas, TX 75201
Sylvia Jones, LCDC, (972) 270-9142, 689 LBJ Freeway, Suite 410, Dallas, TX 75214
Harold Jones, PhD, (214) 814-3621, 48764 Mockingbird, Suite 206, Dallas, TX 75206

I recommend you contact one of these providers, or another provider of your choosing, as quickly as possible to schedule an appointment. With your written consent, I will consult with any professional of your choosing and will forward the file or a summary of your treatment to my successor.

Your primary discharge diagnosis is: 296.32 Major Depression, recurrent.

(continued)

(Continued)

This termination is not due to any personal reasons but solely due to my desire for you to achieve the highest possible level of mental health wellness and social and occupational functioning. I believe referring you to one of the providers listed above presents the best possibility for this to occur. I wish you success and want you to know that I will make myself available for consultation with anyone you choose to work with, in order to make this transition as easy as possible.

Sincerely,

_____

Anthony Kindheart, LPC

I acknowledge receipt and review and accept and understand the terms of this termination letter, dated the 17th day of July, 20_____ .

_____   _____
Kevin Jones   Date

                                                   _____
                                                   Social Security Number

FIGURE 11.1   Sample Form: Client Termination Letter

- Review the ethical guidelines of your profession concerning termination. Make sure you have scrupulously followed them. Many providers belong to several national organizations and have multiple licenses. A provider who has a license or belongs to a national organization is bound by the ethical code of that specific organization or all organizations in which he or she has a membership. If the provider belongs to a subspecialty group within an organization, the guidelines of the subspecialty group also bind the provider.

Termination Letter Checklist

- Include the client's name (no "Dear Client" form letters).
- Identify the date when therapy began.

- Note the termination date.

- Relate the primary and secondary diagnosis.

- Describe the reason for termination.

- Summarize treatment, including any need for additional services.

- List three or more referrals or referral sources, including addresses and phone numbers.

- Draft a statement that the client understands what termination of treatment is, and accepts the responsibility to personally seek further treatment if appropriate.

- Include signature lines for both the therapist and the client, with a date line for each signature.

- If mailing, include two copies with a self-addressed, stamped envelope. Indicate "Enclosure" at the bottom of the termination letter.

Note: The preceding checklist is a modification of a published telephone interview with the author appearing in Psychotherapy Finances, V. 25, N. 3, Issue 299, March 1999, John Klein, Editor *(published by Ridgewood Financial Institute, Inc., 13901 U.S. Highway 1, Ste. 5, Juno Beach, FL 33408, 561-624-1155).*

Maintaining the Clinical File

A carefully drafted intake and consent form (perhaps lawyer drafted to protect the therapist) sets out the steps and procedures for termination and will authorize the mental health professional to contact the client should termination occur by any means other than a mutual agreement and exit interview. Then, as the final notation in the file, the clinical case notes must reflect the circumstances of termination, the termination process, and the fact that therapy has been successfully concluded before the file is officially closed.

After the participatory therapist–client relationship has been terminated, the file must be properly stored and preserved for the length of time required by both statute and ethical canons for adults and minors. In many cases, the client may return for future therapy, and the current clinical file will be of tremendous value. In this sense, "termination" does not really mean "termination." Rather it means abatement. The client is on therapeutic "hold." The file will be preserved in a safe, secure, and

Clinical case notes must reflect the circumstances of termination, the termination process, and the fact that therapy has been successfully concluded before the file is officially closed.

After the participatory therapist–client relationship has been terminated, the file must be properly stored and preserved for the length of time required by both statute and ethical canons for adults and minors.

confidential manner for at least so long as required by law and as set forth in state ethical codes. If sufficient storage facilities are available, perhaps forever.

Is Termination the End of Therapy?

Once the therapist and client mutually agree to end therapy and the file is closed, what happens? Theoretically, the therapist could move, retire, leave the profession, or change from private practice to another means of making a living. Does the phrase or maxim "once a client always a client" hold true in these situations? Probably not, but on the other hand licensing boards have strange and variable statutes of limitations. Should an unhappy client, as evidenced by Sam earlier in the chapter, call the therapist years later, the situation should be confronted rather than ignored. Probably, the pique can be ameliorated or defused with a minimum of effort, leaving a content former client. Joining in combat might create a licensing board complaint. When this happens, the board usually has state or national resources behind the complainant, the former client, whereas the mental health providers are on their own, financially and emotionally.

Malpractice versus Ethical Violations Regarding Termination

A malpractice suit is litigation for money damages filed in the civil justice system.

A malpractice suit is litigation for money damages filed in the civil justice system. Such damages may be awarded by a judge or jury who determine what amount of money, if any, will compensate the plaintiff for the damages caused by, in this case, the defendant's (the therapist) negligent termination of the therapeutic relationship.

An ethical violation begins with a complaint filed with a licensing board.

An ethical violation, on the other hand, begins with a complaint filed with a licensing board. The board considers the complaint and, if it is justified, can revoke or suspend a license or put restrictions on the practitioner. The result can ruin a career, especially if a license is absolutely necessary to practice.

Malpractice is determined by a judge, jury, or both. An ethics violation is determined by a licensing board or, if the complaint is submitted to a national organization, to the complaints committee of the national organization. As stated elsewhere in this book, the profession's ethics code can be introduced into evidence in either case to indicate the minimum standards of the profession. Practitioners must justify any deviation from these standards, especially if some harm damages a client.

Malpractice insurance can protect the therapist from a malpractice suit (see Chapter 19). There is no ethics violation insurance. If covered at all, the malpractice insurance policy will cover a few thousand dollars in attorneys' fees to defend against an ethical complaint, *but the provider cannot be protected by insurance against having a license revoked.*

Malpractice insurance can protect the therapist from a malpractice suit.

There is no ethics violation insurance.

Ethical Flash Points

- When therapy is no longer benefiting the client, the therapeutic relationship must be terminated.

- Therapy has to be reviewed and possibly terminated when the technique used is not working. It might be the therapist–client mix, some hidden or subtle agenda of the therapist or client, or something else. Not every therapist can successfully treat every client who makes an appointment. And the factors for an unsuccessful client-therapist relationship may not be obvious to either party.

- Ethical termination requires a termination checklist and meticulous attention to the details of a termination interview and letter, which the therapist and client should sign.

- The therapist should always offer to be available personally or to cooperate with a subsequent professional if needed.

- Document carefully the circumstances of every termination, but be especially diligent whenever a client is angry or threatening. Offer help and referrals. Defuse the situation and document the actions taken. Be kind!

- Consult the canons of ethics in your jurisdiction together with any national organizations to which you belong. Make sure you have complied with all the requirements of local codes and national guidelines. If they are in conflict, adhere to the most restrictive guidelines.

- Review the checklist and termination letter carefully at least twice to make sure nothing has been omitted. Have a lawyer review the letter and your procedures as well to save yourself a headache down the road!

- Consider termination the final but necessary and eventual step in the treatment plan.

- Review the ethical circumstances of *appropriate termination,* such as client's failure to benefit from treatment, services no longer required, services that no longer serve the client's needs or interests, client's failure to pay the fees charged, or agency or institution limits against provision of further counseling services. Make sure the appropriateness of the termination is fully documented.

Summary

A carefully drafted intake and consent form (perhaps lawyer drafted to protect the therapist) sets out the steps and procedures for termination and will authorize the mental health professional to contact the client should termination occur by any means other than a mutual agreement and exit interview. Then, as the final notation in the file, the clinical case notes must reflect the circumstances of termination, the termination process, the fact that therapy has been successfully concluded and the file closed.

After the participatory therapist–client relationship has been terminated, the file must still be properly be stored and preserved for the length of time required by both statute and ethical canons for adults and minors, for future therapy may be appropriate and the current clinical file will be of tremendous value and a treasure-trove of information when offering future treatment by either this or a subsequent therapist. Thus "termination" does not really mean "termination." Rather it means abatement. The client is on therapeutic "hold." The file will be preserved in a safe, secure and confidential manner for so long as required by law and as set forth in state ethical codes. And, if storage facilities are available, perhaps forever.

PART TWO

ETHICS CODES AND LICENSING

12

Areas of Ethical Complaints

The authors are repeatedly asked for facts, statistics, and opinions about which kinds of ethical misconduct are most often reported to the licensing boards and other disciplinary committees. What infractions should be carefully monitored in the daily life of the practicing professional? What red warning flags indicate a violation that is bound to come to the attention of the disciplinary authority?

We regularly review reports of mental health licensing boards' sanctions in our home state of Texas, as well as those reported by other states and national organizations where available, and are familiar with the offenses for which therapists are being sanctioned. In addition, having been in private law practice consulting with and working with mental health professionals for many years, we are aware of many wrongful actions by therapists that, although unethical, were never reported to a licensing board. Perhaps after consulting with us, the client never filed a formal complaint or the therapist who consulted with us revealed problems or unethical activities that, although revealed to an attorney, remained protected by the attorney-client privilege and continued to be strictly confidential. Not every ethical infraction or violation is reported to the board and not every client with a grievance chooses, after mature afterthought, to become involved in the grievance process. For some clients, sharing a legitimate complaint with a lawyer or with another professional is sufficient airing of the situation and further pursuit is unnecessary.

It has proven difficult to verify whether our Texas experience was representative and consistent throughout the United States. A few state licensing boards that we contacted did share limited complaint data that confirmed the information and opinions set out in this chapter. Insurance trusts and most licensing boards chose not to respond to our requests or declined to provide us with statistics. There is a need for better sharing and compiling of ethical violation information on a national level. The good news is that very few therapists have complaints filed against them and even fewer are sanctioned by their respective boards. According to Shrinksonline.com (an interactive Web site exclusively dedicated to mental health), there are approximately 738,240 licensed mental health professionals in the United States. Their numbers according to discipline, along with organizational membership figures are listed in Table 12.1.

It appears that in any given year less than 2 percent of all mental health professionals are the subjects of an ethical complaint.

It appears that in any given year less than 2 percent of all mental health professionals are the subjects of an ethical complaint. With such a low number, there is a danger that most therapists will have the attitude that there really is nothing to worry about. However, if the actual number amounted to just 1 percent, over 7,000 complaints would be filed in a calendar year. One unethical act is one too many and 7,000 represent a lot of injured clients and patients. With the growing awareness possessed by educated and sophisticated consumers relating to ethical mental health services and the zealousness of our licensing boards and national organizations in policing the professions, the possibility of an ethical complaint is greater today than ever before.

Our experience has shown that the number of complaints filed each year is increasing. A therapist can ill afford a relaxed attitude about ethical issues and practice. Constant vigilance is the price of professional practice, and mental health professionals should be ever mindful of the constantly changing plethora of codes, statutes, and professional responsibilities that govern their profession.

Table 12.1   Number of Licensed Mental Health Professionals in the United States

Psychologist (Ph.D., Licensed)	102,215 (13.8 %)
	APA (incl. MA level) 159,000
Social Workers	320,508 (43%)
	NASW 192,814
Marriage and Family Therapists	52,874 (07.2%)
Professional Counselors	128,143 (17.4%)
School Counselors	90,000 (12.2%)
	ASCA 12,000
Psychiatric Nurses	4,000 (< 1%)
Psychiatrists	40,500 (5.5%)
	American Psychiatric Ass. 40,500
Total	738,240

So what unethical acts are therapists committing? The following list ranks unethical behavior in order of frequency illustrated by the data and as experienced by the authors:

- Sexual exploitation.
- Dual relationships.
- Boundary violations.
- Breach of confidentiality/refusal to provide records.
- Fraudulent billing.
- Financial exploitation of a client.
- Provision of services while impaired.
- Violations of reporting statutes.
- Miscellaneous acts.

Sexual exploitation leads the way in frequency. To make matters worse, we know from firsthand experience that many sexual exploitation complaints go unreported. The exploited person may not want to go public by making the complaint a matter of community gossip and placing a sordid affair in the public domain. Interestingly, many complaints are filed, yet by the time the case works its way through the investigative mill, the importance of the situation has retreated, life's circumstances have changed, or the complainant no longer wishes to proceed. We have also learned that although most complaints in this category are filed against male therapists, female therapists sexually exploit their clients in greater numbers than are being reported. Our practice has shown that men are not as likely to report their therapists for a sexual relationship as female clients are likely to report male therapists.

Sexual exploitation leads the way in frequency.

We have grown weary preaching that sex with clients, former clients, and any person in a close relationship with a client is prohibited. There is not a therapist in the country that does not know this ethical restriction, yet it still happens with alarming frequency. On many occasions, a therapist who has attended one of our ethics workshops and did not heed the message has been forced to contact us for representation. There is zero tolerance for sex with clients by either licensing boards or national organizations.

There is zero tolerance for sex with clients by either licensing boards or national organizations.

Avoiding dual relationships is a lesson preached in every educational program in the country as well. Many therapists cross this line for personal benefit or out of a misguided desire to help a client. Only one relationship is tolerated: the professional therapeutic relationship. Entering into a business deal with a client or trading services with a client may seem harmless in a particular instance, but the risk of exploitation is too great to tolerate such arrangements under any circumstances.

Therapists are being sanctioned for their failure to maintain therapeutic boundaries, for personally violating them, and for allowing a client to do so.

Boundary violations occur in much the same way as dual relationships and sometimes the terms are used interchangeably. Therapists are being sanctioned for their failure to maintain therapeutic boundaries, for personally violating them, and for allowing a client to do so. The therapist is responsible for establishing and maintaining the high protective wall between the client and the therapist. Continuing to provide services to a client who refuses to respect boundaries has resulted in sanctions against many therapists. We recommend that in the very first intake interview, when all contact is above board and before any relationship is established, the therapist determine the nature of the relationship and firmly set all the boundaries. The therapist should impress on the client that boundaries are serious, provide for no exception, and that any violation will lead to immediate termination of the relationship.

Despite being well aware of the need to preserve client confidentiality, many therapists directly and sometimes inadvertently disclose confidential information about their clients. Failure to provide security for client files has resulted in sanctions against therapists who did not directly disclose the information (e.g., a snooping husband entered a therapist's office at night with a cleaning crew and perused his wife's clinical file). On the flip side of this issue, therapists who failed to disclose information or provide copies of records when legally required to do so have been sanctioned. This seems to occur most often in family law cases when a parent wants to review a child's records and the presenting parent does not want the information disclosed to the other parent.

Greed motivates some therapists to bill fraudulently but we have learned that simple economic survival has pushed several mental health professionals to cross the line of honesty.

Economic crimes and unethical acts are as old as mankind and the mental health profession has seen its fair share. With managed care driving fees downward and competition for clients increasing, fraudulent billing activity probably will increase, too. Greed motivates some therapists to bill fraudulently but we have learned that simple economic survival has pushed several mental health professionals to cross the line of honesty. No matter how disgusting one might find managed care or a particular payor of benefits, the risk in this area is too great. Civil, administrative, and criminal penalties are being leveled against the guilty.

Occasionally, a mental health professional takes advantage of the professional relationship to financially exploit a client, although the frequency is not as great as with sexual exploitation. Greed is usually the motivating factor and is inexcusable. It seems to be more prevalent among professionals providing services to elderly clients in nursing homes and assisted living settings.

Many therapists continue to provide services while they are impaired, most often due to substance abuse or addiction. We are aware of cases, however, where a therapist continued to practice when a physical disability impaired the therapist's ability to provide services (e.g., deafness). Alcohol and illegal drug use occurs in all mental health disciplines as it does in all walks of life. Every mental health organization makes assistance available to impaired professionals, who recognize their impairment and seek help. Assistance cannot be imposed on providers.

Failure to report child abuse, threats by a client, elder abuse, or ethical violations by another mental health professional are actionable ethical violations for which therapists are sanctioned not just by licensing boards but often by the criminal justice system. Therapists have a general ethical duty to follow the law at all times with respect to their professional activities. Mandatory reporting statutes make this obligation much more specific under certain circumstances and cannot be ignored.

Under miscellaneous acts, we see such things as falsifying educational records, academic documentation, supervision records, and licensing applications; assisting the evasion of board rules; keeping sloppy records; practicing outside the scope of a license; poorly preparing expert testimony; and having felony convictions unrelated to the practice. Somewhere, sometime, somehow some mental health professionals have violated one or more of the ethical canons. Hopefully better education of ethical issues will keep future violations to a minimum.

Ethical Flash Points

- Even if only 1 percent of all licensed mental health professionals are reported to state licensing boards that still represents over 7,000 complaints annually.

- The number of complaints filed each year appears to be increasing.

- Having a casual attitude about ethics is almost sure to lead to an ethical violation.

- Most therapists who violate ethical canons know the rules.

- Sexual exploitation is the most frequently filed complaint and everyone knows it is improper.

- Education and knowledge are not enough. Self-discipline and self-control are equally important to remain ethically compliant.

- Which category of violation is most often violated matters little. What really matters is that no violations occur.

Summary

Knowing the ethics canons of the national organizations and the licensing board rules in one's state is just the first step to becoming ethically compliant. Educating mental health professionals regarding their ethics is the goal of this book, but we have learned that even therapists who know the rules violate them. Self-control and discipline are necessary to resist the temptation to bend or break the rules that will surely confront every mental health professional at some point in his or her career. Be knowledgeable, be strong, and don't become a statistic!

13

Ethics Codes as Evidence

Jane, a white, married, elected city council member living in a small southern community has carried on a two-year affair with a black school principal. Racked by guilt, Jane sought treatment for depression with a local psychologist, Dr. Kindheart. Aware of the sensitivity of the information received from Jane, Dr. Kindheart does not record any specific information in Jane's file. Session notes are limited to entries such as "explored pressures impacting client's depression." After several months of therapy, Dr. Kindheart leaves on a well-deserved European vacation arranging for a colleague to cover for her in her absence. While Dr. Kindheart is on vacation, Jane's husband sues her for divorce, schedules a temporary custody hearing, and issues a subpoena for Dr. Kindheart to testify and produce Jane's records on her return. Jane, extremely distraught by the pending litigation, contacts Dr. Kindheart's office and schedules a session with the colleague. When she presents herself for the therapy session, Jane is unable to advise the colleague about her affair with the principal but does indicate she is upset over the custody hearing and the subpoena issued for Dr. Kindheart. The colleague, who knows nothing about the affair, tells Jane she has nothing to worry about and to get a good lawyer and relax. Later that evening, Jane commits suicide by running her automobile in the enclosed garage of her family home. She leaves a note apologizing to her husband and children. Her 12-year-old daughter discovers the body when she opens the garage door. When the husband sues the psychologist for malpractice due to negligent record keeping, can the ethics code provisions be used as evidence to support his case? On judicial scrutiny will Dr. Kindheart's records be found deficient of significant facts and statements and inconsistent with minimum ethics requirements? Will the race of the principal be a significant fact or would its inclusion in the progress notes indicate the treating therapist had some prejudice or tendency toward discrimination? Can community bias cloud clinical objectivity? In trying to protect Jane, did Dr. Kindheart make herself vulnerable?

Proving Malpractice

Malpractice has been defined as the unreasonable lack of skill or misconduct by a health care provider.

Malpractice has been defined as the unreasonable lack of skill or misconduct by a health care provider. The plaintiff in a malpractice lawsuit must show that the defendant had the duty to conform to a certain standard of conduct and failed to do so, and this failure caused the injury (*Watts v Cumberland County Hosp.*, 75 N.C. App. 1, 300 S.E. 2d 242 [1985]).

Generally, the plaintiff must prove four elements in a malpractice case: (1) that the health care provider had a duty to conform to a certain standard of care, (2) that the health care provider in question breached the standard of care, (3) the plaintiff suffered an injury, and (4) that there is a causal connection between the breach of the standard of care and the injuries suffered (*Pennington v Brock*, 841 S.W. 2d 127, 129 [Tex. App.-Houston (14th District) 1992, *no writ*]). Further, the plaintiff must prove the standard of care in the locality where the treatment occurred, breach of the standard of care, and proximate cause by expert testimony (*Duff v Yelin*, 721 S.W. 2d 365, 373 [Tex. App.-Houston (1st Dist) 1986], *aff'd*, 751 S.W. 2d 175 [Tex. 1988]).

Of these four elements, the easiest to establish is the standard of care, thanks in part to ethics codes. In a malpractice case, the ethics codes promulgated by a therapist's national and state organizations and by state statute or licensing board regulations can be used to help establish the standard of care that will be applied to the therapist. When presented to the court, the judge may admit them into evidence as indicating a standard of care. The weight to be given to the ethical codes depends on the judgment of the judge or the jury.

National Guidelines for Using Ethics Codes in Malpractice Litigation

APA Ethical Principles of Psychologists and Code of Conduct

Introduction:

The Ethics Code is intended to provide standards of professional conduct that can be applied by the APA and by other bodies that choose to adopt them. Whether or not a psychologist has violated the Ethics Code does not by itself determine whether he or she is legally liable in a court action, whether a contract is enforceable, or whether other legal consequences occur. The results are based on legal rather than ethical rules. However, compliance with or violation of the Ethics Code may be admissible as evidence in some legal proceedings, depending on the circumstances . . .

NASW Code of Ethics

The NASW Code of Ethics is to be used by NASW and by individuals, agencies, organizations, and bodies (such as licensing and regulatory boards, professional liability insurance providers, courts of law, agency boards of directors, government agencies, and other professional groups) that choose to adopt or use it as a frame of reference. Violation of standards in this Code does not automatically imply legal liability or violation of the law. Such determination can only be made in the context of legal and judicial proceedings . . .

Establishing Compliance with Standard of Care

Once the plaintiff establishes that the defendant owed a duty to the plaintiff to comport with the applicable standard of care, the plaintiff must then introduce evidence as to the applicable standard of care. The duty is proved by the relationship between the plaintiff and the defendant. If Jane's husband proves that Jane entered into a therapeutic relationship with Dr. Kindheart, her duty to provide services consistent with the applicable standard of care arises.

In examining the facts in Dr. Kindheart's case, the obvious question presented is whether Dr. Kindheart had a duty to record the information regarding Jane's affair with the black school principal. Was "black" an issue at all? Should race, religion, or sexual orientation, and so forth be entered into a clinical record because of community bias and the feelings of the client or the therapist toward that bias? Section 1.23 of the APA Ethics Code states:

> (1) Psychologists appropriately document their professional and scientific work in order to facilitate provision of services later by them or by other professionals, to insure accountability and to meet other requirements of institutions or the law.

Did Dr. Kindheart appropriately document Jane's file to facilitate her colleague's provision of services while she was on vacation? This is the standard of care to which Dr. Kindheart should have complied. Arguably she did not. Her colleague probably would have taken the events of the divorce and subpoena much more seriously had she known *all* the information Jane shared with Dr. Kindheart. She may have perceived that Jane might contemplate suicide over these events if the consequences and nature of the affair were made public. On the other hand, a minority colleague may have considered race to be a non issue.

The law requires Dr. Kindheart to possess and exercise the degree of skill and learning ordinarily possessed and exercised under similar circumstances by other psychologists in good standing, and to use ordinary and reasonable care and diligence, and her best judgment, in applying her skill to the case (70 *CJS Physicians and Surgeons* Sec. 41 [1951]). Ordinary and reasonable skill, learning, and care involve knowing and complying with the ethical provisions of the psychological organizations of which Dr. Kindheart is a member and those state boards that have issued her the licenses to practice. Pursuant to the APA Ethics Code, ordinary care requires Dr. Kindheart to appropriately document her file to facilitate the provision of mental health services later by her colleague. Dr. Kindheart failed to do this. On the other hand, arguably, the affair could be considered the issue and race a non issue. This is why there are judges and juries in civil trials and grievance committees and complaints committees for licensing boards to make these hard decisions regarding the appropriate documentation in clinical notations. Appropriate documentation is not a science and no universal rules apply in all cases.

Having used the APA Ethics Code to establish the standard of care (i.e., that psychologists properly document their cases), Jane's husband could establish that she breached the standard of care by introducing into evidence Dr. Kindheart's inappropriately documented file. The husband has therefore satisfied two of the four elements of proof necessary to recover a money judgment against Dr. Kindheart.

Establishing the Connection between Breach of Standard of Care and Injury

In many malpractice cases brought against therapists, it is difficult to establish injury and the causal connection between the breach of the standard of care and the injury, particularly where there is no physical injury.

Some courts still hold that absent physical injury there can be no recovery for mental suffering:

> Mental suffering is more difficult to estimate in financial terms, and no less a real injury. . . . Where the defendant's negligence causes only mental disturbance, without accompanying physical injury, illness or other physical consequence, and in the absence of some other independent basis for tort liability, the great majority of courts still hold that in the ordinary case there can be no recovery. . . . (W. Keeton, *Prosser and Keeton on Torts,* Sec. 54, at 361)

In Dr. Kindheart's case, there was a suicide and therefore physical injury as well as mental injury to Jane's family. It is conceivable that Dr. Kindheart's colleague would bridge the causal connection between Dr. Kindheart's failure to appropriately document Jane's case file and Jane's suicide. The colleague could testify that had she known about the potentially explosive affair as Jane perceived local community standards she would have appreciated the risk involved to Jane and possibly recommended inpatient care or immediately called in a psychiatrist who could have appropriately prescribed antidepressant medication.

Could Dr. Kindheart plead ignorance of the applicable APA ethics provisions? Would this be a defense to the malpractice action or limit the damages awarded in the case? Absolutely not. Therapists are required to be familiar with their ethics codes. Ignorance will not excuse unethical conduct. Section 8.02 of the APA Ethics Code states:

> Psychologists have an obligation to be familiar with this Ethics Code, other applicable ethics codes, and their application to psychologists' work. Lack of awareness or misunderstanding of an ethical standard is not itself a defense to a charge of unethical conduct.

The authors present workshops and seminars throughout the country stressing the importance of ethical standards, canons, and codes and are amazed by how many seasoned professionals have not reviewed their associations' ethics codes since graduate school or their licensing examinations. Judging by the questions asked during the question-and-answer period following each presentation, therapists prefer to receive this knowledge through seminars rather than a careful examination of the codes. Don't wait to familiarize yourself with any applicable ethics codes. You need to know their provisions *before a problem arises, not after.*

================= *Ethical Flash Points* =================

- Therapists are required to be familiar with their ethics codes. Ignorance of ethics code provisions is not a defense to unethical acts or omissions and will not lessen damages awarded.

- Ethics codes can be used to establish the minimum standard of care in a malpractice action.

- Once a plaintiff establishes violation of an ethics code provision, the only real issue remaining is to decide the amount of monetary damages.

- Finding the appropriate provision in the canons of ethics is easy. Usually the canons are brief, to the point, and carefully thought out. Interpreting them is often difficult and the licensing boards and national organizations will offer general advice, but usually will not comment on specific questions. The therapist customarily determines what to document, as in the case used for illustration.

Summary

Ethical codes must be carefully reviewed and digested by every therapist. They are potent ammunition for a plaintiff in a malpractice case and therefore knowledge and compliance are a strict necessity for every practicing therapist. Proving a departure from an ethical requirement can relegate a malpractice case to a single issue, "How much money will compensate the client for the harm caused by the ethical violation?"

14

Licensing Board Procedures

Albert, a licensed professional counselor in private practice for over 12 years, received a certified letter from his state licensing board. Although he had never before received a certified letter from the board, he instinctively knew it was not good news. As he suspected, it was not. For the first time in a stellar career as a helping professional, Albert was facing a complaint and investigation by his licensing board. Albert broke out in a cold sweat when he realized he did not know what to do. He had never been advised in school or at any ethics continuing education seminar what action to take if an unhappy client filed a complaint with his licensing board. He was unsure whom he could call or wanted to call. After all, he really did not want to share the information about the complaint. After a couple of days, he finally discussed the matter with a psychologist who practiced in the same building and whom he occasionally joined for lunch. The psychologist calmed his fears with a few stories from his own practice in which he had responded to complaints with long letters to his board, which then dropped the matter completely. Albert, following the psychologist's advice, dashed off a five-page letter to his board letting them know about all the great things he had accomplished in the past 12 years.

Thinking the matter resolved, he put the original letter and the answer out of his mind until a second certified letter came three months later. This time, the licensing board advised him that based on their initial investigation, he had violated several sections of the state licensing act and they were pursuing a hearing before an administrative law judge to seek revocation of his license. At this point, Albert contacted an attorney. Did he wait too long and violate the maxim: "The law aids the vigilant, not those who slumber on their rights"?

∼

Dr. Sellers practiced for years. She was incensed when a client complained about not receiving a copy of her file in a timely fashion. She was so mad she refused to respond to a complaint notice from the board. Big mistake. The board then proceeded with a complete investigation, discovered discrepancies *in billing practices and procedures and followed with a revocation hearing. Only after engaging a lawyer at $200 per hour did Dr. Sellers understand her precarious situation. Had she respectfully responded, perhaps with a half-hour attorney consultation, the matter might have been dropped.*

~

A therapist responding to a complaint filed with his licensing board for having sex with a client ended his five-page self-laudatory biography by saying: "Besides, I only did it once." Once was once too much. With a zero tolerance sensitivity for sex with clients, the board revoked his license. A thoughtful lawyer would have struck that remark from the letter if asked to review it. Although the admission might have come out in future testimony had the case gone to trial, it would not have come from the therapist.

National Licensing Board Trends

The national trend is toward state licensing of all mental health disciplines.

The national trend is toward state licensing of all mental health disciplines. By their nature, licensing acts are an effort to regulate an industry or profession, protect the public at large, and create minimum standards of conduct and professional practice for a given profession. The mistake many mental health professionals make is to assume that the licensing board that bestowed a license on them is their friend. This may be true until a complaint is filed. A licensing board's mission is to regulate the mental health profession and to sanction mental health professionals when necessary. Simply put, they tell you what you can do, when you do it, how you can practice, and what will happen if you violate their rules.

Not only do therapists misperceive their licensing boards' attitudes and mission, but they have little or no knowledge of complaint procedures and the administrative process. This chapter provides an overview of both actions.

Administrative Law

Administrative law involves the study of agencies, the decision-making parts of our government that are neither legislatures nor courts.

Most citizens are familiar with the civil and criminal justice systems either through personal interaction or what they acquire and assimilate through the media. There is a third system or body of law known as *administrative law* that is not as well known nor understood even by most attorneys. Administrative law involves the study of agencies, the decision-making parts of our government that are neither legislatures nor courts. We are familiar with numerous federal agencies, such as the Social Security Administration, the Food and Drug Administration, the Federal Communications Commission, and the Federal Trade Commission. Licensing boards are agencies. In the context of mental health, licensing boards are primarily state agencies, created by the states to regulate and police mental health providers.

Licensing Boards as State Agencies

Agencies are legislative creations enacted through statutes that are often referred to as their *enabling acts*. These enabling acts do not always establish the agency's precise procedures but do set forth the agency's mission or reason for existence. Procedure is dictated in part by a more general set of laws governing all agencies known as an *administrative procedure act*. The federal government's version is entitled the Administrative Procedure Act, 5 U.S.C. Sections 551–808. State administrative procedure acts can differ greatly but a Model State Administrative Procedure Act has been promulgated that many states have adopted totally or substantially follow in enacting particular state laws.

An agency generally has wide discretion when creating the policies and procedures to fulfill its legislative mission. First, they make lots of rules. In addition to rule making, agencies have an adjudicative function by which they enforce the rules they adopt or promulgate. Courts have a very small role in supervising agency conduct. If a licensee strikes out (i.e., is disciplined at the agency level), generally very little help is available through the courts. To appeal an administrative hearing (i.e., a determination lost at the hearing level) is difficult, cumbersome, and expensive, and is an uphill process.

A state mental health licensing board is an agency governed by administrative law. It is created by the state legislature and given the mission to regulate the particular discipline through the licensing of those who practice that discipline. It passes rules, issues licenses based on qualifications it establishes, and enforces punishment if a licensee violates the licensing act or its ethics codes and board rules. The state's administrative procedure act provides some procedural guidelines, and each board generally has wide discretion in creating detailed and specific procedures. Boards establish their own complaint and informal resolution procedures, but formal resolution, involving a hearing before an

Every state has written rules and regulations, in addition to informal understandings that can guide both the boards and the licensee.

administrative law judge, is usually controlled by the state's administrative procedure act. Although it is not possible in one chapter to set out the complaint procedures for each state, we will discuss a representative procedure. Every state has written rules and regulations, in addition to informal understandings that can guide both the boards and the licensee. Understanding these "understandings" is helpful when developing a defense to a complaint.

The Complaint Procedure

The first step of a complaint procedure involves the receipt and an initial review of a complaint filed with the board by a client, another professional, any member of the public, or the board itself. Most state licensing boards require their licensees to provide information to each client on how and where to file a complaint against them with the licensing board. Some boards require the provider to post prominently, the address and a toll-free number to contact the licensing board. Either an individual or a committee may make the initial complaint review, but the introductory inquiry concerns whether on its face the board has jurisdiction over the matter or parties complained of and, if so, whether the complaint states a violation of the licensing act, the ethics code, or a board rule. If the board does not find it has jurisdiction, it usually dismisses the matter and forwards information regarding the allegation and its findings (e.g., the board lacks jurisdiction over the matter or the complaint does not state a specific violation) to the licensed mental health provider and the complaining party.

Most state licensing boards require their licensees to provide information to each client on how and where to file a complaint against them with the licensing board.

To be a valid complaint, it must indicate that a board rule was violated.

Numerous complaints are filed with licensing boards from clients who are dissatisfied with the result of the therapy. Mental health professionals do not guarantee results. To be a valid complaint, it must indicate that a board rule was violated. Clients filing a complaint state the facts as they perceive them; the board then determines whether a rule has been violated.

Finding a Violation

If the board finds that the provider has violated a rule, he or she will receive notice of the complaint and will be asked to respond to the allegations within a prescribed period. The initial time for responding is usually short but most boards are willing to extend the time for filing the response upon a timely and reasonable request.

If the reviewer or committee that studies the therapist's response still perceives a likelihood that a violation has occurred, they may move directly to their adjudicative stage. If there is still doubt, the board may continue the investigation. An investigator may interview the parties or other witnesses and possibly check public records for relevant documentary evidence. Some investigations are conducted secretly. If the board concludes either (1) no jurisdiction or (2) no violation after the investigation is concluded, they will dismiss the matter and notify each party. Otherwise, the board moves on to the adjudicative stage.

The Adjudicative Stage

The adjudicative stage occurs when the licensing board attempts to enforce the licensing act, ethics code, or its rules either through informal resolution or formal adjudication. The board thus fulfills its mission to protect the public from inappropriate, unfit, negligent, or fraudulent practitioners and harmful practices. Informal adjudication could be likened to plea bargaining in a criminal case. Here the board determines that although an ethical, licensing act, or board rule violation has occurred, the matter can be best resolved informally by agreement with the therapist. This is the usual procedure for less serious violations, such as failure to promptly forward copies of a client's file upon request, maintaining slightly incomplete records, or other minor infractions. Informal adjudication may be handled over the phone, by correspondence, or through a face-to-face settlement conference. Letters of instruction, public or private reprimands, education, and additional supervision are all techniques implemented for informal resolution. If an agreement cannot be achieved, the board will move on to formal adjudication.

The adjudicative stage occurs when the licensing board attempts to enforce the licensing act, ethics code, or its rules either through informal resolution or formal adjudication.

Formal adjudication customarily means seeking revocation of a license through an administrative hearing.

Formal Adjudication

Formal adjudication customarily means seeking revocation of a license through an administrative hearing governed by the rules and procedures of the state's administrative procedure act. The administrative procedure acts require the affected person to be given specific notice of the hearing time, date, place, nature of the hearing, the legal authority for convening the hearing, and information on the issues presented (see Federal Administrative Procedure Act, Sec. 554[b]). These matters are usually set forth in the original complaint. Since agency proceedings are civil cases (one can't be sentenced to jail), the charged therapist need only be given reasonable notice of the violation (*Savina Home Industries v Secretary of Labor,* 594 F.2d 1358 [10th Cir. 1979]). In criminal cases, the complaint against an individual must be very specific regarding the crime and the charge. A civil case does not require same specificity. The therapist should always file a written response to the complaint with the licensing board prior to the hearing to set the tone for the defense. Providers should always consult a lawyer prior to filing their response to a complaint. It is easier for an attorney to create an effective defense in a letter than it is to explain away an admission once it is reduced to writing by an unwitting and naive provider.

The therapist should always file a written response to the complaint with the licensing board prior to the hearing to set the tone for the defense.

The Hearing

An administrative law judge conducts the hearing and hears testimony under oath through direct and cross-examination, allows documentary information into evidence, makes evidentiary rulings, and enters an order (Federal Administrative Procedure Act, Sec. 556). The hearing closely resembles a civil trial without a jury. The licensing board has the burden of proof (Federal Administrative Procedure Act, Sec. 556[d]), which means it is up to the board to introduce evidence of a violation.

Since the board's original complaint may be general in nature, how can a mental health professional prepare for the hearing? Most administrative procedure acts, including the federal act, make little mention of discovery except for subpoenas. Many states allow depositions with either the administrative law judge or the agency itself having the power to compel appearance. Record disclosure laws may mandate that the board provide the therapist with copies of its file prior to the hearing. These tools should be actively employed in preparing for the hearing. An active, participatory, but nonabrasive defense is essential.

An active, participatory, but nonabrasive defense is essential.

Burden of Proof

• Preponderance of the evidence.

• Clear and convincing evidence.

• Beyond a reasonable doubt.

As a result of the media coverage of the O.J. Simpson murder trial and the popularity of Court TV, Americans have become well acquainted with the burden of proof in a criminal case: *beyond a reasonable doubt*. In civil cases, there are two burdens of proof: *clear and convincing evidence* and *preponderance of the evidence*. The federal administrative procedure act and many state acts fail to include a standard of proof to be applied by the administrative law judge in an administrative law hearing. In *Steadman v S.E.C.* (450 U.S. 91 [1981]), the Supreme Court held that absent a statutory requirement or an agency rule or practice, the burden of proof to be applied in agency proceedings is *preponderance of the evidence*. This is obviously the easiest of the three legal burdens to employ, which may be a chilling thought for a therapist accused of an ethical or licensing act violation.

Taking the Fifth

When facing a licensing board complaint, can a therapist claim a fifth amendment right against self-incrimination and refuse to release copies of records or to give testimony if called to do so? Professor K.C. Davis in his book, *Administrative Law* (Casenotes Publishing Co., Beverly Hills, CA, 1977) sets out five situations in which the fifth amendment cannot be used in response to a request for records including "(4) records that are required to be kept by statute or agency regulation" (p. 567). A therapist is unable to withhold records by asserting the fifth amendment for two reasons. First, a therapist is generally required by the licensing act or the ethics code adopted by the licensing board to keep client records and notes. As the board has this requirement, therapists must turn over the records to the board if ordered. Second, if the complaining client consents and directs the therapist to turn over copies of his or her files, the therapist is obligated to surrender them usually pursuant to state statute or ethics code.

A therapist may invoke the fifth amendment and preclude oral testimony; nevertheless, in all but the rarest cases refusing to testify will

A therapist may invoke the fifth amendment and preclude oral testimony.

make defending the complainant's allegations extremely difficult. Failing to testify will make it hard to rebut the complainant's statements, which will be taken as true if there is no contradicting evidence. The board must prove a violation of its licensing act, and they can meet the preponderance of evidence burden of proof with just the complainant's testimony. A therapist who holds his or her tongue may not be holding on to his or her license very much longer.

A therapist who holds his or her tongue may not be holding on to his or her license very much longer.

Sometimes, however, the therapist also faces a criminal prosecution in which a long-term jail sentence is a possible outcome, such as when a therapist sexually exploits a client. If criminal prosecution is likely or certain, asserting a fifth amendment right and losing a license could be a necessity.

Prehearing Settlement Conference

Most licensing boards and administrative procedure acts favor informal resolution even after a hearing has been requested. Often referred to as a *prehearing settlement conference,* it can be an opportunity to persuade a licensing board to rescind its request for the formal hearing. In practical terms, this means the therapist attempts to persuade the board not to revoke the license and either dismiss the complaint or agree to a lesser sanction.

A prehearing settlement conference can be an opportunity to persuade a licensing board to rescind its request for the formal hearing.

Judicial Review

Once the administrative law judge has entered an order, there are few grounds on which to base a request for court or judicial review. Such grounds set out in administrative procedure acts include a decision that was arbitrary and capricious or unsupported by the great weight of the evidence, or an abuse of discretion (Federal Administrative Procedure Act, Sec. 706). The opportunity for a *de novo* (new) hearing on the merits before a civil or appellate judge after agency adjudication is available in very few states. Convincing a court to undo an agency result is possible but not very probable. It is critical then for therapists to be aware of the board's complaint procedure and to put on the best possible case throughout its proceedings.

Ethical Flash Points

- When a complaint is received, seek peer and legal advice before finalizing *any* response. Be cautious about talking with your peers. Colleagues may have some obligation to report infractions to the board. Any consultation with a board or a colleague should be theoretical, hypothetical, and about "another" person.

- Many lawyers are unfamiliar with administrative law, and even fewer mental health professionals are familiar with board rules and regulations. Consult with colleagues on practice issues, but engage an attorney familiar with board procedures and mental health law to defend you.

- Responses to complaint letters should be succinct, *addressing only the issues raised by the complaint or the board.* Attorney review prior to submission is recommended.

- Don't wait for the board to seek revocation through a formal hearing before retaining competent legal assistance. There is an old saying in law that a lawyer who represents himself has a fool for a client.

- Be sure your malpractice insurance policy provides benefits for licensing board representation and costs. Defending against a complaint by a licensing board can cost thousands of dollars.

- Notify your malpractice insurance carrier the minute a complaint is filed; don't wait until a revocation hearing is requested. Policies contain specific notice provisions that, if not followed, can cause the loss of coverage.

- Vigorously pursue whatever discovery is available (e.g., depositions, letters, or other documents sent to the board) and take advantage of all statutes allowing access to the board's file, especially interboard communications and memoranda.

- Mount a good defense but be courteous and respectful of the board and its staff at all times. Even if the result is favorable, those people will monitor your activities for a long time. A hearing before the board or an administrative judge is not the same as a full adversary hearing before a court. It is less dramatic and more conversational and conciliatory.

- Utilize every opportunity for informal resolution of the complaint even after a formal revocation hearing has been requested.

- Even though the board has the burden of proving a violation by a preponderance of the evidence, approach the case as if the burden is shifted and *prove* innocence or compliance beyond all reasonable doubt. This will help ensure high energy and a strong defense.

- Assert the fifth amendment right against self-incrimination only if absolutely necessary.

- Familiarize yourself with the board's complaint procedure before a complaint is filed and develop a response plan to implement a defense the minute notification of a complaint is received.

- Don't rely on the fact that you have never had a complaint filed against you. Many complaints that are filed are without merit. Even the most consciously ethical practitioner has the risk that an unhappy client may file a complaint.

- There is no risk to a client when filing a frivolous complaint. Only the practitioner is at risk.

Summary

With the increasing number of complaints filed against mental health professionals annually and the increased knowledge of consumers with respect to mental health practice issues, no therapist is immune from an ethical or licensing act violation allegation. Board complaint procedures involve administrative law with which most therapists are totally unfamiliar. Competent legal assistance and direction is critical. Life and liberty may not be at risk before the licensing board but a license revocation could certainly impact a therapist's pursuit of happiness. Practice ethically, but be informed and prepared to defend against a specious and fabricated allegation. Take every complaint seriously.

Take every complaint seriously.

15

Reporting Statutes

Cheryl scheduled an afternoon counseling session with Dr. Kindheart, a child psychologist, after receiving a referral from a school counselor. Cheryl suspected her second husband had sexually molested her 12-year-old daughter, Susan. After the initial session with Susan, Dr. Kindheart told her mother there was a strong probability Susan was abused. Cheryl assured him she would contact the child welfare authorities and make a report. Dr. Kindheart practiced in a state that requires reporting suspected child abuse. Relying on Cheryl's assurance that she would file a report, Dr. Kindheart scheduled a second appointment for Susan three days later. Cheryl went home and, fearful of the unpredictable outcome of a report, did not call child welfare. The night before the second appointment, Susan's stepfather sexually assaulted her again. When the police investigated the case, they found out that neither Cheryl nor Dr. Kindheart had reported the suspected prior abuse. Criminal charges were filed against each of them for failure to comply with the reporting statute. They each pleaded guilty to the misdemeanor offense, paid fines, and performed community service. The lead detective on the assault case against the stepfather also filed a complaint with the state board responsible for disciplining and licensing psychologists. Dr. Kindheart received a public reprimand that was published in the board's newsletter.

~

After becoming romantically and sexually involved with a recently terminated client, Kevin, a licensed social worker, confided in Jerome, also a licensed social worker, and a longtime friend. Jerome counseled Kevin regarding the obvious inappropriateness of the relationship and strongly urged Kevin to discontinue seeing the client. Kevin decided to do just that and told the client about his conversation with Jerome and the advice he received. The client was devastated about the breakup, but later became incensed and filed a complaint with the social work licensing board. When she spoke with the board's investigator, she told him about Kevin's conversation with Jerome that precipitated the breakup. The licensing board sought and secured the revocation of Kevin's license and simultaneously sanctioned Jerome for failing to report sexual exploitation under a state reporting statute and ethics code provision. Jerome was placed on two years' probation, a fact he was required to disclose to each client and on every malpractice renewal application along with the ethics code provision he had violated.

~

John, Richard, and Carolyn, licensed professional counselors, shared office space together for over 10 years. They maintained separate practices but contributed equally to common office expenses, referring clients to one another and covering for each other during absences. After experiencing a difficult marital breakup, Carolyn began to drink excessively. Her alcohol abuse became evident to John and Richard, and they became concerned for her. They made excuses for her with clients and suggested repeatedly that she take some time off. Richard even tried to convince her that she needed help for substance abuse. Carolyn politely thanked them each time they tried to help her but kept insisting she was going to be all right. She just needed some time. Late one afternoon, Carolyn screamed obscenities at a client and physically pushed her out of her office and out the front door of the building. The client immediately called the state licensing board. When an investigator interviewed John and Richard, they honestly shared how they had been concerned for some time regarding Carolyn's drinking and erratic behavior. They indicated this was not the first time she had been intoxicated and abusive to a client. To their surprise, the board sanctioned them for failing to report unethical conduct by another licensed counselor. Most state ethical canons provide procedures concerning impaired colleagues. At a minimum, call the licensing board anonymously and seek guidance.

What Is a Reporting Statute?

Every state has laws that will circumvent or supersede general principles of confidentiality. The general perception of American consumers, that information shared between a client and a therapist is sacrosanct and absolutely privileged, is erroneous. The belief in this myth must be dispelled by a therapist as part of informed consent (i.e., informing a client about the numerous and well-known exceptions to confidentiality).

Reporting statutes include some of the exceptions to confidentiality that must be disclosed to a client. The typical matters that most often fall within a statutory obligation to report are child abuse and neglect, elder abuse, abuse of the physically or mentally impaired, sexual exploitation by a mental health professional, and imminent danger to a client or a third party. The mechanics of each statute and the authorities to whom a report should be made vary with each state and statute. Therapists are sometimes compelled by their professional duties and obligations to disclose confidential information that ordinarily would be protected by the mental health privilege and ethical concepts of confidentiality. The law has determined that in these instances society's right to protection outweighs a client's right to confidentiality.

National Guidelines for Breaching Confidentiality

ACA Code of Ethics and Standards of Practice

Standard of Practice Nine (SP-9) Confidentiality Requirement. Counselors must keep information related to counseling services confidential unless disclosure is in the best interest of clients, is required for the welfare of others, or is required by law. When disclosure is required, only information that is essential is revealed and the client is informed of such disclosure.

B.1.   Right to Privacy . . .

c. Exceptions. The general requirement that counselors keep information confidential does not apply when disclosure is required to prevent clear and imminent danger to the client or others or when legal requirements demand that confidential information be revealed . . .

AAMFT Code of Ethics

2.1 Marriage and Family Therapists may not disclose client confidences except: (a) as mandated by law; (b) to prevent a clear and immediate danger to a person or persons . . .

NASW Code of Ethics

1.07   Privacy and Confidentiality . . .
(b) Social workers should protect the confidentiality of all information obtained in the course of professional service, except for compelling

The typical matters that most often fall within a statutory obligation to report are child abuse and neglect, elder abuse, abuse of the physically or mentally impaired, sexual exploitation by a mental health professional, and imminent danger to a client or a third party.

professional reasons. The general exception that social workers will keep information confidential does not apply when disclosure is necessary to prevent serious, foreseeable, and imminent harm to a client or other identifiable person or when laws or regulations require disclosure without a client's consent . . .

Know the Codes

Mental health professionals are obligated to know all exceptions to confidentiality, including mandatory reporting statutes. Ignorance is not an excuse and will not provide a defense. When legally required to disclose confidential information, a mental health professional is under a legal and ethical obligation to do so. Too many times, mental health professionals are reluctant to make reports because of uncertainty or a reluctance to get involved in what may turn out to be a very messy or nasty legal matter. In most instances, the therapist cannot rely on a client or a third party to make the report. Ethically and legally, it is the provider's responsibility to report such behavior. Just as importantly, the therapist should document the report to prove compliance with the statute and ethics code.

In the first vignette, Dr. Kindheart relied on her client to report the child abuse to the proper authorities. Cheryl failed to do so, and it was easily argued that had Dr. Kindheart fulfilled her legal and ethical duty to report the suspected abuse, Susan's stepfather would not have had an opportunity to continue the abuse. The liability under these facts is threefold. First, the authors are unaware of any state that does not impose criminal penalties for failure to report child abuse. Second, the damages suffered by the child make a civil lawsuit highly probable. Third, failing to report as required by law is an ethical violation that could lead to licensing board sanctioning. It is foolish to fail to report when one considers the potential consequences as well as that most statutes provide for civil and criminal immunity from prosecution for reports made in good faith.

In the second vignette, Jerome failed in his legal duty as well as his ethical obligation to report Kevin's sexual relationship to the state licensing board as required by the statute dealing with a mental health professional's sexual exploitation of a client. A sanction against Jerome was entirely appropriate. A mental health professional cannot afford to protect friends and colleagues by ignoring ethical obligations.

Ethics codes require reporting ethical violations to state or national organization ethics committees and to state licensing boards. In the third vignette when Richard and John knew Carolyn was seeing clients while intoxicated and therefore impaired clinically, they had an ethical duty to report her after they had confronted her and she refused to take steps to correct her problem.

Ethics codes require reporting ethical violations to state or national organization ethics committees and to state licensing boards.

National Guidelines for Reporting Ethical Violations

APA Ethical Principles of Psychologists and Code of Conduct

8.04 Informal Resolution of Ethical Violations

When psychologists believe that there may have been an ethical violation by another psychologist, they attempt to resolve the issue by bringing it to the attention of that individual if an informal resolution appears appropriate and the intervention does not violate any confidentiality rights that may be involved.

8.05 Reporting Ethical Violations

If an apparent ethical violation is not appropriate for informal resolution under Standard 8.04 or is not resolved properly in that fashion, psychologists take further action appropriate to the situation, unless such action conflicts with confidentiality rights in ways that cannot be resolved. Such action might include referral to state or national committees on professional ethics or to state licensing boards.

NASW Code of Ethics

2.11 Unethical Conduct of Colleagues

(a) Social workers should take adequate measures to discourage, prevent, expose and correct the unethical conduct of colleagues.

(b) Social workers should be knowledgeable about established policies and procedures for handling concerns about colleagues' unethical behavior. Social workers should be familiar with national, state, and local procedures for handling ethics complaints. These include policies and procedures created by NASW, licensing and regulatory bodies, employers, agencies, and other professional organizations.

(c) Social workers who believe that a colleague has acted unethically should seek resolution by discussing their concerns with the colleague when feasible and when such discussion is likely to be productive.

(d) When necessary, social workers who believe that a colleague has acted unethically should take action through appropriate formal channels (such as contacting a state licensing board or regulatory body, an NASW committee on inquiry, or other professional ethics committees).

ACA Code of Ethics and Standards of Practice

H.2 Suspected Violations . . .

d. Reporting Suspected Violations. When an informal resolution is not appropriate or feasible, counselors, upon reasonable cause, take action such as reporting the suspected violation to state or national ethics committees unless this action conflicts with confidentiality rights that cannot be resolved.

Interpreting the Ethics Codes

These provisions impose an affirmative duty on mental health professionals to informally take action and if necessary formally report and prevent unethical conduct by other mental health professionals. Mental health professionals must report dual relationships, unethical sexual relationships, substance abuse, billing fraud, exceeding competence levels, and so forth even if the offender is a close friend or colleague. Providers are obligated to self-police the profession and failing to take action as required is itself an ethical violation.

Providers are obligated to self-police the profession and failing to take action as required is itself an ethical violation.

These cited provisions should cause every practicing professional to be careful when consulting with colleagues about ethical concerns or violations. To do so may impose an ethical dilemma on the friend and colleague concerning whether to report you. A better course would be to consult with a knowledgeable attorney or a person outside the profession who is not under an ethical duty to report a therapist's misconduct. If providers do consult other colleagues about an ethical concern, they should ensure the conversation is agreed to be an academic, hypothetical, or theoretical situation. In that way, real circumstances are not discussed and no one would feel obligated to report questionable behavior.

================ *Ethical Flash Points* ================

- Confidentiality must be breached when legally required by law.

- A mental health professional must be knowledgeable regarding all exceptions to confidentiality including mandatory reporting statutes, and these exceptions must be explained to the client before therapy begins. It is an ethical part of informed consent.

- Ignorance is not an excuse or defense and mandatory reporting statutes must be strictly observed.

- Document all reports to prove compliance.

- It is the therapist's obligation to report abuse or possible harm to the client or a third party.

- Criminal, civil, and administrative penalties can be imposed for failing to strictly comply with reporting statutes.

- Ethics codes impose a duty on practitioners to self-police and report unethical conduct by other members of the discipline.

- Failure to report a close friend's or colleague's unethical conduct is itself an ethical violation.

- Consulting with a knowledgeable attorney or another person outside the profession regarding unethical conduct may be safer than talking to colleagues since the outsider generally does not have an obligation to report you.

Summary

Although confidentiality is the backbone of therapy, there are numerous times when confidential information must be disclosed. It is absolutely essential for a mental health professional to be thoroughly knowledgeable about all reporting statutes and ethics code provisions which mandate a report of client information or unethical conduct by another mental health professional. Reporting statutes and provisions are designed to protect societal interests, whether it be to protect a child from abuse by a parent or step parent or an unsuspecting client from misconduct by a therapist.

Strict compliance is ethically demanded and failure to do so will lead to serious criminal, civil and administrative (disciplinary) penalties.

PART THREE

PRACTICE CONSIDERATIONS

16

Billing

Susan, a recently retired licensed professional counselor, was unexpectedly subpoenaed to appear at an attorney's office and give a deposition in a divorce case involving a couple she had seen for marriage counseling three years earlier. After reading the subpoena, she immediately contacted her attorney to represent her in a fruitless effort to quash the subpoena. After a court hearing in which she was ordered to appear for the deposition and give testimony, she became inordinately anxious. When her attorney asked her why she was so upset, she advised him that the subpoena required her to produce her case file for this couple, including her billing records. The billing records were her main concern. Although she saw the couple for marital therapy, she billed the husband's insurance company as if she were providing the husband individual counseling for depression because his employer-provided insurance did not pay for marriage counseling. At the time, both husband and wife were happy with the arrangement since it meant they would not have to pay for their marital or family therapy. Now that the couple was in the midst of a custody fight, the husband might not be as excited about a billing record that suggested he was treated for depression. Susan was justifiably frightened about the consequences of her billing practices and her questionable creativity in receiving third-party payments.

~

When Carol missed her third scheduled therapy appointment without calling to cancel, Robert, her licensed psychologist, sent her a billing statement charging her for the three missed appointments. On receiving the invoice, Carol became incensed and called Robert demanding an explanation. When Robert advised her he felt justified in billing her, she swore she would never pay him. Several months, several invoices, and several disparaging notes from Carol later, Robert filed suit against Carol in small claims court for $300. Carol immediately filed a complaint with the state licensing board accusing Robert of failing to inform her that she would be billed for skipped appointments, for not advising her on a procedure for canceling appointments, and for causing

*her stress and aggravation that only exacerbated the mental and emotional
condition for which she was being treated. Robert brought a lot of grief on
himself for three hundred dollars.*

~

*Jane, a suburban housewife, had a secret affair with her next-door neighbor,
the husband of her close friend, for over a year. Overwhelmed with grief,
shame, and depression, she contacted Sarah, a licensed professional counselor,
for help. Jane didn't want anyone to know she was seeking counseling and told
Sarah she wouldn't be in a position to pay her until the end of the month without her husband finding out. They agreed to five sessions over the next thirty
days, at the end of which Sarah would bill Jane and Jane would come in and
pay cash.*

*Thirty days later, Sarah sent Jane a bill for her services. The return address
on the envelope contained an address without any name or description identifying Sarah. By chance, Jane's husband, George, came home early and removed the mail from the family mailbox. Glancing at the envelope from
Sarah, he became curious but did not open it. Instead, he wrote down the return address and the next day on the way to his attorney's office found the address and learned it was the office of Sarah, LPC. He was meeting with his
lawyer to finalize divorce pleadings and strategy. When he mentioned Sarah
and the envelope, his attorney had a subpoena issued for Sarah, together with
Jane's records, for the temporary hearing scheduled to decide temporary custody and exclusive use and possession of the family home.*

*Sarah was served with the subpoena the night before the hearing, and when
she attempted to call Jane at home, her husband answered each time and
Sarah hung up without identifying herself. When Sarah walked into the courtroom the next morning, Jane shrieked. Sarah was ordered to testify and turn
over her file to the opposing attorney for examination. This file contained information about Jane's affair. Jane lost temporary custody and was ordered to
move out of the family home.*

*Jane was furious with Sarah and filed a complaint with the licensing board
alleging breach of confidentiality and failure to obtain written consent to forward billing or any other information to Jane's home. Sarah did not lose her
license over this matter, but she was sanctioned by her licensing board.*

Billing Practices

It may be hard to believe that billing clients for services can create ethical
issues and lead to ethical violations, but it is true. Mental health professionals practice in a climate of consumer protectionism. As consumers,

clients must be adequately advised about how they will be charged and billed for services provided, as well as their obligation to pay. Informed consent must be obtained to bill for services rendered, as well as for appropriate billing of missed and noncanceled appointments, sometimes called "no shows."

It is not improper to bill a client for a missed appointment that was not canceled within a proscribed period of time. It is only inappropriate if the client was not previously informed of the cancellation policy and procedure. Likewise, late fees can be billed to a client for payments not received within a set period so long as the practice is disclosed before providing the services. Ethical charges include no-show fees, late fees, interest on past-due accounts, and even attorney's fees and court costs if the account is placed in the hands of an attorney for collection, as long as these charges are disclosed in advance and are part of the signed informed consent in the intake contract.

A therapist providing services to a client pursuant to a provider contract with a managed care entity or insurance company must be aware, however, of any contractual restrictions or limitations. Some provider contracts prohibit the provider from charging and billing the client for any fee except a copay. Under those circumstances, the therapist is not free to bill for skipped or noncanceled appointments. There is no "standard" or "uniform" managed care contract. Each contract is unique, carefully drafted by and for the protection of the managed care entity and must be read carefully.

Informed consent must be obtained to bill for services rendered, as well as for appropriate billing of missed and noncanceled appointments, sometimes called "no shows."

Protecting Client Confidentiality

The client's right to confidentiality also poses an ethical concern for the therapist with regard to billing. Billing for services requires at a minimum a description of the service provided (i.e., a treatment plan), the date of service, and if submitted to a third-party payer, a diagnosis together with an ongoing and updated prognosis. When the billing is submitted to a third-party payer, it will be reviewed by a person other than the therapist and the client. Consent to submit the information required by the third party should be obtained from the client on intake and when treatment begins, and should be documented before a bill is ever submitted for payment.

Therapists should obtain a specific address, phone number, e-mail address, fax number, and so forth where they can contact clients. Therapists should be able to forward billing and other information to them using

Billing records contain confidential information that therapists usually can share only with client consent. Informing a third party that a person is a client is a breach of confidentiality.

Allowing a third party to learn an individual is a client through a return address or caller ID on the telephone can be a breach of confidentiality.

It is improper to intentionally misstate or miscode a diagnosis on billing statements. Such misrepresentations are considered ethical violations and are punishable offenses.

these contact methods with the client's advance permission. Billing records contain confidential information that therapists usually can share only with client consent. Informing a third party that a person is a client is a breach of confidentiality. Such information must be carefully guarded and protected. Confidential information includes all information concerning a client, including whether or not a person is a client.

Allowing a third party to learn an individual is a client through a return address or caller ID on the telephone can be a breach of confidentiality. If the client consents to contact by mail at a particular address or at a specific telephone number, he or she bears the risk and the sole blame and responsibility if a breach of confidentiality occurs. All authority for disclosure can easily be included in an intake and consent form.

Misrepresenting Treatment for Billing Purposes

It is improper to intentionally misstate or miscode a diagnosis on billing statements. Such misrepresentations are considered ethical violations and are punishable offenses. Accuracy and truth in connection with billing records are absolutely required. Failing to be accurate and truthful not only can lead to ethical violations and licensing concerns but also may lead to criminal charges for fraud or theft. Governmental and private insurance payers are not hesitant to seek criminal prosecution for fraudulent billing practices. The right to audit the provider's accounts, billing records, and procedures is usually included in every managed care contract. Many managed care companies routinely spot-check providers to ensure that billing practices meet company standards.

Susan, the LPC who thought she was doing her clients a favor and helping her cash flow at the same time, by miscoding her billing invoices, risked serious consequences for her actions in billing for depression and providing marital therapy. She advised her attorney that she had done this with many clients and could name at least 10 colleagues who had submitted similar bills in the past. Susan was lucky because her billing records, although subpoenaed, were not specifically requested by either attorney when she gave her deposition. Her ethical violation in providing one treatment and billing for another did not come to light and she undoubtedly is still having sleepless nights hoping no one else decides to subpoena, audit, examine, or review her records.

More than one unlucky health care provider has been caught billing for services not actually provided. Accuracy dictates that only services actually performed can be billed and collected. Criminal prosecution is a real probability for this kind of billing practice (e.g., substituting clients or including skipped appointments as if services were rendered).

National Guidelines for Billing Practices

AAMFT Code of Ethics

7.4   Marriage and family therapists represent facts truthfully to clients, third party payers, and supervisees regarding services provided.

APA Ethical Principles of Psychologists and Code of Conduct

1.26 Accuracy in Reports to Payers and Funding Sources.
In their reports to payers for services or sources of research funding, psychologists accurately state the nature of the research provided, the fees or charges, and where applicable the identity of the provider, the findings and the diagnosis.

Ethical Flash Points

- Accuracy and honesty are essential ethical requirements when billing a client.
- Intentionally miscoding a diagnosis to secure payment for services by a third-party payer can lead to criminal prosecution for fraud or theft.
- Billing for services not actually provided is also unethical and can lead to criminal prosecution.
- Confidentiality should be a concern for every therapist each time mail or e-mail is sent or calls are placed directly to the client. (Beware of messages delivered to answering machines or call notes.)
- Forward billing to a client only at an authorized address. Follow the same procedures with mail, e-mail, telephone, or other communication.
- Remember, even a casual "You can call me any time," or "just send the bill to my home (office)" should be noted in the file.

  Written consent is best. Note the sage words: "An oral contract is not worth the paper it is written on." This is true now more than ever.
- Document the client's contact authorization in writing.

NASW *Code of Ethics*

3.05 Billing

Social workers should establish and maintain billing practices that accurately reflect the nature and extent of services provided and that identify who provided the service in the practice setting.

Summary

As with sexual exploitation most billing sins are obvious and blatant ethical violations which may lead to criminal prosecution if committed with intend to defraud a third party payor. Good judgement and honest behavior will insure ethical billing practices. Inadvertent breaches of confidentiality may be more innocent but certainly can cause a lot of trouble for a mental health professional. Thoughtful and accurate billing procedures will contribute to a healthy and long term mental health practice and career.

17

Closing a Practice

Dr. Stern has been in practice for 35 years and is ready to retire. His office lease, yellow pages ad, and managed care contracts are all up at the end of the year. His malpractice insurance will also run out on December 31. All his client files are in order and he has maintained them for 10 years, although he also kept his first client's file for sentimental reasons. Now that he has decided to retire, Dr. Stern is unsure what to do first.

∼

Alice Gump is a play therapist. Over the past few years, she has had an active practice treating children and young adolescents using the latest techniques and some advanced theories she has developed herself. Because of her cutting-edge therapy, several clients whose children she treated have filed complaints with the licensing board, others have written to the national organization of play therapists, and one has retained a lawyer to file a malpractice suit. Ms. Gump has ample insurance, but she feels she can do better financially and live a more happy and carefree life if she changes professions. "Mental health had its opportunity," she says with resignation. "Dealing with unhappy clients makes the practice not worth the effort." She decides to close her office and focus on the very successful family business.

∼

Drs. Tom, Dick, and Harry have leased office space together, use the same stationery, share a sign on the door, and use the same general telephone number with individual extension numbers. To some extent, they cooperate when managed care and insurance are concerned, and they have a lawyer-drafted contract that provides that any unhappy professional can withdraw at any time on 60-days' notice. It also provides that the person leaving is fully accountable for all contracts that extend beyond the withdrawal date. Dick becomes ill, and his physician insists he retire. Can he simply shake hands with Tom and Harry, wish them well, and retire on his income disability insurance? What must he do?

∼

Dr. and Dr. Puente are a husband-and-wife therapy team both licensed by the state and operating a thriving business consisting primarily of private pay clients. He deals principally with marriage and family problems, whereas she is a highly regarded play therapist. After a routine physical and additional testing, they discover he has Alzheimer's, a debilitating disease that will become progressively worse with time. His wife is not able to incorporate her husband's clients into her practice. What do the Puentes do now?

Deciding to Close a Practice

There are many reasons for closing a practice. In two-career families, the mental health professional's spouse might be transferred or offered a position in another city "too good to resist." Or, after years of practice, the therapist may feel "burned out" and ready to take up a new career. Some practitioners have attended risk management workshops and concluded that, in the age of consumerism, the risk of continuing in a private practice is not worth the income rewards received. Some entrepreneurial therapists have sold their practices to large organizations for significant profit and closed their therapeutic doors. Then there are the fortunate ones who over the years have accumulated a substantial nest egg, built a thriving practice and are ready now to retire and bask in the good memories of thousands of satisfied and paying clients.

There are ethical provisions for terminating a professional practice, and therapist–client relationships can become legal problems if ignored or followed incorrectly.

Whichever way it comes about, a mental health professional with client files; former and current clients; listings and memberships in local, state, and national organizations; and state-issued licenses cannot simply wait until a lease is up, buy a sign that says "gone fishing" or "retired" or "call 123-4567 if you need assistance," insert a new message on the answering machine, and disappear. A therapist, social worker, counselor, psychologist, addictions specialist, or mental health professional who leaves a practice for any reason—personal or business, expressed or implied, forced or voluntary—must follow correct procedures. There are ethical provisions for terminating a professional practice, and therapist–client relationships can become legal problems (i.e., a malpractice suit) if ignored or followed incorrectly. Lawyers may introduce an ethics violation into evidence to demonstrate that a provider breached his or her duty to the client and damaged the client by not following the ethical provisions for closing a practice. Ethics and law are intertwined to a significant degree when it comes to malpractice allegations.

Covering All the Bases

For some therapists, closing their practice is the result of a carefully conceived, orchestrated, and thought-out plan in which the practitioner has consulted the licensing board, national organization, attorney, accountant, professional colleagues, and malpractice carrier. Armed with the knowledge and input from all these sources, the therapist gradually and systematically shuts down the practice. These therapists have made all preparations, met all deadlines, and considered the termination dates of all agreements. They have appropriately referred all clients, made arrangements for the security and confidentiality of the files, and taken steps to retrieve the files on a selective basis if needed. No client is abandoned or neglected.

On other occasions, the end of the road is not predictable. Therapists sometimes cannot predict when they will retire. Sickness or sudden mental or physical disability may impair therapists to a degree that prevents them from continuing their practice. To do so would be inappropriate and unethical in itself and might lead to negligence and malpractice actions.

Sometimes a practice is closed because a licensing board has revoked the therapist's license to practice. Numerous board complaints may have accomplished the same result by inhibiting the therapist's ability to obtain malpractice insurance, attract or maintain clients, or gain hospital privileges. Complaints may also make it difficult to obtain referrals or associate with colleagues.

Still other mental health professionals simply find the paperwork, approval procedures, or complexities of dealing with insurance companies for third-party reimbursement too cumbersome. They decide they are no longer willing or able to confront and process the mountain of necessary forms and paperwork and opt instead to retire or pursue a different career.

The reasons for retirement or withdrawal are not important. A practitioner who chooses to withdraw from the practice for any reason may do so, but to do so ethically, he or she must consider certain concerns and hazards.

Things to Consider When Closing a Practice

A therapeutic practice is not like a bookstore or grocery chain where the owner simply has to gather the remaining inventory, sell it to the public

Therapists cannot turn to their professional guidelines for a precise and recommended course of action to follow in transitioning into retirement or a new profession.

When closing a mental health practice, therapists need to consider potential legal liabilities, contractual obligations, and ethical and moral dilemmas.

or donate it to charity, and then close shop. Therapists have numerous long- and short-term obligations to colleagues, their profession, clients, and business associates. In addition, therapists must honor their contractual agreements with individuals, corporations, and partnerships. Therapists cannot turn to their professional guidelines for a precise and recommended course of action to follow in transitioning into retirement or a new profession. The ethics codes do not delineate a definitive retirement sequence or a critical path to retirement heaven.

Ethical and Legal Obligations

When closing a mental health practice, therapists need to consider potential legal liabilities, contractual obligations, and ethical and moral dilemmas. They must also decide what to do with client files and how long to maintain them. Should they be stored in a closet or garage, put through a shredder, or sent to the dumpster?

Although some professional obligations are contractual and legal, they may also have ethical overtones:

- Leases are contractual obligations. If they continue after the projected date of retirement, they must be considered and negotiated either by paying an agreed amount or by fulfilling the balance of the lease term. Leases cannot be abandoned without legal consequences.

- Advertising and listing contracts with the telephone company, newspapers, magazines, and yellow pages are often for long terms that must be honored. Therapists must make arrangements for responding to potential clients who answer these advertisements.

- Mental health professionals often belong to associations, partnerships, joint ventures, corporations, and limited partnerships. The precise terms of these organizational structures may contain the process and procedure for termination and withdrawal. Each contract and agreement must be reviewed and analyzed. The terms of the agreements voluntarily entered into years ago bind the retiring or withdrawing individual.

- External contracts between the individual and organizations may be continuing and long term. Not only leases, but contracts with managed care entities, insurance companies, hospitals for in- or outpatient services, and contracts to provide mental health treatment to groups for extended periods have to be considered and honored. Walking away from these and other long-term obligations can easily lead to licensing board complaints, as well as a malpractice suit. In general, malpractice policies will not cover contractual defaults.

- Review malpractice policies to ensure that acts of commission or omission covered during practice continue to be covered after retirement.

- In some situations, professional guidelines are not specific concerning retirement, relocation, the total and complete closing of a practice, and future absolute unavailability of the therapist. When this occurs, the client's best interest should always be considered and reasonable steps taken to protect the client, client records, and the client's future needs.

Planning for Retirement

An ethical complaint can be filed after retirement as can a malpractice suit. Continuing insurance coverage is desirable in the event of either of these unpleasant events. Likewise litigation, ethical complaints, and current contracts "in the mill" have to be legally, ethically, and contractually honored and concluded.

An ethical complaint can be filed after retirement as can a malpractice suit. Continuing insurance coverage is desirable in the event of either of these unpleasant events.

Planning for all obligations to terminate on a given date is impossible. Leases have different termination dates. Clients likewise recover at different times. Therapists planning to retire need to consider when to start declining additional clients. Group practices must be terminated in an orderly fashion, with consideration given to colleagues, clients, and business associates.

The perfect blend is a detailed retirement plan that considers the needs of the retiring professional, the requirements of the consumer or the client, and the general reputation of the profession. Retiring and closing a practice with dignity is achievable, although complex. It requires thorough and careful planning.

National Guidelines for Closing a Practice

NASW Code of Ethics

1.15 Interruption of Services

Social workers should make reasonable efforts to ensure continuity of services in the event that services are interrupted by factors such as unavailability, relocation, illness, disability, or death . . .

3.04 Client Records

(d) Social workers should store records following the termination of services to ensure reasonable future access. Records should be maintained for the number of years required by state statutes or relevant contracts.

APA Ethical Procedures for Psychologists and Code of Conduct

4.08 Interruption of Services

(a) Psychologists make reasonable efforts to plan for facilitating care in the event that psychological services are interrupted by factors such as the psychologist's illness, death, unavailability, or relocation or by the client's relocation or financial limitations. (See also Standard 5.09, Preserving Records and Data.)

4.09 Terminating the Professional Relationship

(c) Prior to termination for whatever reason, except where precluded by the patient's or client's conduct, the psychologist discusses the patient's or client's views and needs, provides appropriate pretermination counseling, suggests alternative service providers as appropriate, and takes other reasonable steps to facilitate transfer of responsibility to another if the patient or client needs one immediately . . .

5.09 Preserving Records and Data

A psychologist makes plans in advance so that confidentiality of records and data is protected in the event of the psychologist's death, incapacity, or withdrawal from the position or practice.

ACA Code of Ethics and Standards of Practice

A.11. Termination and Referral

a. Abandonment Prohibited.
Counselors do not abandon or neglect clients in counseling. Counselors assist in making appropriate arrangements for the continuation of treatment, when necessary, during interruptions, such as vacations, and following termination . . .

Ethical Flash Points

THE RETIRE-IN-PEACE CHECKLIST AND SUMMARY

1. Executory Contracts (Contracts to be performed in the future):

   - Contracts with managed care, hospitals, insurance companies, and businesses have to be terminated. For example, many professionals have long-term contracts to provide mental health treatment to clients, employees, and staff. These must be terminated and other providers substituted, if possible.

   - Rental agreements and contracts for telephone and fax services, yellow pages advertisements, Web pages, and other services must be timed to end on the retirement date or negotiated so they do not carry postretirement obligations.

   - Cancel utilities, phone, and other services where appropriate.

2. Client Obligations:

   - Inform clients as soon as practicable of your intention to close your practice.

   - If not accomplished in the intake form, obtain authorization from the client to deliver the client record to another competent professional.

   - Prepare transfer summaries where needed and, with client permission, call the therapist taking over the file to discuss the case in more detail.

   - All case notes, client files, and progress notes must be up-to-date. All correspondence that pertains to a file should be answered.

   - Check with your national and state organization, as well as the licensing board, and then call the malpractice carrier. Make sure you have scrupulously followed all the prerequisites for closing a practice.

   - Client files are confidential and this obligation continues postretirement. Most state licensing laws as well as civil statutes indicate the number of years a file must be maintained, secured, and preserved. Clients have a right to view these files for the number of required years and afterward as long as they are in existence and in the possession of the therapist or a successor therapist. In case of any complaint, the preserved file is the first line of defense.

   - Even retired therapists can sue and be sued, and may be subpoenaed into court at any time, either with or without the file. Therefore the file must be accessible as well as secure. The retained file protects both the provider and the consumer. *A well-preserved, complete file that cannot be located is no file at all.*

   - Although a therapist may terminate the therapeutic relationship and retire at any time without obtaining client permission, there remains an ethical obligation to cooperate with a subsequent therapist in a meaningful manner. An available file will ensure that the information offered will be accurate and helpful to a subsequent therapist as well as the client.

(continued)

===== *Ethical Flash Points* =====

(Continued)

- Continuing clients normally are entitled to an exit interview. The client should be advised of additional community resources, other competent providers, and be provided with written posttreatment recommendations. A termination letter would be appropriate.

- Individual client needs or circumstances may require a therapist to provide therapy even after all other clients are terminated. As with any termination, careful consideration must be given to the client's emotional and psychological condition and to timing the termination properly.

- For former clients who are only now discovering the therapist has retired, a recorded message should direct them to a relief therapist who has not reviewed their file but has access. Confidentiality should be maintained.

- Client obligations continue for the statute of limitations period even after therapy has terminated. Confidentiality continues until the file is destroyed.

- Since death, disability, relocation, forced retirement, and other unforeseen circumstances are always a possibility, the intake form should contain a clause that permits the therapist to arrange for the transfer of the clinical record to another competent professional if any of these circumstances should occur. Thus the client would give the provider or the professional permission in advance to store and preserve the file in a protected facility with a licensed professional in charge. Arrangements could then be made between professionals to make the files accessible.

3. The Clinical File:
   - Files should be summarized, indexed, and itemized so that they can be located.
   - If boxed, each box must be clearly marked and labeled.
   - The storage facility must be secure, locked, dry, and free of mildew and rodents. Storing files after therapy has terminated and postretirement is a necessary expense.
   - Access to client records must be limited to such individuals with a legal right to know the contents and a legal right of entry. All access should be on a "need to know" basis.

4. Mail, Phone, E-Mail, and other Correspondence:
   - Mail addressed to a retired therapist should be forwarded to the therapist for response, if possible. Otherwise, a designated responsible professional should send a prepared letter to the addressee explaining the therapist's retirement and nonavailability and suggesting alternative resources. Some arrangements have to be made to access the file if therapeutically warranted or if desired by the client.

═ Ethical Flash Points ═

- A telephone message must notify callers of the therapist's retirement and list alternative sources for treatment.
- If e-mail is used as a treatment option, it should be recognized in the intake and consent form and an "all points" e-mail should be sent announcing the retirement and outlining alternative treatment options. Confidentiality is as important with e-mail as it is for other addresses and phone numbers. *Client information must be safeguarded regardless of the communication medium involved.*

5. Terminating Business Relationships:
   - Most business entities have termination provisions and procedures established by contract. Before retirement, these must be reviewed to determine whether the parties have terminated in the prescribed manner. Litigation of any type should be avoided. Mediation, if needed, can be a big help to parting (soon to be former) associates.
   - Many technical details must be taken care of to dissolve a partnership, corporation, limited partnership, professional association, and other created entities and relationships. Therapists should employ a lawyer and banker, as well as an accountant and financial planner to facilitate the dissolution.
   - Usually a lawyer-drafted written termination or dissolution agreement is appropriate.
   - A handshake, pat on the back, and good wishes do not comprise a sound legal dissolution.

6. Memberships, Licenses, and Subscriptions:
   - Continuing professional memberships should be terminated. Send notices to professional groups and organizations as needed. It is better to have a termination letter in the professional association's file than for the provider to be finally dropped from the association because of delinquency or nonpayment of dues.
   - If your license is to lapse or terminate, make sure it is properly handled according to licensing board requirements.
   - Ongoing subscriptions can either lapse or be stopped if a refund is possible. Some subscription contracts for advertisements and magazines have automatic renewal clauses, so canceling such subscriptions in writing is preferred.
   - Malpractice insurance may terminate on the date of retirement; however, it is important to obtain continued coverage for claims made due to past actions. Check with the insurance professional and seek out all the options. Generally, it is a good idea to purchase a "tail," a continuing policy that offers the provider coverage for all the years of practice whether or not any claim is or has been made or threatened. Such a policy enables the mental health professional to sleep at night knowing that past activities are covered by insurance to the extent of the policy coverage and limits.

18

Kickbacks, Bartering, and Fees

Over several years, Sharon, a school counselor and licensed professional counselor, referred more than 100 clients to Dr. Kindheart, a licensed marriage and family therapist and a member of Sharon's church. As an expression of gratitude, Dr. Kindheart bought two tickets to a series of musicals, a $300 value, and sent them with a card to Sharon. When Sharon shared her delight with the unexpected gift with another school counselor, she was surprised by her colleague's response. She was advised that accepting the gift was unethical and that it was unethical and perhaps illegal for Dr. Kindheart to send the gift.

~

When Carol, a recently licensed social worker, answered an advertisement regarding office space for lease, the psychiatrist who owned a small office building offered her a terrific deal. He offered her a corner office without a fixed rental payment. He suggested that Carol simply pay him 20 percent of all fees she collected from her clients and an additional 10 percent of any fees collected from clients referred to her by the psychiatrist. Without an established practice, Carol found the offer very appealing, moved in, and began paying the appropriate percentages to the psychiatrist. Two years later when the psychiatrist was investigated for insurance fraud, Carol came under investigation by state law enforcement officials for an illegal fee-sharing arrangement. She was also challenged by the state licensing board.

~

Cheryl, a discontented and separated housewife, offered a psychologist a piano in payment for therapy. After much deliberation, the psychologist, a pianist of some accomplishment, agreed to provide 20 hours of therapy at the normal session rate of $90 per hour in exchange for the piano. Six months later, Cheryl and her husband reconciled thanks in part to improvements achieved through Cheryl's therapy. When Cheryl's husband moved back into the marital residence, he was shocked to see his piano missing. He became furious when he learned Cheryl had traded it for $1,800 worth of therapy. The piano had been purchased for $15,000. He filed suit and judgment was entered *against the psychologist for $13,200 plus attorney fees. The husband also filed a complaint with the therapist's licensing board.*

~

Dr. Mortale is spending a long overdue and well-deserved secluded summer vacation in Big Bucks Point, Florida, when the call comes in. He has published widely in the field of suicide prevention and caters to a wealthy clientele of retired, but unhappy and bored, mature children of the "old money" generation. Mrs. Frantic finally reaches him on her cell phone. She is calling from the suspension bridge over the bay, where her husband (who has tried and conspicuously failed three times so far to commit suicide) is threatening to jump. Knowing that a therapist should not treat a client without first negotiating a fee, and that the fee should be within the client's ability to pay, and knowing that this client (Mrs. Frantic) can pay just about any fee charged, he quotes, and she accepts, a $1 million fee to talk-by-cell phone to Mr. Frantic, who will talk only to Dr. Mortale. Thirty minutes later, a more relaxed and relieved Mr. Frantic comes down from the bridge, hugs his wife without feeling, and glumly returns home. Can Dr. Mortale send the bill for $1 million or is the transaction unreasonable? After all, the expert saved Mr. Frantic's life, as well as incredible public exposure and embarrassment.

Kickbacks

Most therapists sense that paying a referral source for making referrals is wrong or at least questionable. The ethics codes leave little room for doubt. When a psychologist pays, receives payment from, or divides fees with another professional other than in an employer-employee relationship, the payment to each is based on the services (clinical, consultative, administrative, or other) provided and not on the referral itself.

The payment of referral fees is an acceptable practice in many other industries but is not tolerated in the delivery of mental health services. Why not? Why shouldn't we allow therapists to develop and cultivate referral sources to enhance income and increase a practice? Isn't that consistent with good American business principles? Isn't it appropriate and in good character to thank people appropriately for a kindness rendered? In the mental health field, it is not good business or acceptable because the potential for abusing the client is too great.

Mental health professionals have an obligation to make referrals to the *best possible sources of care for their clients*. If a payment were made to

Mental health professionals have an obligation to make referrals to the best possible sources of care for their clients.

a referring party a question would arise concerning why the referral was made. Was it made so a referral fee could be collected or because it was the best possible source of care? This is another area in which the mental health profession strives to avoid even the hint or appearance of abuse or the risk of exploitation. Making a referral is a clinical decision, and a decision based even in small part on an actual or potential referral fee would have a difficult time passing muster against a challenge of clinical objectivity.

Are arrangements whereby a mental health professional pays a percentage of fees earned and collected in lieu of rent permissible? Fees can be split if the shared fee is reasonably and rationally related to the services actually provided by the nontreating person or entity. It may be difficult to establish the reasonable and rational relationship between the fees paid to a landlord and the value of the space provided to the treating therapist. The burden will be on the mental health professional to establish the relationship. Such arrangements, although not absolutely forbidden, should be avoided.

National Guidelines for Accepting Kickbacks

AAMFT Code of Ethics

Paragraph 7.1 of Section 7. *Financial Arrangements*
Marriage and Family Therapists do not offer or accept payment for referrals.

APA Ethical Principles for Providers and Code of Conduct

Paragraph 1.27 of Section 1. *Referrals and Fees*
When a psychologist pays, receives payment from, or divides fees with another professional other than in an employer–employee relationship, the payment to each is based on the services (clinical, consultative, administrative, or other) provided and is not based on the referral itself.

National and State Statutes

Federal and state statutes make kickback arrangements in connection with health care criminal acts subject to fine and imprisonment. They are typically much broader in scope than just criminalizing fee-sharing or fee-splitting arrangements. According to national and state statutes, offering or accepting a seemingly innocent and thoughtful gesture such as musical tickets in connection with one or more referrals would be a criminal as well as an unethical act. Doing more than offering a verbal thank-you is prohibited. Receiving more than the verbal appreciation from the professional to whom the referral was made is also prohibited. Anything more would constitute a reward and bring the act within the purview of criminal statutes.

Vernon's Texas Statutes Annotated

Section 161.091. *Prohibition on Illegal Remuneration*

(a) A person commits an offense if the person intentionally or knowingly offers to pay or agrees to accept any remuneration directly or indirectly, overtly or covertly, in cash or in kind, to or from any person, firm, association of persons, partnership or corporation for securing or soliciting patients or patronage for or from a person licensed, certified, or registered by a state health care regulatory agency.

Bartering

Mental health professionals should also avoid bartering for services. A trade has potential for unfair advantage since the playing field is never level. Bartering leaves a mental health professional open to allegations of abuse and the risk of exploitation. Bartering is an ancient and long-accepted method of exchanging goods and services. It was a necessity when there was no monetary system to drive and facilitate commerce. It is common today in many countries with devalued currency. However, due to the potential for exploitation, bartering is not a recommended practice by any of the mental health disciplines.

If bartering is accepted, it not only has to be the client's suggestion but must not be exploitative, must be documented by written informed consent, and must be an accepted practice among professionals where the therapist is providing services. It will be a very unusual and rare circumstance that can meet this burden. Even though bartering, just as fee sharing, is not absolutely prohibited, payment for services rendered in cash, by check, or by credit card appears to be the most ethically sound and defensible practice.

According to national and state statutes, offering or accepting a seemingly innocent and thoughtful gesture such as musical tickets in connection with one or more referrals would be a criminal as well as an unethical act.

Bartering leaves a mental health professional open to allegations of abuse and the risk of exploitation.

National Guidelines for Bartering

NASW Code of Ethics

Section 1.13 Paragraph (b) *Payment for Services*

Social workers should avoid accepting goods or services as payment for professional services. Bartering arrangements, particularly involving services, create the potential for conflicts of interest, exploitation, and inappropriate boundaries in social workers' relationships with clients. Social workers should explore and may participate in bartering only in very limited circumstances when it can be demonstrated that such arrangements are an accepted practice among professionals in the local community, considered to be essential for the provision of services, negotiated without coercion, and entered into at the client's initiative and the client's informed consent. Social workers who accept goods or services from clients as payment for professional services assume the full burden of demonstrating that this arrangement will not be detrimental to the client or the professional relationship.

ACA Code of Ethics and Standards of Practice

Section A.10. *Fees and Bartering*

c. *Bartering Discouraged.* Counselors ordinarily refrain from accepting goods or services from clients in return for counseling services because such arrangements create inherent potential for conflicts, exploitation, and distorting of the professional relationship. Counselors may participate in bartering only if the relationship is not exploitative, if the client requests it, if a clear written contract is established, and if such arrangements are an accepted practice among professionals in the community.

Fees

What can a mental health professional charge for professional services? In the United States and within its free enterprise system, is it not what the market will bear? In these days of $100 million professional sports contracts, why shouldn't the therapist be able to charge whatever the client is willing to pay? The ethics codes require fees to be reasonable and not excessive.

The ethics codes require fees to be reasonable and not excessive.

The sky is not the limit in setting fees even if the therapist by virtue of education, experience, and skill is considered to be the top practitioner in the community. A "reasonable fee" is dependent on the client's ability to pay and what other therapists in the community are charging. Therapists should avoid even the appearance of exploitation.

Fees, including late charges, the use of collection agencies and charges for responding to record requests or subpoenas to give testimony, must be disclosed prior to beginning therapy (see Chapter 6). Nevertheless, providing clients with all necessary information concerning fees and obtaining informed consent does not excuse an excessive or unreasonable fee. The unequal power positions of the mental health professional and the client in the therapeutic relationship necessitate special consideration and divergence from free market concepts in the areas of setting fees and bartering. The intent of ethics codes is to protect the client from monetary exploitation by mental health professionals. The ACA even expects its members to assist clients in finding affordable services if the counselor's reasonable fee is beyond the client's ability to pay. Charging an excessive fee even if the client agrees to it is an ethical violation subjecting mental health professionals to the full range of sanctions and consequences.

A "reasonable fee" is dependent on the client's ability to pay and what other therapists in the community are charging.

National Guidelines for Setting Fees

AAMFT Code of Ethics

7.2   Marriage and family therapists do not charge excessive fees for services.

NASW Code of Ethics

1.13 *Payment for Services.* (a) When setting fees, social workers should ensure that the fees are fair, reasonable, and commensurate with the services performed. Consideration should be given to client's ability to pay.

ACA Code of Ethics and Standards of Practice

Section A.10 *Fees and Bartering*

a. Advance Understanding. Counselors clearly explain to clients, prior to entering the counseling relationship, all financial arrangements related to professional services including the use of collection agencies or legal measures for nonpayment.

b. Establishing Fees. In establishing fees for professional counseling services counselors consider the financial status of clients and locality. In

Ethical Flash Points

- Paying or receiving referral fees is unethical and illegal.
- Never give or receive more than a hearty verbal "thank-you" (a cordial note is also acceptable) in connection with the referral of a client.
- Clients are to be referred to the best possible sources for care and treatment consistent with their ability to pay.
- Splitting fees in lieu of rent is problematic and could be construed as illegal fee sharing.
- Bartering, although not absolutely prohibited, should be avoided. The therapist has the burden of establishing that the transaction is ethical.
- Bartering must be requested by the client; must not be exploitative; must be documented in the form of written, informed consent; and must be practiced by professionals in the community.
- Only rarely is bartering considered ethical.
- Fees must be reasonable and not excessive.
- The mental health professional cannot charge whatever the client will pay even after obtaining informed consent. The client's agreement to pay does not make the fee ethical.
- Reasonableness is a function of what is charged in the locality and the client's ability to pay.

the event that the established fee structure is inappropriate for a client, assistance is provided in attempting to find comparable services of acceptable cost.

Summary

Regardless of the fee arrangement the burden will always be on the mental health professional to establish that the fee was reasonable, appropriate in the community where the services were rendered and adequately disclosed in advance of therapy to the client. Establishing that the client was not exploited becomes problematic when high fees are charged or bartering takes place in lieu of exchanging money for services. The free enterprise, whatever the market will bear mentality, is not acceptable in the delivery of mental health care services.

19

Malpractice Insurance

Allen, a licensed marriage and family therapist, became sexually involved with the 32-year-old daughter of a retired couple he saw for marital therapy. She lived with her parents and became acquainted with Allen when she provided transportation for her parents to and from therapy sessions after her father broke his hip and was unable to drive. It was several months before the parents noticed the strange way their daughter and Allen looked at each other when they met in the reception area of Allen's office. When they pressed their daughter on the way home about these unusual glances, she laughed and told them she had been dating Allen and was in love with him. The parents were upset and immediately called Allen to confirm the news. The next day they filed a complaint with the state licensing board and consulted an attorney regarding a malpractice lawsuit. Should Allen be comforted by the fact that he faithfully paid all his malpractice insurance policy premiums?

Susan is a licensed social worker. She made a practice of miscoding billing statements to bring her services within the coverage scope of her clients' insurance policies. Her clients were delighted with this practice and Susan made a decent living until an insurance provider investigated, discovered the deception, and reported Susan to the district attorney's office and the state licensing board. In addition, the insurance provider brought a civil action to recover thousands of dollars in payments made to Susan over the years. Can Susan relax, secure in the knowledge that her malpractice insurance carrier will take care of these problems for her?

Scott, a psychologist under investigation by his state licensing board for sexual misconduct, agreed to a license suspension. In need of income, he continued to see a few direct-pay clients during the board's investigation and during the period of his license suspension. One of the direct-pay clients filed a malpractice case against Scott in connection with his diagnosis and treatment for repressed memories. Eventually the licensing board cleared Scott of the sexual misconduct charges, but when he turned the malpractice complaint over to his malpractice insurance provider, was he assured of a defense? Scott assumed he was covered since he had kept his premiums current during the board's investigation.

Why Have Malpractice Insurance?

In today's litigious society, a mental health professional would be foolish to practice without obtaining and retaining "professional liability" (i.e., malpractice) insurance coverage. Disgruntled clients can file claims with relative ease and impunity even if there is no merit to the allegations. The cost of defending these claims can run into thousands of dollars. A professional liability insurance policy provides benefits for defending claims asserted while the professional is practicing his or her licensed profession and for the payment of damages.

What Is Malpractice Insurance?

The typical professional liability insurance policy provides benefits including the cost of defense, settlements, and judgments within the stated policy limits.

The typical professional liability insurance policy provides benefits including the cost of defense, settlements, and judgments within the stated policy limits. Most policies provide a benefit for representation and defense before licensing boards. This is the good news. The bad news is that these same policies contain between 15 and 20 stated policy exclusions (see specimen policies in Appendixes I and II). Complaints regarding certain ethical violations are not covered by the policy leaving the offending mental health professional exposed to damage awards that must be paid from personal assets or future earnings.

Malpractice Exclusions: Practicing without a License

A license is generally a prerequisite to coverage.

A license is generally a prerequisite to coverage. Scott, the psychologist, would not be covered by his APA-sponsored professional liability insurance policy because the malpractice action was brought against him for professional services he rendered while his license was suspended. It is irrelevant that his license was fully reinstated and that he was cleared of the misconduct charges and any ethical violations. When the services were rendered that constituted the basis of the action, his psychologist's license was suspended and he was prohibited from practicing psychology. Consider the exclusions contained in the following sample professional liability policies:

American Home Assurance Company, Social Workers Professional Liability Insurance Policy (offered through the NASW Insurance Trust)

VI. EXCLUSIONS FOR ALL INSURING AGREEMENTS

We shall not defend or pay any **claims** against **you** under Insuring Agreements A, B, and C . . .

17. Arising from any lawful act committed while you did not have a license required by law or while your license was suspended . . .

TIG Insurance Healthcare Professional And Liability Supplemental Insurance Policy (offered through the AAMFT Insurance Trust)

V. EXCLUSIONS

This Insurance does not apply to any **Claim, Incident,** or **Suit** arising out of . . .

4. The **Insured's** rendering of or failure to render professional services while his or her license is suspended, restricted, revoked or terminated, or arising out of an **incident** occurring while the **Insured** is on probation . . .

Chicago Insurance Company, Psychologists Professional Liability Claims-Made Insurance Policy (offered through the APA Insurance Trust)

VI. EXCLUSIONS

This Insurance does not apply . . .

5. to **Bodily Injury** or **Property Damage** based on or arising out of the practice of the **Insured's** professional occupation unless the **Insured** is properly licensed, exempted or certified by the laws of the state(s) in which the **Insured** practices, or is otherwise qualified to practice the **Insured's** professional occupation in the absence of such laws . . .

Malpractice Exclusions: Sexual Misconduct

Most professional liability insurance policies contain exclusions for therapists' sexual misconduct with clients and family members or persons in close relationship to clients. Sexual misconduct is a clear ethical violation and can lead to substantial damages being awarded against the

Most professional liability insurance policies contain exclusions for therapists' sexual misconduct with clients and family members or persons in close relationship to clients.

mental health professional (see Chapter 10). Plaintiffs' lawyers often refer to sexual exploitation cases as "slam dunk" lawsuits. Once the plaintiff establishes the sexual relationship, the only question remaining for the jury to decide is how much money to award.

Some policies provide a limited liability benefit whereby the insurance company will pay damages awarded up to a maximum of $25,000 or pay defense costs up to a maximum of $25,000 without any obligation to pay for damages assessed. Allen, the licensed marriage and family therapist, would be entitled to a defense under the AAMFT-sponsored professional liability insurance policy, but once $25,000 in legal fees and expenses were incurred, coverage would cease. If a judgment were entered against Allen or if he decided to settle the case, regardless of the amount agreed on, Allen must pay the money from his personal assets or out of his future earnings.

Because many state statutes criminalize sexual exploitation by mental health professionals, ethical violations of this type involving direct sex or sex once removed are doubly excluded from the policy coverage.

Typical professional liability insurance policies also contain provisions that exclude claims arising out of ". . . the willful violation of a penal statute or ordinance committed by or with the knowledge or consent of the **Insured** . . ." (Chicago Insurance Company, Psychologists Professional Liability Claims-Made Insurance Policy offered through the APA Insurance Trust). Because many state statutes criminalize sexual exploitation by mental health professionals, ethical violations of this type involving direct sex or sex once removed (i.e., family, friends, or business associates) are doubly excluded from the policy coverage. The message has always been clear—avoid sexual relationships with clients and those in close relationships with clients. A mental health professional engaging in this kind of misconduct will stand alone, unprotected by the insurance carrier and its policy. Sex of this nature is unprotected sex from any perspective.

Consider the clauses related to sexual misconduct in the following sample policies:

American Home Assurance Company, Social Workers Professional Liability Insurance Policy (offered through the NASW Insurance Trust)

VIII. SEXUAL MISCONDUCT PROVISION

A. **Our** Limit of Liability shall not exceed $25,000.00 in the aggregate for all damages with respect to the total of all **claims** and **suits** against **you** involving any actual or alleged erotic physical contact, or attempt threat or proposal thereof:

  1. By **you** or by any other person for whom **you** may be legally liable; and

2. With or to any former or current client of **yours,** or with or to any relative or member of the same household as any said client, or with or to any person with whom said client or relative has an affectionate personal relationship.

2. In the event that any of the foregoing are alleged at any time, either in a complaint, during discovery, at trial or otherwise, any and all causes of action alleged and arising out of the same or related courses of professional treatment and/or relationships shall be subject to the aforesaid $25,000 aggregate Limit of Liability and shall be part of, and not in addition to, the Limits of Liability otherwise afforded by this Policy.

3. **We** shall not be obligated to undertake nor continue to defend any **suit** or proceeding subject to the $25,000 aggregate Limit of Liability after the $25,000 aggregate Limit of Liability has been exhausted by payment of judgments, settlements and/or other items included within the Limits of Liability . . .

TIG Insurance Healthcare Professional and Liability Supplemental Insurance Policy (offered through the AAMFT Insurance Trust)

V. EXCLUSIONS

This Insurance does not apply to any **Claim, Incident,** or **Suit** arising out of . . .

7. Physical abuse, threatened abuse, sexual abuse or licentious, immoral or sexual behavior whether or not intended to lead to, or culminating in any sexual act, whether caused by or at the instigation of, or at the direction of, or omission by any **Insured.** However, the Company will defend any civil **Suit** against an **Insured** seeking amounts that would be covered if this exclusion did not apply. In such case, the company will only pay **Fees, Costs and Expenses** of such defense up to per $25,000 per **Incident** . . .

Chicago Insurance Company, Psychologists Professional Liability Claims-Made Insurance Policy (offered through the APA Insurance Trust)

VI.   EXCLUSIONS

This Insurance does not apply . . .

7. to any **Claims** made or Suits brought against any **Insured** alleging, in whole or part, sexual assault, abuse, molestation, or licentious, immoral or other behavior which threatened, led to or culminated in any sexual act whether committed intentionally, negligently, inadvertently or with the belief, erroneous or otherwise, that the other party is consenting and has the legal and mental capacity to consent thereto, that was committed, or alleged to have been committed by the **Insured** or by any person for whom the Insured is legally responsible . . .

However, notwithstanding the foregoing exclusion, the **Insured** shall be entitled to a defense as provided under the terms of the policy as to any **Claim** upon which suit is brought for any such alleged behavior, unless a judgment or final adjudication adverse to any **Insured,** or admission by any **Insured** accused of such behavior, shall establish that such behavior caused, in whole or part, the injury claimed in such **Suit.** The Company shall not be required to appeal a judgment or final adjudication adverse to the **Insured** . . .

Making Sense of the Policies

The APA-sponsored policy provides a $0.00 dollar benefit for payment of assessed damages but does provide for a defense. What this means is that the insurance carrier will retain an attorney and pay court costs and legal expenses incurred in defending the suit against the psychologist but will not be obligated to fund any resulting settlement or judgment. The NASW-sponsored policy provides for payment of damages up to a maximum of $25,000, while the AAMFT-sponsored policy only pays costs of defense incurred up to a maximum of $25,000.

Malpractice Exclusions: Billing

The NASW Code of Ethics Section 3.05 "Billing" states, "Social workers should establish and maintain billing practices that accurately reflect the nature and extent of services provided and that identify who provided the service in the practice setting." Susan, while trying to assist her clients and maximize her income violated her canon of ethics, which enabled her insurance carrier to deny coverage under her professional liability insurance policy. Under these facts, her insurance carrier would not even provide a defense and she must hire and pay her own attorneys and costs. And the fees? Most lawyers charge a minimum of $150 per hour. Thus, an 8-hour day in court can cost at least $1,200 in addition to preparation time, which may consist of hours waiting for the trial to begin or waiting for the jury to reach a decision. Hiring an attorney is not for the faint of heart.

Consider what the following professional liability insurance policies say about billing issues and coding insurance claim forms:

American Home Assurance Company, Social Workers Professional Liability Insurance Policy (offered through the NASW Insurance Trust)

VI.   EXCLUSIONS FOR ALL INSURING AGREEMENTS

We shall not defend or pay any **claims** against **you** under Insuring Agreements A, B, and C . . .

4. For matters involving overbilling, miscoding, reimbursement requests, and other fee related matters or inquiries, unless the action involves an actual disciplinary proceeding where **your** license or your ability to practice is threatened; . . .

Malpractice Insurance: Other Exclusions

Other ethical violations are excluded in malpractice policies. For example, professional liability insurance policies exclude coverage for claims arising from wrongful acts committed while under the influence of an illegal substance or drug or while intoxicated. Ethics codes also prohibit dual relationships. Professional liability insurance policies exclude coverage for claims arising out of any business relationship or venture with any prior or current client. Ethics codes prohibit discrimination. Professional liability insurance policies exclude coverage for claims arising from discrimination.

Professional liability insurance policies exclude coverage for claims arising from wrongful acts committed while under the influence of an illegal substance or drug or while intoxicated.

Regardless of the alleged complaint, offense, or negligent act, some other interesting exclusions come into play. This is true even if the alleged wrongful acts of commission or omission are covered under the policy. What follows are some examples of additional exclusions included in malpractice policies:

TIG Insurance Healthcare Professional and Liability Supplemental Insurance Policy (offered through the AAMFT Insurance Trust)

V. EXCLUSIONS

This Insurance does not apply to any **Claim, Incident,** or **Suit** arising out of . . .

3. **Bodily Injury** that arises solely out of humiliation or other emotional distress and that does not arise out of a physical intrusion or other physical event that first causes a physical injury or physical sickness to the person suffering the emotional distress or illness . . .

In this case, the policy suggests that the provider is not covered for emotional distress or mental anguish damages. Suicide and homicide cases excepted, in the majority of suits brought against a mental health professional, there is not going to be physical injury. Mental and emotional distress constitute the harm suffered by the plaintiffs, and this policy seems to exclude payment and coverage for such damages. In the past, most states excluded the award of "psychic" or psychological damages in lawsuits if they did not flow from a physical injury. The trend now is to allow these damages, and they are being recovered in lawsuits all around the country. The exclusion cited in the AAMFT-sponsored policy significantly reduces the coverage and increases the risk to the mental health professional.

American Home Assurance Company, Social Workers Professional Liability Insurance Policy (offered through the NASW Insurance Trust)

VI.   EXCLUSIONS FOR ALL INSURING AGREEMENTS

We shall not defend or pay any **claims** against **you** under Insuring Agreements A, B, and C . . .

13. For any **wrongful act** committed with knowledge by you that it was a **wrongful act**. . . .

This same policy defines wrongful act as "any actual or alleged negligent act, error, or omission, or any actual or alleged **defamation.**" Mental health professionals are presumed to know the ethical canons promulgated by their national and local organizations and their licensing boards. *One could argue then that any violation of an ethical canon constitutes a wrongful act committed with knowledge thereby eliminating the insurance carrier's obligation to defend and pay claims.*

Malpractice Insurance: Punitive Damages Provision

Punitive or exemplary damages are often excluded from the coverage of a professional liability insurance policy.

Intentional, malicious, or particularly offensive misconduct can lead to the imposition of damages against the defendant that are intended not to compensate the plaintiff for loss or harm but to punish the defendant. These are called *punitive* or *exemplary* damages. Sexual misconduct or financial exploitation of a client could easily lead to the award of punitive damages. These types of damages are often excluded from the coverage of a professional liability insurance policy or the coverage is severely limited. Consider the following policy provisions:

American Home Assurance Company, Social Workers Professional Liability Insurance Policy (offered through the NASW Insurance Trust)

IX.   PUNITIVE DAMAGES PROVISION

We shall not pay for fines or penalties or punitive, exemplary or multiplied damages; wherever permitted by law **we** shall pay up to $25,000 in the aggregate for all damages with respect to the total of all **claims** and **suits** against **you** involving punitive, exemplary or multiplied damages as part of and not in addition to the applicable Limits of Liability of this Policy.

It is not hard to imagine a jury awarding millions of dollars in punitive damages against a mental health professional for conspicuous exploitative conduct even if the plaintiff's actual damages are nowhere near as great. A jury, riled up or angry after a lawyer's stirring emotional appeal, can easily award significant punitive damages, especially if the sensitivity of the moment makes them generous with the therapist's money.

Ethical Flash Points

- Practical considerations make acquiring professional liability insurance a necessity for the mental health professional.
- The cost of defense of even a fabricated claim could bankrupt an uninsured therapist.
- The professional liability insurance coverage purchased should include defense of licensing board complaints and administrative hearings. *Read each insurance policy carefully and determine individually if coverage is provided for attorneys while representing the mental health professional before the licensing board or before a national organization.*
- Although professional liability insurance policies provide needed coverage, the typical policy contains between 15 and 20 policy exclusions.
- Sexual offenses result in severely limited policy coverage.
- Coverage for punitive damages is often greatly restricted.
- Many ethical violations are not covered by professional liability insurance policies.
- Knowledge of and compliance with ethics codes are critical to a successful mental health practice.
- If operating in an agency, school, managed care setting, or other venue where malpractice insurance is provided as part of employment, the same rules apply. The policy must be read, understood, and digested. Only then can the line provider truly understand the nature and extent of the coverage. Coverage for representation before a disciplinary board of any type is not universal or required.
- In the authors' perspective, an appearance before a disciplinary committee without representation is not a wise move. As soon as a complaint of any type from any source is determined, consult with an attorney familiar with mental health rules and regulations.

Awarding another's cash seems easier than awarding one's own. Under the aforementioned policy language, the carrier is limiting its exposure to $25,000.

Summary

Each mental health discipline presumes therapists are thoroughly familiar with their profession's ethics codes, and ignorance has never been an excuse for violations. An ethical violation not only will lead to licensing board complaints, malpractice lawsuits, and criminal prosecutions but also can result in the assertion of a policy exclusion to deny professional liability insurance benefits. Knowledge of and compliance with ethics code provisions are as critical to a mental health practice as obtaining a professional liability insurance policy.

Ethical violations can limit or in many cases eliminate an insurance carrier's obligation to defend and pay claims under a professional liability insurance policy. Sexual misconduct is not the only violation excluded from coverage. A knowing violation of any ethical canon that gives rise to a claim can leave the unfortunate mental health professional in the undesirable position of having to pay for the defense and damages from personal assets or future earnings. As with all insurance policies, beware the fine print and be sure to read and understand all of the policy's stated exclusions and definitions.

As with all insurance policies, beware the fine print and be sure to read and understand all of the policy's stated exclusions and definitions.

Authors' Note

In this chapter, the authors have reviewed some of the more common policy clauses contained in malpractice insurance policies utilized by mental health practitioners. The authors understand that a malpractice insurance carrier might, under numerous circumstances, interpret the policy differently. When a question arises concerning coverage under a policy of insurance of any type, it is helpful to contact the insurance carrier itself, communicate in writing with a knowledgeable officer of the company or employee, and obtain the position of the company. Insurance companies are ready, willing and able to clarify possible or potential ambiguities in their policies. All the insured has to do is ask. The authors have no authority to speak on behalf of any insurance carrier.

20

Record Keeping

After many years in private practice, Bob, a licensed psychologist, developed an adversarial attitude when it came to the legal profession and attorneys' seemingly endless demands to access client records for litigation. Bob began to believe that his profession's exceptions to confidentiality were compromising his clients' rights to privacy and impeding the therapeutic process. He devised a method to combat the legal system's intrusions into his files and to protect his clients' privacy and the confidentiality of their work together by keeping minimal notes of his sessions. He limited his note-taking to documenting the date a session occurred, the payment, and a phrase such as " worked toward client's stated goals utilizing agreed therapeutic techniques." When one particular attorney secured a court order for one of Bob's client's files, he was appalled at what he considered inadequate record keeping. The attorney filed a complaint against Bob with the state board. Are Bob's stated intentions sufficient to prevent a licensing board sanction?

∽

Carol, an unusually skittish social worker, made an extraordinary effort to record in her session notes virtually everything her clients told her. At the end of each day, she had a habit of reviewing her notes and fleshing them out when she remembered the content of discussions she did not have time to record earlier. In the context of one therapy session, a client mentioned that she and her husband had seen a married neighbor, a local judge whom she mentioned by name, coming out of a gay bar with a very young-looking man on her arm. Carol dutifully recorded the remark and the judge's name in her notes. Two years later, the client and her husband became ensnared in a messy, media-centered divorce and custody case. The husband successfully subpoenaed Carol's file and introduced her notes into evidence at their final custody hearing. Before long the courthouse was buzzing with delicious gossip about the recorded remarks concerning the judge and the gay bar. The judge in question was furious. Carol's records were admitted into evidence *and became part of the public record. Does he have grounds to complain against Carol for recording the remarks?*

⌢

When Bill, a licensed professional counselor, decided to retire, he moved all his client files home and stored them in the garage. But Bill had forgotten about two boxes of files on the top shelf of his basement storage room. When the building manager sent in a cleaning crew to prepare the office space for lease to a new tenant, they discovered the boxes and began reviewing their contents. One unsavory cleaning person recognized the name on one of the files as belonging to a local television news anchor person. He took the file home that night and attempted to blackmail the anchor person who contacted the police. The cleaning person was ultimately arrested and charged with criminal offenses. Bill faced a licensing board complaint as well as a malpractice lawsuit.

⌢

Sheila has been Dr. Blanque's client for three years. One day she reports to Dr. Blanque's office for her usual therapy session and is informed that Dr. Blanque has committed suicide. In a panic, Sheila calls Dr. White, another competent therapist in Dr. Blanque's office. When Dr. White reviews Dr. Blanque's clinical record of Sheila's treatment, he should be able to determine with reasonable accuracy the status of Sheila's treatment.

⌢

Dr. Stanford, a professional counselor, kept meticulous records of all clients. The statute in his state mandated that records be maintained for 10 years before they could be destroyed. Every year, Dr. Stanford shredded his 11-year-old files. Out of the blue, a client filed a complaint that Dr. Stanford had sex with her during treatment 12 years ago. Dr. Stanford had no file, and could not even remember whether she had ever been a client. Of course, he denied having sex with any client, but he was vulnerable when forced to defend a credible story without any documentation to prove the client wrong.

⌢

Mary Lou, a social worker, worked with several managed care panels. With the approval of her managed care gatekeeper, she treated clients and was reimbursed for the services provided. One day the managed care auditor called wanting to inspect Mary Lou's files to determine if the treatment offered was consistent with what the company had authorized and if the diagnosis was consistent with the treatment plan (i.e., when a covered diagnosis was indicated, were the clients receiving the authorized treatment and was this reflected in the progress notes?) Mary Lou would be responsible for reimbursing the managed care company for any treatment that the company paid for but did not authorize.

~

Tom and Mary brought their 5-year-old, acting-out son to Rosemary for therapy. Rosemary visited with the son for about a year, and then the therapy was terminated by mutual agreement. All parties signed a termination letter that contained the clause: "Should further treatment be needed, Tom and Mary will call Rosemary." How long should this file be preserved? According to the Texas statute, the file must be maintained until the child turns 25 (i.e., until the child turns 18, plus 7 years). In most jurisdictions, files must be maintained at least until children reach their majority.

Why Keep Records?

Mental health professionals have always maintained records for their practice. Before licensing boards and professional associations published their sophisticated canons of ethics and codes of conduct, clinicians maintained records of appointments, pricing and billing procedures, and financial records concerning income and disbursements for tax purposes and to determine the profitability of their practice. Therapists can make sound business decisions only if they maintain accurate records according to normally accepted accounting procedures.

Clinical records are another matter. For years, mental health providers resisted generating copious clinical notes, and most were unfamiliar with medical professionals' standard practice of charting. Although therapists jotted down occasional notes to record significant facts or events, in general clinicians were not taught or inclined to record information that might be harmful or embarrassing to them or their clients in the future.

The authors attended a cocktail party during which they talked about record-keeping procedures with a psychiatrist. The authors argued for maintaining accurate files in case another therapist assumed responsibility for a client's treatment. The psychiatrist said she had been practicing for 30 years and had never been sued nor had her clinical records been audited. She was unwilling to change her method of documenting treatment and preserving files. She did not contemplate dying or becoming incapacitated soon and was not worried if she did. Later, the authors discussed privately the psychiatrist's incredible vulnerability should any of her patients have committed suicide or homicide, or had any patient made an unjustifiable claim against her. It is unlikely a judge or jury

A client record may be the only tangible evidence available to a licensing board or a jury in assessing an alleged ethics code violation or malpractice allegation.

would have taken the psychiatrist at her word. Without evidence to corroborate her testimony, they would assume whatever she said to defend herself, was self-serving dialogue to "win" the case. Most judges and juries rely on the maxim, "Absence of evidence is evidence of absence." Without evidence that the psychiatrist did anything appropriate or helpful to the client, they can assume the psychiatrist did nothing.

A client record may be the only tangible evidence available to a licensing board or a jury in assessing an alleged ethics code violation or malpractice allegation. The file is the therapist's first line of defense. Licensing boards and ethics committees usually review the clinical record under scrutiny to determine if the complaint is valid. The authors have defended numerous providers whose records were examined and who were disciplined, not because the complaint was valid, but because the record, as considered and examined by a professional board of peers, was found not to be adequate or in accordance with professional ethical standards. Thus, if for no other reason than self-interest or self-preservation, good record keeping makes common sense. Even if a therapist believes that meticulous, thorough, and complete record keeping is unnecessary and doesn't make good sense, the ethics codes of the mental health disciplines at both the state and national level require it.

Licensing boards and ethics committees usually review the clinical record under scrutiny to determine if the complaint is valid.

Maintaining Clinical Files

The clinical file serves many purposes, and many parties have a stake in its contents. Thus, maintaining accurate records is important for more than just the provider's sake.

For clients, the clinical file serves as a permanent record of their mental health history.

For clients, the clinical file serves as a permanent record of their mental health history. Although the file may be destroyed after a certain number of mandated years, when preserved, it is an accurate information source and an invaluable record of the client's diagnosis, treatment plan, and therapeutic outcome. A well-organized and faithfully maintained file indicates the client's baseline condition and treatment goals. Clients may review their files and may request that they be shared with subsequent mental health providers.

Therapists use progress notes from the client file to refresh their memories between therapy sessions.

Therapists use progress notes from the client file to refresh their memories between therapy sessions. Often clients visit therapists with intense frequency, then drop out of treatment only to return months or years later. Only a complete and up-to-date record will provide the needed background for continuing treatment. This is especially true when therapists retire, become ill, disabled, or die. The new clinician will be more informed if treatment was thoroughly documented and the file is still available. In fact, if the new clinician does not review an available file, it might be grounds for a malpractice action or an ethical complaint. Perusing the file can indicate to the therapist what helped a particular client and what methods did not work. Knowing either or both would be helpful.

To insurance companies and managed care organizations who audit provider records, the clinical files or case notes indicate whether the provider is offering the authorized therapy in the proscribed manner. The authorized treatment is usually stated in a diagnosis and projected treatment plan. The recorded treatment must conform to that diagnosis and plan. If not, insurance companies may refuse payment, or if they have already paid for treatment, the insurance company may bill the provider for reimbursement.

To disciplinary boards, ethics committees, courts, and juries, the clinical records or case notes reflect what transpired between the patient/client/consumer and the provider/clinician/therapist. In their minds, what is recorded is what happened, and what is not recorded did not happen. When providers are called to account for professional actions, the first records examined are the clinical case notes, the intake history, and the informed consent. If the case notes reveal unethical or negligent conduct on their face, disciplinary action will follow and the vulnerable provider will be even more vulnerable. Thus, therapists should maintain clinical records beyond the state-mandated limits. It is worthwhile to spend a few dollars a month for a secure storage facility. Defending a claim without proper documentation is difficult.

What Constitutes a Well-Documented Client Record?

Conscientious record keeping requires more than jotting down a few descriptive notes about a session. A well-documented client file should include:

1. Diagnosis: What the problem is.
2. Treatment Plan: What the therapist is going to do about it.
3. Prognosis: As a result of what is done, what is expected to happen.

As these three elements change, the case notes must evolve accordingly. A diagnosis can shift slightly as time progresses or can turn dramatically. A treatment plan, once thought effective, may have to be altered, changed completely, or disregarded if it is not efficacious. A prognosis, which depends on the correct diagnosis and treatment plan, may have to be updated to reflect the client's changing situation. The clinical file should include the facts, as stated by the client, the reactions, as determined by the professional, and all the necessary times, dates, and information to obtain a complete mental picture of a particular client.

National Guidelines for Record Keeping

Ethical Standards for School Counselors: ASCA

A8. Student Records.

The professional school counselor:

> maintains and secures records necessary for rendering professional services to the counselee as required by laws, regulations, institutional procedures, and confidentiality guidelines.

Texas State Board of Professional Counselors Subchapter C Code of Ethics

681.32 General Ethical Requirements.

(p) For each client, a licensee shall keep accurate records of the dates of counseling treatment intervention, types of counseling treatment intervention, progress or case notes, and billing information. Records held by a licensee shall be kept for seven years for adult clients and seven years beyond the age of 18 for minor clients. Records held or owned by governmental agencies or educational institutions are not subject to this requirement.

Note. The preceding extract (p) is a concise statement of the minimum records that should be maintained and the minimum length of time for preservation in Texas. Check state regulations for each jurisdiction.

NASW Code of Ethics

Section 3.04 Client Records

(a) Social workers should take reasonable steps to ensure that documentation in records is accurate and reflects the services provided.

(b) Social workers should include sufficient and timely documentation in records to facilitate the delivery of services and to ensure continuity of services provided to clients in the future.

(c) Social workers' documentation should protect clients' privacy to the extent that is possible and appropriate and should include only information that is directly relevant to the delivery of services.

(d) Social workers should store records following the termination of services to ensure reasonable future access. Records should be maintained for the number of years required by state statute or relevant contracts . . .

ACA Code of Ethics and Standards of Practice

a. Requirement of Records.

Counselors maintain records necessary for rendering professional services to their clients and as required by laws, regulations, or agency or institution procedures.

b. Confidentiality of Records.

Counselors are responsible for securing the safety and confidentiality of any counseling records they create, maintain, transfer, or destroy whether the records are written, taped, computerized, or stored in any other medium.

c. Counselors obtain permission from clients prior to electronically recording or observing sessions. (See A.3.a.)

d. Client Access.

Counselors recognize that counseling records are kept for the benefit of clients and, therefore, provide access to records and copies of records when requested by competent clients unless the records contain information that may be misleading and detrimental to the client. In situations involving multiple clients, access to records is limited to those parts of records that do not include confidential information related to another client. (See A.8., B.1.a., and B.2.b.)

e. Disclosure or Transfer.

Counselors obtain written permission from clients to disclose or transfer records to legitimate third parties unless exceptions to confidentiality exist as listed in Section B.1. Steps are taken to ensure that receivers of counseling records are sensitive to their confidential nature.

APA Ethical Principles of Psychologists and Code of Conduct

1.23 Documentation of Professional and Scientific Work.

(a) Psychologists appropriately document their professional and scientific work in order to facilitate provision of services later by them or by other professionals, to ensure accountability, and to meet other requirements of institutions or the law.

(b) When psychologists have reason to believe that records of their professional services will be used in legal proceedings involving recipients of or participants in their work, they have a responsibility to create and maintain documentation in the kind of detail and quality that would be consistent with reasonable scrutiny in an adjudicative forum.

1.24 Records and Data.

Psychologists create, maintain, disseminate, store, retain, and dispose of records and data relating to their research, practice, and other work in accordance with law and in a manner that permits compliance with the requirements of this Ethics Code . . .

5.04 Maintenance of Records.

Psychologists maintain appropriate confidentiality in creating, storing, accessing, transferring, and disposing of records under their control, whether these are written, automated, or in any other medium. Psychologists maintain and dispose of records in accordance with law and in a manner that permits compliance with the requirements of this Ethics Code . . .

Commonalities among Ethics Requirements for Record Keeping

- Every mental health discipline requires a clinical record for both business and therapeutic purposes but the exact information to be recorded remains within the clinician's discretion.

- The length of time a record must be maintained differs from discipline to discipline and from jurisdiction to jurisdiction.

- State guidelines have to be checked meticulously. They are altered and amended from time to time.

- Although records may be destroyed after a certain number of years, a better practice would be to preserve them for a greater length of time, perhaps forever. (Some ethics complaints have no statute of limitations. Some malpractice actions have a discovery rule: the statute of limitations does not begin to run until the client "discovers" that the actions of the therapist were negligent. That could occur 20 years after the negligence or bad conduct arose.)

- Clinical records may be written, computerized, or automated but all must be preserved according to statute.

- A disposition cycle may be established.

- Confidentiality of clinical records survives the death of the therapist and the client.

- Client records should only contain information pertinent to the client's treatment.

Avoiding Ethics Violations

A therapist can commit an ethical violation related to record keeping in several ways. First, therapists are professionally obligated to generate and maintain complete, accurate, thorough, and professionally competent client records. Records must be meaningful and essentially establish a road map of the therapeutic process. The notes should make obvious what has transpired in therapy and where the process is headed. A subsequent therapist should be able to review a file and determine the goals, progress to date, and current needs of the client (diagnosis, treatment plan, and prognosis) at any given time. If this information is not in a client record, the record is inadequate and the therapist has violated the records provisions of the applicable ethics code.

Records must be meaningful and essentially establish a road map of the therapeutic process.

Thus, in the first vignette, Bob, although well intentioned, violated the APA Ethics Code by failing to thoroughly document his client sessions. Not only did he fail to document therapy so that he or another therapist could easily continue the client's treatment later, his concern that the legal system might compromise his client's rights of privacy and confidentiality caused him to take action exactly the opposite of what was ethically required. As a psychologist, he had an ethical obligation to "create and maintain documentation in the kind of detail and quality that would be consistent with reasonable scrutiny in an adjudicative forum" (APA Ethical Principles of Psychologists and Code of Conduct, Sec. 1.23[b]). Bob's record keeping did not rise to the level of this standard and he was subject to licensing board sanctions.

*Another way
therapists may
violate ethics
codes is by failing
to secure client
files and
maintain,
preserve, and
protect
confidentiality of
client records.*

Another way therapists may violate ethics codes is by failing to secure client files and maintain, preserve, and protect confidentiality of client records. Even accidentally leaving behind a box of files during a move violates ethical requirements. Bill, the licensed professional counselor mentioned earlier, violated the ACA ethics code since he was "responsible for securing the safety and confidentiality of any counseling records" (ACA, Code of Ethics and Standards of Practice B.4.b) he created. It doesn't matter what medium is used to create the record. The therapist has full and complete responsibility to ensure that prying eyes do not obtain access to the files. Locked file cabinets and password-protected computers are a minimum practice to protect records. Allowing anyone access to client files without client consent is a breach of confidentiality and an ethical violation. Files must be protected from the cleaning staff, temporary help, and others who are not involved in clients' treatment, including other curious clients who have a tendency to peer over a counter or around a door, or other therapists or friends who visit the office. Only those individuals who need to know about a file should perceive that a particular client file even exists.

*Therapists must
preserve not only
a file's
confidentiality but
also the physical
integrity of the
file itself.*

Therapists must preserve not only a file's confidentiality but also the physical integrity of the file itself. Each state requires records to be maintained for various lengths of time, typically 5 to 7 years for adults and for 5 to 7 years past the age of 18 for a minor client. Files must be safeguarded from fire, theft, flood damage, and disintegration or decay. Special care should be taken with files kept on audio- or videotape and computer tape or discs. These mediums may be more sensitive to temperature, humidity, and air pressure variations than paper records.

Other concerns exist for preserving computer files. First, the professional codes do not specify an exact length of time for storing these types of files. Second, with technology evolving at a fast pace, therapists may be unable to access some files that were preserved using outmoded processes and hardware. The therapist bears total responsibility for maintaining the client file and its physical integrity for the requisite period, even if it means converting files from one type to another to keep pace with technology. Failure to do so is an ethical violation.

Maintaining Accuracy

Client records must be accurate and reflect the services provided. Incorrectly recording information, even inadvertently, can be an ethical violation. Each entry should be reviewed and any errors should be corrected. A simple change from "he" to "she" can alter the entire meaning of an entry, and pronouns are easy to miss in the editing process. Too often, errors are discovered only after a file has been copied and provided to a third party for review. Once that happens, an ethical complaint is sure to follow.

Inaccurate entries should be crossed out, corrected, dated, and initialed, so that the record clearly reveals what was recorded, the new entry, the date the new entry was made, and the person making it. The same is true for computer files. Never delete information. Client records must reveal the new corrected entry *and* the former inaccurate documentation.

Inaccurate entries should be crossed out, corrected, dated, and initialed, so that the record clearly reveals what was recorded, the new entry, the date the new entry was made, and the person making it.

The Danger of Overdocumentation

Can a therapist violate an ethics code for recording too much information? Carol, the social worker who recorded her client's remarks about the local judge, seemingly violated the NASW ethics code provision that states the social workers should record only information that is "directly relevant to the delivery of services" (NASW Code of Ethics, Sec. 3.04[c]). The information about the judge had no direct relevance to the therapeutic services Carol was providing to her client. When case notes include information irrelevant to treatment, therapists may face licensing board sanctions for recording too much information.

Summary

Record keeping is critical from an ethical perspective as well as for the therapist's personal protection. Conceptualizing the file as the first line of defense against an accusation of an ethical violation or a suit for malpractice should motivate mental health professionals to keep thorough records. Therapists should consider the client file a road map of the therapy that can fully inform subsequent therapists of the client's problems, progress, and therapeutic needs and ensure a successful therapy transition.

Ethical Flash Points

- Documenting therapy in client records and files is a basic tenet of therapy. Being cavalier about the clinical file is unwise, unprofessional, and unethical.

- Entries in a clinical file should be timely made, at or near the time of the service. Notes are always suspect when they are added as an afterthought, days, weeks, or months later.

- Laziness or concern for client confidentiality is not an acceptable excuse for a sloppy or incomplete record.

- Recording irrelevant information in a client file can lead to an ethics code complaint.

- The therapist bears complete responsibility to maintain the confidentiality of the client file. Locked file cabinets and password-protected computers are a minimum protection for client files.

- It is important to preserve the physical integrity of the client file at least for the length of time proscribed by law. Make a record of all files destroyed. Better still, cull files rather than destroying them. Preserve informed consent and intake forms along with other significant documents including the termination interview, memo, or letter. Create a summary of the file's contents. This can reduce the preserved file to a few pages. Keep culled files permanently.

- The therapist is responsible for the accuracy and completeness of all information in the client file. While all disciplines require providers to maintain clinical files, they are vague in stating exactly what to include in each file.

- Files should be reviewed periodically for accuracy and ethical compliance. Any corrections to client records should be documented and initialed and the inaccurate information crossed out *but not deleted.*

- When files are requested, review them first. If entries require clarification or explanation, add the additional description or information as a dated addendum to the file. Do not delete information before surrendering files.

- When an ethical complaint is filed or registered, the clinical record is often the first item requested by the disciplinary board.

- Insurance companies can audit clinical records for completeness and accuracy, and to verify that the authorized treatment took place. Auditors may report inconsistencies to disciplinary boards.

- If the therapist makes a referral to a psychiatrist or vice versa, and medication is needed, the file should reflect the coordination between therapy and the medication. Case notes should reflect consultations between the two mental health disciplines.

- Always keep the original file if the client requests a copy or if the client transfers to another therapist. Send out copies only with a signed release of information form.

PART FOUR

PROFESSIONAL ISSUES

21

Drug and Alcohol Use

Suzanne, a therapist in private practice, had a reputation for being a fine clinician. Her colleagues also knew her to be a liberal drinker although her criminal and professional records were clean. A gossipy cloud seemed to follow Suzanne in this small town, but no one could find hard evidence of a drinking problem. One day, on the way to her office, she stopped in a bar to have a Diet Coke with friends. Suzanne did not take so much as a sip of alcohol, but when she left for the office, her clothing had picked up the smoky smell that permeated the bar along with the odor of stale beer. Ten minutes into her first session, her client accused her of coming to the office drunk and stormed out of the office in a fit of rage. How does Suzanne defend herself if a complaint is filed? What does she do now?

~

Jack, a therapist for 20 years, has just had major dental surgery. His dentist has prescribed pain medication, which he warned could make Jack a little woozy. Jack has a client scheduled for a weekly appointment and knows the client becomes very upset if appointments are canceled. Just as he is about to go into the session, the pain becomes severe. His options: take a pill before his client arrives, cancel the session, or conduct the session without medication while trying to hide the pain that is affecting his concentration. Which option is most acceptable? Does Jack have other options?

Substance Abuse and Ethics

Using drugs and alcohol, individually or in any combination that impairs the clinician's judgment, constitutes an ethical violation, and disciplinary action will follow a substantiated claim. In addition to the two case vignettes, what other circumstances might generate complaints of ethical infractions to licensing boards and state and national organizations?

Using drugs and alcohol, individually or in any combination that impairs the clinician's judgment, constitutes an ethical violation, and disciplinary action will follow a substantiated claim.

The inappropriate use of drugs or alcohol is a recurring problem to which mental health providers, like any other professionals, are not immune. Professional publications, especially state licensing board and bar association reports, list the names and circumstances of professionals who injure clients or patients while under the influence of drugs or alcohol or while their clinical or legal judgment is impaired. Intemperate drug or alcohol use compromises their competent, learned treatment of clients. Clients suffer when drugs, alcohol, or a controlled substance have become an inappropriate part of the provider's life and adversely affect his or her therapeutic skills.

Mental health professionals, like other substance abusers, will often deny a problem exists. Inappropriate use of alcohol or drugs can take many forms, including:

- Taking a controlled substance without a prescription.

- Taking a higher dosage of prescription medication than is recommended or combining it with other medications.

- Consuming an amount of alcohol that impairs judgment.

- Using alcohol in a manner that might lead clients to *think* that the provider is under the influence and therefore the therapy offered *appears* to be unsound.

- Having alcohol (even if disguised by enormous amounts of breath spray or mouthwash) on one's breath during a session.

- Using a combination of medication and alcohol (both legal) in a manner that causes an overall harmful effect on the clinician's judgment.

- Practicing while under the influence of a legally prescribed medication that impairs judgment in any way.

When to Say "No"

Some drugs are totally acceptable in reasonable dosages, including all prescription drugs taken according to a physician's order. Drinking alcohol is also legal under most circumstances, including having a drink in one's home. Drinking alcohol or taking prescribed medication becomes a problem for therapists only when it impairs their clinical and professional judgment. Pilots, for example, have strict rules concerning the length of time they should abstain from alcohol before flying. Likewise, therapists should not have so much as one drink before a session if it will even slightly impair their judgment. This is a self-policing policy. Only the individual can know his or her limits as far as drinking and driving or carrying on a conversation are concerned.

This is a self-policing policy.

Therapists must raise the bar when thinking about taking alcohol or medication while seeing clients, who are often vulnerable, dependent, and hypersensitive. Even a hint of a lack of concentration when coupled with a whiff of alcohol could create a situation that would compromise the entire therapeutic relationship. If the client perceives an impairment, real or imagined, and files a complaint with either the licensing board or a national organization, the therapist could face serious repercussions. Thus, **mental health providers should never use any alcohol, drug, or controlled substance that might in any way, no matter how slight, affect their judgment while dealing with clients.**

Mental health providers should never use any alcohol, drug, or controlled substance that might in any way, no matter how slight, affect their judgment while dealing with clients.

National Guidelines for Recognizing Impairment

ACA Code of Ethics and Standards of Practice

Section C: Professional Responsibility

g.   Impairment

Counselors refrain from offering or accepting professional services when their physical, mental or emotional problems are likely to harm a client or others. They are alert to the signs of impairment, seek assistance for problems, and, if necessary, limit, suspend, or terminate their professional responsibilities. (See A.11.e.) . . .

Standard of Practice Nineteen (SP-19) Impairment of Professionals

Counselors must refrain from offering professional services when their personal problems or conflicts may cause harm to a client or others. (See C.2.g.)

AAMFT Code of Ethics

3.   Professional Competence and Integrity

3.1   . . . (f) are no longer competent to practice marriage and family therapy because they are impaired due to physical or mental causes or the abuse of alcohol or other substances . . .

3.2 ... Marriage and family therapists seek appropriate professional assistance for their personal problems that may impair work performance or clinical judgment.

APA *Ethical Principles of Psychologists and Code of Conduct*

1.13 Personal Problems and Conflicts

(b) In addition, psychologists have an obligation to be alert to signs of, and to obtain assistance for, their personal problems at an early stage, in order to prevent significantly impaired performance.

(c) When psychologists become aware of personal problems that may interfere with their performing work-related duties adequately, they take appropriate measures, such as obtaining professional consultation or assistance, and determine whether they should limit, suspend, or terminate their work-related duties.

NASW *Code of Ethics*

2.09 Impairment of Colleagues

(a) Social workers who have direct knowledge of a social work colleague's impairment that is due to personal problems, psychosocial distress, substance abuse, or mental health difficulties and that interferes with practice effectiveness should consult with that colleague when feasible and assist the colleague in taking remedial action.

(b) Social workers who believe that a social work colleague's impairment interferes with practice effectiveness and that the colleague has not taken adequate steps to address the impairment should take action through appropriate channels established by employers, agencies, NASW, licensing and regulatory bodies, and other professional organizations.

Texas State Board of Examiners of Professional Counselors

681.35 Drug and Alcohol Use

A licensee shall not:

(1) Use alcohol or drugs in a manner which adversely affects the licensee's ability to provide counseling treatment intervention services;

(2) Use illegal drugs of any kind;

(3) Promote, encourage, or concur in the illegal use or possession of alcohol or drugs.

State of Arkansas—Social Work Licensing Board

The Social Work Licensing Act and the Regulations for the Administration of the Social Work Licensing Act

XI: Definition of Unprofessional Conduct: (17-46-203)

Unprofessional conduct in the practice of social work shall include, but shall not be limited to the following: . . .

S. Offering medication, prescription or otherwise, controlled substances or alcoholic beverages to a client, or accepting these substances from a client.

Ethical Responsibilities

Clients are entitled to effective treatment from educated and well-functioning therapists. Thus, therapists should be aware at all times of their physical and mental condition. If at any point, regardless of the cause, the therapist feels unable to provide effective therapy, or the ability to provide therapy is limited or impaired in any way, treatment must be terminated or suspended. Any act that interferes with the goal of effective treatment could easily be considered unethical, inappropriate, and subject the provider to disciplinary action.

If the therapist feels unable to provide effective therapy, or the ability to provide therapy is limited or impaired in any way, treatment must be terminated or suspended.

The following are practice guidelines regarding misuse of alcohol or other substances:

• The impaired professional must seek professional help.

• Until professional help is obtained and the problem of impairment overcome, professional responsibilities must be limited, suspended, or terminated.

• Each mental health professional is individually responsible for determining whether drugs, alcohol, or some other substance, controlled or not, affects professional competence.

• The abuse of any controlled substance as well as the intemperate use of alcohol can lead to an ethical disaster.

- The earlier the professional discovers the impairment and seeks help the better.

- If the client is injured, it is both unethical and grounds for a malpractice suit. The treatment of clients while impaired is unethical whether or not drugs or alcohol led to personal problems or personal problems led to the substance abuse. The client's perception of the therapist's condition will be given great weight The provider is the vulnerable person. (*Note. Recently, a state licensing board member indicated that complaints took about one year to process. The threat of disciplinary action*

Ethical Flash Points

- Impairment can come from many sources. Use of a substance, even a legal substance such as prescription drugs or alcohol, may represent an ethical infraction if it impairs the clinician's ability to function effectively.

- "Functioning effectively" is in the eyes of the consumer of mental health services. Perception is everything. If the client perceives the therapist is "under the influence" as that phrase is commonly understood, the therapist could be disciplined if a complaint is filed.

- As soon as an impairment is detected, arrangements must be made to protect clients and client records. Other competent therapists must be consulted to carry the client load so that all clients are served and protected on a continuing basis.

- If impairment is permanent, proper termination procedures must be followed. The impaired therapist may have to close the practice (see Chapter 17).

- If impairment is temporary, the therapist must make arrangements for clients while the therapist is receiving treatment.

- If therapy is terminated or suspended, the therapist should consider and address clients' abandonment issues, especially if the client requires continuous care and treatment.

- An act can be unethical and still be legal.

- An illegal act is generally unethical, although this depends on the circumstances. (A clinician might drive while under the influence—an illegal act—but if all clients are seen while the clinician is sober and functioning perfectly, the clinician has not committed an ethical violation.)

- Ethical conduct requires that the client receive competent, effective treatment. Any drug or alcohol use that dilutes therapeutic effectiveness is unethical.

- If the clinician feels "woozy," impaired, or unable to function in any way, cancel the session, regroup, consider the options, and consult any applicable ethical standards.

- Taking chances courts ethical disaster.

hanging over a therapist's head is unpleasant and produces anxiety. Even a dismissal may not be a finding of innocence. It may simply indicate that the case could not be proved to the satisfaction of the ruling body. The black cloud of suspicion could follow the provider for the rest of his or her career.)

- Malpractice and unethical conduct are determined by two different systems. Injury must be proved in a malpractice suit. In a complaint for unethical conduct, the board need only find that the practitioner practiced while impaired thus endangering clients while not necessarily injuring them.

- Therapists have an ethical obligation to help impaired colleagues and to report evidence of unethical conduct resulting from their impairment. But that obligation is not as clearly defined as a lawyer would wish.

- A clinician should never take a client out for a drink and should never accept an invitation to go for a drink from a client.

Summary

Not all drugs are forbidden. Over the counter drugs are legal as are prescription drugs and all the "natural" supplements found in health food stores. What is unethical is taking medication or any drug or substance which prevents the mental health professional from performing with 100 percent clarity and efficiency and thereby *potentially* injuring a client in the process. Legitimate medications can become inappropriate when taken in higher than physician recommended dosages or when taken in combination with other substances that cause impairment

Other substances are illegal and defined as such by state and federal penal codes. The clinician who takes a controlled substance which alters his ability to function is acting unethically in addition to acting criminally.

Alcohol is generally legal and the mental health professional who has wine or champagne with dinner or imbibes within tolerable limits is free to exercise his or her right to drink with impunity. Unethical conduct only takes place when any illegal substance is used or when the active provider is adversely affected by alcohol intake while practicing as a professional. Clients take a dim view of the provider/clinician who comes to the office with the odor of alcohol surrounding him/her or enveloped in a haze of marijuana smoke. The authors' advice: Don't see clients after a champagne dinner or a one martini lunch.

Providers are skating on thin ethical ice if they use alcohol, drugs, or controlled substances of any type, especially if they use them in a manner which adversely affects the provider's ability to provide effective therapeutic services or treatment. Also, it is unethical, as well as illegal, to use illegal drugs of any kind or to promote, encourage, or concur in the illegal use or possession of illegal drugs.

Strange as it may seem, there is a small but impressive roster of therapists who have lost their licenses because of their inability or unwillingness to seek and receive the help offered by well-meaning friends and colleagues. "I don't have a problem," they said. But they did, and the board disciplined them for their problem because it adversely affected their clients.

Denial, in the therapeutic sense, is not limited to clients.

22

Duty to Warn

An agitated client began a fourth therapy session with Karen, a licensed psychologist, with the statement, "If my boss doesn't get off my back soon, I don't know what I'm going to do!" When Karen asked him what he meant, he responded, "You know. Like those post office cases." Control went downhill from there. Karen learned the client had a state-issued concealed handgun permit and several firearms and knew how to use them. Karen tried to get the client to agree to contact her or present himself to a hospital emergency room if he felt sudden homicidal urges coming over him. She tried to obtain the commitment that he would immediately see a psychiatrist on leaving her office. Karen also asked him to allow another family member to take possession of his guns and his permit for the weapons. She even sought consent from the client to notify his boss that he might be in danger. The client refused all her requests, and after 30 frustrating, frightening, and unproductive minutes, he abruptly ran out of the office. After 45 more uncomfortable and difficult minutes of contemplation, Karen elected to breach confidentiality. She phoned the client's boss and warned him of the threats. The boss was so frightened by the warning that he terminated the client's employment immediately and sent a telegram to the client's home to advise him of the fact. Is Karen free from any liability for breaching confidentiality?

∼

Sylvia is a patient in marital and individual therapy with Kevin, a licensed marriage and family therapist. She told Kevin in an individual counseling session that she was on the verge of killing herself. She said that her marital problems, her kids, and her job were all more than she could handle at one time. After an extended therapy session, Sylvia said she felt much better and did not feel suicidal. She contracted with Kevin to call him should she become overwhelmed again and said she would see her family doctor the next day and ask for a prescription for an antidepressant. After Sylvia left the office, Kevin *phoned her husband and advised him to watch Sylvia very closely because she had indicated she felt like killing herself. The husband called his lawyer and told him to proceed with a divorce and custody lawsuit and to subpoena Kevin and his wife's records. When Sylvia learned that Kevin had called her husband, she was incensed and promised to pursue all legal remedies against the therapist. Does Kevin have anything to worry about?*

Case Law Regarding "Duty to Warn"

In 1976, the California Supreme Court opined that society's need for protection outweighed a client's right to confidentiality.

In 1976, the California Supreme Court established what many perceived to be the national standard for mental health professionals when a client poses a threat to an identified person. In *Tarasoff v Regents of the University of California* (17 Cal. 3d 425, 551 P2d 334, 131 Cal. Rep. 14 [1976]), the highest California state court ruled that the psychotherapist of a potentially violent patient had a duty to protect the intended victim from the patient's threatened violence. The California Supreme Court opined that *society's need for protection outweighed a client's right to confidentiality.* Over the past several decades, the trend around the country has been to follow the ruling of *Tarasoff* although it has by no means been universally applied. Courts in states such as Texas and Florida have specifically rejected the holding in *Tarasoff*. Therefore, whether Kevin and Karen, the mental health professionals named in the previous vignettes, acted appropriately depends on the state in which the practice is located.

National Guidelines Regarding "Duty to Warn"

National ethics codes lean in the direction of the *Tarasoff* holding, requiring a breach of confidentiality to prevent harm by the client to third persons or to the client, but fall short of imposing the *obligation* to contact the identified potential victim.

AAMFT Code of Ethics

2.1 Marriage and family therapists may not disclose client confidences except: (a) as mandated by law; (b) to prevent clear and immediate danger to a person or persons . . .

APA *Ethical Principles of Psychologists and Code of Conduct*

5.05 Disclosures.
(a) Psychologists disclose confidential information without the consent of the individual only as mandated by law, or where permitted by law for a valid purpose, such as ... (3) to protect the patient or others from harm ...

ACA *Code of Ethics and Standards of Practice*

Section B: Confidentiality
B.1.   Right to Privacy ...
c. Exceptions. The general requirement that counselors keep information confidential does not apply when disclosure is required to prevent clear and imminent danger to the client or others or when legal requirements demand that confidential information be revealed ...

NASW *Code of Ethics*

1.07 Privacy and Confidentiality ...

(c) Social workers should protect the confidentiality of all information obtained in the course of professional service, except for compelling professional reasons. The general expectation that social workers will keep information confidential does not apply when disclosure is necessary to prevent serious, foreseeable, and imminent harm to a client or other identifiable person or when laws require disclosure without a client's consent. In all instances, social workers should disclose the least amount of confidential information necessary to achieve the desired purpose; only information that is directly relevant to the purpose for which the disclosure is made should be revealed ...

Mandated Disclosure versus Duty to Warn

These provisions allow for disclosure of confidential information when the client or a third party is in imminent danger but do not specifically provide authority for contacting the identified potential victim. Each code states confidentiality must be breached when "mandated by law" or

It is apparent that in situations that involve danger to self and others that calling the family in a suicide situation or the identified potential victim in a homicide possibility, can possibly cause confidentiality to be breached.

"when laws require disclosure." These codes create a situation whereby the mental health professional must be cognizant of the specific state statutes and the case law of the state in which the mental health services are being provided.

It is apparent in situations involving danger to self and others, that calling the family in a suicide situation or the identified potential victim in a homicide possibility, can possibly cause confidentiality to be breached. What is not clear and is not universal is the *duty to warn* and which person or persons should be warned or contacted. Does the therapist have a duty to contact the identified victim? Can the therapist contact the identified victim? Can the therapist contact medical or law enforcement personnel? The answers to these questions vary from state to state, although the consensus is that imminent danger to a client or another person generally gives rise to an exception to confidentiality. The following is a sampling of states that have imposed a duty by statute on mental health professionals to warn identifiable potential victims: Alaska (Alaska Stat. Sec. 08.86.200, 1986), California (Cal. Civ. Code Sec. 43.92, West Supp. 1988), Colorado (Colo. Rev. Stat. Sec. 13-21-117, 1987), Indiana (Indiana Code Ann. Sec. 3.4-4-12.4-1, Burns Supp., 1988), Kansas (Kan. Stat. Ann. Sec. 65-5603. Supp. 1987), Kentucky (Ky. Rev. Stat. Ann. Sec. 202A400, Baldwin, 1987), Louisiana (La. Rev. Stat. Ann. Sec. 9:2900.2, Supp. 1989), Minnesota (Minn. Stat. Ann. Sec. 148.975, West Supp., 1989), Montana (Mont. Code Ann. Secs. 27-1-1101, 2, 3, 1987), New Hampshire (N.H. Rev. Stat. Ann. Sec. 329:31), Utah (Utah Code Ann. Sec. 78-14a-102, Supp., 1986), and Washington (Wash. Rev. Code Ann. Ch. 212 and 301, Cum. Supp. 1987).

Many of these statutes require notification of the identified potential victim as well as local law enforcement personnel. Many require that the client, whose right of confidentiality has been superseded by state law, be advised of the information disclosed and the identities of the person(s) to whom disclosure was made. More states impose a *Tarasoff* duty than do not. Many experts in the area believe that, regardless of specific state statutes, the *Tarasoff* holding is a national standard. Robert I. Simon, in his treatise, *Clinical Psychiatry and the Law* (Simon, 1987), writes, "practitioners should practice as if the *Tarasoff* duty to protect is the law . . . the duty to protect is, in effect, a national standard of practice" (pp. 312–313). The authors would pose two questions to a therapist practicing in a state that does not follow *Tarasoff* or that does not have a "duty to warn" statute:

1. Would I prefer to be sued for breaching confidentiality, by warning the potential victim or a family member if the client is suicidal, and perhaps saving a life or preventing harm?

2. Would I prefer to be sued for not breaching confidentiality and allowing harm to be suffered by a third party or my client?

Any clear-thinking person would pick the first question as the lesser of two evils, but courts and legislatures are still debating these issues.

Exceptions to the Tarasoff Rule

The threats of imminent danger by a client to himself, herself, or a third party creates an immense ethical conflict for therapists. When state law clearly defines the therapist's duty, the correct course of action is obvious. The therapist follows the statute and warns each person to whom warnings are required to be given. Ethics codes impose a duty on therapists to breach confidentiality when mandated by law. Failing to do so to preserve confidentiality under those circumstances is an ethical violation that could lead to sanctioning by a licensing board or professional organization. This would be true even if the client or a third party suffers no harm and no civil or criminal action is brought against the therapist. Failure to follow the law is an ethical violation. When state law is not specific or in fact precludes contacting identified potential victims, the therapist's resolution of the ethical conflict is not clear.

As stated earlier, *Tarasoff* is not universally applied. Texas has clearly departed from the holding of the California Supreme Court in the *Tarasoff* case. Texas statutory law gives a mental health professional the option of notifying medical or law enforcement personnel if the mental heath professional reasonably believes that the client or a third person is in imminent physical danger or the client is in imminent emotional danger. The statute doesn't authorize disclosure or warning to the identified victim. It uses the word "may" in connection with notifying medical or law enforcement personnel so it does not even create a duty to notify those persons. (Texas Health and Safety Code Sec. 611.004(a)(2).) One of the Texas Licensing Boards has incorporated this provision into its licensing act and substituted the word "may" for "shall" (State Board of Examiners of Licensed Professional Counselors, Texas Administrative Code, Chapter

681, Sec. 681.32 [m]). Even among mental health disciplines in Texas, there is a variance on the duties imposed on mental health professionals when a client threatens violence.

On June 24, 1999, the Texas Supreme Court, in *Thapar v Zezulka* (994 S.W.2 635) (Texas 1999), reversed a lower court's decision imposing a duty on mental health professionals to warn identifiable victims when a client reveals an intention to harm a third party. In this case, a psychiatrist was sued when one of his patients, after threatening to kill his stepfather, did so. The Texas Supreme Court held, "Because the Legislature has established a policy against such a common law cause of action, we refrain from imposing on mental health professionals a duty to warn third parties of a patient's threats." The Court carefully reviewed Texas statutory law on confidentiality and although many exceptions and duties were legislated, a duty to warn identifiable potential victims was conspicuously absent. Because the applicable statute did not impose a duty to contact medical or law enforcement personnel, the Court refused to hold the psychiatrist liable for his failure to do so. The Court held that the legislature had given the mental health professional the option, but not the duty, to contact medical or law enforcement personnel.

Differentiating between Homicide and Suicide Threats

The current national consensus regarding duty to warn seems to favor notifying potential victims when harm is threatened to a third party (potential homicide), or family members in the event of suicidal ideation.

Even states following *Tarasoff* distinguish between cases of threats of homicide and suicide. A therapist's duty to warn is less straightforward when a client threatens to commit suicide. Can a family member be contacted? Is there a duty to warn family members? The therapist may simply have to consider all available information, consult with colleagues, an attorney, the professional liability insurance provider, and the licensing board, and then balance the potential risk of each option in deciding which will best serve the client, the therapist, and society. The current national consensus regarding duty to warn seems to favor notifying potential victims when harm is threatened to a third party (potential homicide), or family members in the event of suicidal ideation. The therapist must be knowledgeable of all applicable laws case precedents and ethics code provisions regarding duty to warn before a client ever walks into the therapist's office. Waiting until a duty-to-warn crisis situation is presented in therapy may be too late to correctly, ethically, and effectively handle the situation.

========= *Ethical Flash Points* =========

- Threats by a client to harm a third party or the client should be taken very seriously.

- National ethics codes do not establish a clear, mandated "duty to warn potential identified victims" but do require confidentiality to be breached when mandated by law.

- Since not all states impose a "duty to warn," the *Tarasoff* case cannot be considered the universal standard of care.

- It is critical to acquire and keep updating thorough knowledge of the statutory law and case law regarding duty to warn applicable in the state in which the therapist provides mental health services. An understanding of the statute and case law must be evaluated in the risk-reward context each time a problem arises.

- Even when potential victims cannot be specifically notified, a therapist is usually authorized to contact law enforcement personnel.

- Since this area of law is not well settled in many states, therapists should annually seek an advisory opinion from their licensing board before a situation raises the question about the duty to warn.

- Depending on the state where services are provided, the failure to warn or warning and breaching confidentiality could each be an ethical violation.

- When state law is not specific or does not authorize warning potential victims, therapists must balance each risk when making a decision concerning what action to take, if any.

- Breaking new ground and becoming a test case is not always professionally helpful.

- Therapists need to keep abreast of current case law concerning duty to warn because such situations constitute an emergency, allowing the therapist little time to reflect and ponder the options. When a client threatens homicide or suicide, the threat is usually immediate, serious, and emotional and requires the therapist to decide quickly what action to take, if any.

- Consent to warn an identifiable or identified potential victim or the family, friends, or physician of a potential suicidal client might be considered by utilizing a carefully drafted intake and consent form. In this form, reviewed by an attorney in each jurisdiction, the client might consent in writing, in advance, waiving confidentiality in the event of possible homicide or suicide dangers.

Summary

Most therapists will practice in a state that either follows *Tarasoff* or has enacted specific legislation that imposes a duty to warn and identifies those persons who are to be contacted. The ethical considerations are less complicated for these particular therapists. For those who do not practice in such states, the therapist is left with choices to ponder and a multitude of options. The Texas *Thapar* case indicates that in some jurisdictions there is *no* duty to warn the identifiable potential victim.

The national consensus seems to favor notifying potential victims when harm is threatened to a third party (potential homicide), or family members in the event of suicidal ideation. Knowledge of all applicable laws and ethics code provisions is essential before a client ever walks into a therapist's office. Waiting until a duty-to-warn crisis situation is presented in therapy may be too late to correctly, ethically, and effectively handle the situation.

23

Interprofessional Issues

A few years ago in a major midwestern city, an argument concerning the relative effectiveness of psychiatry versus psychology became part of the local media scene. Psychiatrists and psychologists were publicly criticizing each other while each profession defended its perceived turf. Eventually the conflict fizzled out, but not until after the debate had sullied the dignity and reputation of both professions in the eyes of the public. What should have been a quiet negotiation ended in a noisy, media-inspired discourse that confused rather than clarified.

~

Johanna consulted an open forum of mental health providers representing members of each of the major mental health professions. She indicated that her marriage was in trouble, she had difficulty keeping a job, her son "might" be using a controlled substance, and her attractive 14-year-old daughter was sexually active and only chuckled when Jane wanted to talk to her about sex. She felt terribly depressed as a result. Jane's insurance covered therapy, but she was confused by her treatment options. Should she consult a social worker, a job counselor, a marriage and family therapist, or a psychologist? She received a different answer from each practitioner's discipline represented.

Alike Yet Different

No one really knows what Sigmund Freud was thinking when he began his quest to understand the human mind. We cannot determine whether he predicted the diverse group of mental health providers or the incredible variety of treatment options available to consumers. Today, there are several major categories of mental health practitioners, and subgroups too numerous to mention within those categories. Therapists practice hypnosis, play therapy, music therapy, and animal therapy. Others offer marriage counseling, substance abuse counseling, or career counseling. To the consuming public in need of mental health help, the options can be mind boggling. If testing is needed, a psychologist should be engaged. If the presenting problem concerns a family, does one call a counselor or a marriage and family therapist? If an addiction surfaces in the middle of couple therapy, should the individual be referred to an addiction counselor or can the marriage and family therapist call in a consultant for the addiction problem and continue to offer counseling to the couple? In the hospital setting, where cost-conscious administrators make every effort to cut expenses, does it make a difference whether a psychiatrist, psychologist, counselor, or social worker is consulted, considering that the hourly rate can vary considerably between and among disciplines? If someone were to examine a well-documented diagnosis and treatment plan, could that person determine to which discipline the mental health provider belonged?

Common Threads: Ethics

Common to all the mental health professions is a responsibility to the public, confidentiality, professional competence and integrity, a responsibility to research participants, and responsibilities to the different professions.

The ethics codes of the various disciplines indicate that the common ground far outweighs the differences among them. Common to all the mental health professions is a responsibility to the public, confidentiality, professional competence and integrity, a responsibility to research participants, and responsibilities to the different professions. Financial arrangements with clients, limits on advertising, the requirements for advanced degrees, and, in most cases, obtaining a license also represent common ground among the professions. There are some differences. For example, psychological testing in some jurisdictions is restricted to psychologists, and addictions counseling in some jurisdictions can be limited to individuals with special background and training, but in general the concepts are the same.

Other commonalities among the professions include:

- A vulnerability to malpractice suits and ethical complaints. In addition, the elements of a malpractice suit (i.e., duty, breach of duty by an act of commission or omission, negligence, proximate cause, and damages) among the disciplines are almost identical.

- Using ethical codes as evidence in a malpractice suit. Licensing board rules and regulations are also admissible evidence in a malpractice suit.

- Malpractice policy exclusions. For example, most policies will not cover, except up to a certain set limit, sexual activities with a client, criminal accusations such as fraudulent billing or insurance claims and appearances before licensing boards.

- Limitations on bragging rights in literature, advertising, introductions, and publicity.
- Specific and general elements of informed consent.
- Limitations on the treatment that can be offered and the need to back up the treatment modality by research, the literature, or sufficient education or experience.
- Prohibitions against kickbacks.
- Prohibitions against boundary violations, dual relationships, or any hint of client exploitation.
- "Duty to warn" provisions for potentially homicidal or suicidal clients.
- Record keeping and documentation procedures.
- Billing records including missed appointments, court appearances, and other services rendered.
- The need to interview clients in person.
- Rules against sexual misconduct.
- Policies for reporting an impaired provider and practicing while impaired.
- Rules for maintaining confidentiality.
- Guidelines for supporting suppressed and recovered memory.
- Policies for addressing special problems within group settings.
- Guidelines for avoiding potential discrimination accusations.
- Procedures for managing turf disputes.
- Policies for reporting colleagues' unethical conduct.

Protecting One's Professional "Turf"

Most mental health practitioners see clear boundaries between the mental health disciplines, but the differences among them may be less clear to the consuming public. Picking and choosing intelligently from among the many types of providers is difficult. The boundaries of the mental health disciplines are not clearly defined for the layperson nor can they be identified with such specificity as to be totally separated.

What might be considered a turf problem actually represents healthy competition for the mental health dollar.

What might be considered a turf problem actually represents healthy competition for the mental health dollar. The number of licensed mental health professionals continues to grow, and many large metropolitan areas are saturated with qualified providers who are seeking their fortune in a managed care—controlled mental health environment in which only the strongest survive. The mental health professions will continue to protect what they perceive to be their turf if they can, but in many cases control of the mental health environment has slipped out of providers' hands and into the hands of insurance companies, conglomerates, and other gatekeepers.

Avoiding Turf Battles

Some differences between mental health disciplines are well recognized. Psychiatrists are able to prescribe medication, whereas most psychologists are not. Other specialties also have protected turf, but most mental health providers practice under a wide umbrella whose services compete with other mental health professionals. Every provider has a proprietary interest in protecting his or her turf. But is it worth it? The last thing the larger mental health profession and its practitioners need is interdisciplinary discord, especially public discord. Mental health professionals should avoid public turf battles. A large segment of society already views the mental health profession and its practitioners with skepticism, cynicism, or uncertainty. Public expressions of mutual respect and support among the disciplines will increase public confidence in the profession and induce more people to seek services.

Ethical Flash Points

- Engaging in public turf conflicts with other mental health professionals can be mutually disastrous and should be avoided.
- To mental health consumers, differences among mental health disciplines are ill defined, unnecessary, and confusing.
- "Bad mouthing" a competitive discipline is unethical and demonstrates a clinician's bad judgment. It could also be libelous, slanderous, or both.
- Personal success makes turf battles unnecessary.

There is also a potential for media involvement if a conflict does arise. Ever vigilant for a juicy story, the media often goad disputing parties to cross the lines of professionalism to heat up their broadcasts. In such cases, practitioners should consider the adage "Stop! Look! Listen!" before jumping into the fray.

Summary

In the field of psychiatry, the difference is clear. Physicians can prescribe medications. Psychologists in some areas are seeking to obtain the same privileges in their field of expertise, but to date the ability of nonmedical people to write prescriptions in not widely supported.

Some specialties have protected turf which is well recognized, acceptable, and accepted. Other mental health providers are under a wide umbrella and provide overlapping services.

Every professional has a proprietary interest in protecting his or her turf. Before entering into the field of protectionism, consider the consequences, and ponder: Is it worth it? The last thing the mental health profession and mental health professionals need is interdisciplinary discord, especially public discord. A large segment of our society already views the mental health profession and its practitioners with limited and controlled skepticism, not to mention cynicism and uncertainty. Public expressions of mutual respect and support will increase confidence in the profession and induce more people to seek services. All disciplines will benefit.

Note. The authors continue to view movies and television programs, ever optimistic that somewhere, somehow, movies will be made and shows will be produced which star a mental health professional as the hero, endowed with mental health healing qualities of profound benefit to the public. There are some. We are still waiting for a ground swell of favorable vignettes to appear.

Hark. The psychologist (or social worker) (or marriage and family therapist) (or professional counselor) to the rescue. And just in time to save the endangered client. The nick of time.

24

Professional Vulnerability

Dick was a therapist in private practice. One of his clients suffered from borderline personality disorder and was needy and vulnerable. Several times during treatment, she directly and indirectly implied that their common interest in art and art history transcended therapy and suggested they attend openings and other cultural events together. Dick always indicated that any relationship other than their professional one was a clear boundary violation, a prohibited dual relationship, and inappropriate as well as unethical. One evening, after a particularly stressful session for Jane, she again suggested a liaison. Without thinking too deeply, Dick replied, "It might be nice, but I can't." Jane only heard the "it might be nice" part and conveniently forgot the rest. Building on that, Jane convinced herself that she and Dick had actually attended an art exhibit together, and although she was fuzzy about the details, she convinced herself that some sort of a sexual encounter had taken place. She was furious when, after a few more sessions, Dick indicated that he had helped her as much as he could and she ought to seek out another therapist. He offered her several competent referral sources should she wish to continue the therapeutic process, all of which she could afford and all of whom were competent, recognized professionals. Jane's fury turned to anger and the anger was channeled into a woman scorned getting even. Jane would show Dick. No one could reject her without consequences. So she lashed out in every direction she could find or create: civil, criminal, and ethical. Even though Dick had done nothing inappropriate, unethical, immoral, illegal, questionable, evil, unprofessional, or indecent, he was still vulnerable.

Criminal Vulnerability

In Dick's state, as in many others, sex with a client is a felony. The legal process begins when a client makes an allegation. If a district attorney or grand jury finds the client's testimony believable, the defendant (in this case, Dick) is indicted. An indictment only means there is probable

The legal process begins when a client makes an allegation. If a district attorney or grand jury finds the client's testimony believable, the defendant is indicted.

cause of guilt. A jury trial would follow. Assuming justice triumphed, Dick would be found not guilty after several years of pending litigation, thousands of dollars in "cash on the barrel head" legal fees, countless hours away from his practice, and colleagues who snickered quietly with "where there's smoke, there's fire" self-righteousness. Even if Dick is found not guilty, the damage to his professional reputation and credibility can never be repaired.

Civil Vulnerability

In our litigious society, civil litigation for money damages in a malpractice suit is common practice. Plaintiff's attorneys usually accept these cases on a contingent fee (i.e., for a percentage of the recovery) and often advance their client's court costs and other litigation expenses. Jane's attorney would have to prove that Jane was one of Dick's clients, thereby acquiring a duty toward her. Further, they must prove that Dick breached his duty to Jane by an inappropriate or negligent proposition and that the proposition caused physical or psychological damage or both to her. If malpractice is determined, the jury then decides what money damages will compensate Jane for the damage she suffered.

Civil litigation for money damages in a malpractice suit is common practice.

As in the criminal trial, Dick's professional reputation will be ruined even if the jury finds for the defendant. He is forced to spend additional time in court, becomes a minor celebrity on the evening news during the trial and receives only limited exposure or publicity when found innocent. Moreover, he must pay the deductible on his malpractice insurance (assuming he had it—otherwise he would have had to pay all the trial expenses) in addition to suffering lost income from spending time out of the office. Finally, he will experience terrible anxiety while waiting for a jury to report the verdict. On the other hand, Jane has nothing to lose by filing suit. Although she does not receive a settlement, she also does not have to pay attorney fees. Nor does she owe Dick anything for the inconvenience and expense to him. She just smirks as she leaves the courtroom and waves her gloved hand to Dick. "Adios," she says.

Ethical Vulnerability

Jane located Dick's local professional organization which indicated it did not have jurisdiction to discipline members. The local organization referred her to the state organization, which referred her to the national organization, which requested that she submit a written complaint to the national disciplinary committee responsible for overseeing complaints and taking action when an ethics violation is determined. By now, conversant with the jargon of the trade and knowledgeable concerning the terminology relative to dual relationships, boundary violations, and sex with clients, she embellished what had never happened finally creating a scenario of sordid events to further her goal: having Dick expelled from the national organization. She also recognized that she was not jeopardized in any way if her complaint were dismissed. Her only reaction could be, "Oops."

The national committee, after reviewing all the "he said" and "she said" evidence, concluded that no infraction had taken place and dismissed the complaint. Finally, after almost a year of interviews, letters, affidavits, and legal expenses, Dick was exonerated. He retained his membership in the national organization and continued to hold office in his supportive local chapter.

Vulnerability to Other Professional Organizations

When a complaint in writing is filed, it is referred to the association's ethics committee and then forwarded to a local committee where the member resides.

Dick belongs to several other national organizations, each with a Code of Ethical Conduct and each with a mechanism in place to discipline members who violate the published ethical standards of the profession. When a complaint in writing is filed, it is referred to the association's ethics committee and then forwarded to a local committee where the member resides. Committee members review the facts and the member's written response and then, if the complaint is sustainable, expel the member from the organization and publish notice of the expulsion in the organization's annual publication and in their quarterly newsletter. Or, they can come to some compromise, mediate the dispute, or both. Jane located all Dick's memberships and wrote to all the parent organizations explaining her situation. The national organizations also investigated, found nothing inappropriate, and dismissed her complaints. Dick had spent agonizing hours defending himself and won the battle, but did he win the war?

Licensing Board Vulnerability

Jane also filed a complaint with Dick's state licensing board, consisting of eight individuals: six professional and two lay members. The board's ethics committee oversees any violations of the canons of ethics issued by the state board of examiners of Dick's discipline. After Jane filed a written complaint, they compared the complaint with the licensing law, board rules, and, in some cases, published ethical opinions of the state's attorney general. If the complaint states a violation, they send it to the licensee who must respond within 10 to 20 days. The board quotes the sections of the licensing law canons on ethics that include the alleged violation and ask the licensee to respond to the alleged violation. Based on their review of the licensee's response, they can dismiss the complaint or continue their investigation if the complaint merits further examination.

Dick answered fully, openly, and completely, and sent his response to the board after sending a rough draft to his attorney for approval (at about $ 200 per hour). After reviewing the circumstances, the rules, the evidence, and the allegations, the board dismissed Jane's complaint.

Media Vulnerability

Each time Jane left the courtroom, reporters besieged her with questions. She was even asked to address various civic organizations concerning therapeutic ethics and the vulnerability of clients when they are in the hands of predatory professionals. With a publicist in tow, she glibly and intelligently answered all questions, offering to the media the picture of a wronged person. Some of her interviews appeared as sound bites on the evening news for a few seconds, and her words often found their way into the print media. As each accusation vaporized and Dick was found not guilty, not culpable, or not liable, media and public interest in her vanished, the speaking invitations were withdrawn, and the visibility of the situation became extinct. But although the media hounded Dick during his ordeal, his vindication received little press. Vindication did not seem to be newsworthy.

Overcoming Professional Vulnerability

Every forum hearing the evidence realized nothing had taken place that was in any way punishable. No evidence of an inappropriate dual relationship, a boundary violation, or a sexual proposition could be proven. Yet examine the damage to Dick. Despite being cleared of any wrongdoing, his problems are not over. He now has trouble applying for hospital privileges and renewing his malpractice insurance, because they always ask if there have been any complaints filed against him alleging ethical violations. He also has to grapple with slyly placed personal questions when considering a new job opportunity or a different association with professional colleagues. There is always a certain skepticism when reading a document that alleges the *absence* of inappropriate conduct. Making an accusation is easy. Explaining it away is much more difficult, and writing a believable exculpatory letter is a Herculean challenge.

In addition, Dick still owes past due fees to his attorney and will be saddled with a public record, a media history, and the apparently unshakable questionable reputation of *did he or did he not* following him the remainder of his professional life. It is unlikely that he will he ever completely recover emotionally, financially, and psychologically from the ordeal. Could he ever recoup the losses he suffered?

Now consider Jane. She is perfectly happy. She achieved her 15 minutes of fame, and now retires with a full scrapbook and memories of how the world is full of voracious therapists, none of whom are ever punished.

Note. For purposes of illustration, Dick is the alleged perpetrator and Jane is the alleged victim. This is not to imply that in such situations men are always the wrongdoers and women are always the victims.

Ethical Flash Points

- As soon as the hint of a personal connection arises, the professional must set the record straight, explain the strict boundaries, and document the event and the method by which it was handled.
- Attach a copy of the ethical standards to the initial intake form signed by the client so the client knows the distances that must be observed between client and therapist.
- Be careful with casual offhand remarks. They may return to haunt you.
- The client who has lunch with his lawyer, plays golf with his banker, and goes sailing with his broker is going to want to blur the boundaries with his therapist. Don't do it!
- For a premium, good malpractice insurance exists. Unethical conduct insurance does not.
- There is no insurance to cover the loss of a license and hence, a career.
- Income disability insurance does not cover the loss of a professional license or reputation.

Summary

There is no professional practice without risk, and many of the risks are detailed in this chapter. These risks include civil liability, criminal vulnerability, and administrative controls such as licensing boards and state enforcement organizations. In addition, professional people join numerous national, state, and local organizations too numerous to mention without thinking of whether or not these organizations have published ethical standards, and without realizing that when a person joins an organization with published standards they are bound by those standards and might be negligent if those principles are not honored.

Then there is the ever intrusive eyes of the free press. This makes every person's life, when that person becomes a "public" figure, the object of an open, publicly viewed, hunting season. A newspaper or television station can fill the pages or the screen with "unsubstantiated allegations" which is a true statement, but when the emotional and hotly contested allegations prove to be totally untrue and absolutely without legitimate foundation, the media is under no obligation to offer equal time to the vindication. All the innocent professional can do is, some day, show his scrapbook to colleagues, family, and friends who are interested.

So in summary: Know the rules, regulations, and ethical codes, practice within those rules, and, when an *ethical flash point* becomes a reality or a potential reality, honor and respect your gut reaction. Take immediate notice and respond seriously. Review the entire file, check the codes, and consult a colleague and a lawyer.

The potential consequences far exceed the obvious.

Remember, poor Dick.

And Dick did nothing wrong.

25

Supervision

Dr. Livingston heads a college campus clinic utilized by both students and faculty who have problems they wish to discuss. On staff are psychology and marriage and family graduate students who see clients under Dr. Livingston's personal clinical supervision. Unknown to Dr. Livingston, his niece, a student at the school, sought counseling and was assigned to one of the graduate student intern counselors for consultation. Dr. Livingston only learned about his niece's therapy after the niece had seen the counselor for three sessions. A fourth session is scheduled. To appropriately supervise the intern, Dr. Livingston must review the clinical file. What should Dr. Livingston do?

~

Jane attends a college that requires psychology students to complete a certain number of supervised hours of clinical training. The supervisor who would normally be assigned to her is a former employer with whom she has had hard feelings. She feels reluctant to enter a supervision relationship with him as she is aware of the control a supervisor has over her future career. What are her options?

~

The graduate school caters to mature adults returning for post master's degrees. Dr. Smythe, an available bachelor, is in charge of the school's counseling program. He supervises a divorced graduate student who, over the period of supervision, appears to show interest in him, although they have never discussed this. Ethically, can Dr. Smythe date her, or even request a date, while she is under his supervision? Would it be ethical to ask her for a date after she completes her supervisory hours? What if he waited to ask her out until she graduates in two years? Would it be better to wait until after she graduates, is employed, and independent? Should Dr. Smythe assume that the risk of seeking a social relationship with a supervisee, current or former, is too risky and unethical and seek a social life elsewhere?

~

Dr. Goldberg is a professor who operates a small private practice on Monday evenings. Joy, a practicum student-intern whom he supervises, calls one day and asks if he will see her as a client as she has some severe personal problems that she believes only he is competent to handle. Joy is an outstanding student, and Dr. Goldberg thinks she will eventually become a distinguished professional colleague. He has consulted with her in his capacity as a caring professor, but is reluctant to take her on as a client. What should he do?

~

Dr. O'Hara supervised Sue while she was in graduate school. They engaged in no inappropriate behavior during supervision, although each could sense the other's attraction. Following graduation, Dr. O'Hara wrote Sue a recommendation letter for a job she ultimately accepted. Soon after, they met coincidentally at a national conference and began to date. The social arrangement ended badly, however, and they went their separate ways. Sue decided to look for a new job, but Dr. O'Hara refused to write another letter of recommendation. Sue complains to the university and the licensing board. Dr. O'Hara would probably be called on the carpet for unprofessional conduct, although there is some doubt. Supervisors are always vulnerable to disciplinary action when they become involved with supervisees or former supervisees.

When Is Supervision Advisable?

In mental health practice, supervision is often part of a future clinical practitioners' initial education. During their training, students treat clients under the watchful eyes of credentialed, savvy, and experienced clinician-supervisors. Later, as individuals apply for state licenses and seek other advanced professional credentials, supervision is often a prerequisite and is or becomes a part of providers' continuing education as they develop and utilize new skills.

The disciplinary committees of many national organizations and licensing boards use supervision to reeducate practitioners who have committed ethical infractions. Their misconduct may not be sufficient to revoke or suspend their licenses, but the committees find that therapists who violate a rule or regulation benefit from additional supervision and ethical training either to increase knowledge, correct a bad habit, or augment their awareness and sensitivity. Thus, boards often discipline providers by requiring additional supervision hours to bring them up to ethical standards. Experienced clinical supervisors are in an excellent

Committees find that therapists who violate a rule or regulation benefit from additional supervision and ethical training either to increase knowledge, correct a bad habit, or augment their awareness and sensitivity.

position to explain and illustrate current ethical principles, review published standards, and relate these rules to the situation at hand or to future problems as they arise.

The Supervisor-Supervisee Relationship

The supervisor-supervisee relationship is one-sided in terms of authority, power, and position. The supervisor oversees the supervisee's work, and the supervisee is expected to learn, emulate, and accept feedback from the supervisor. The supervisor must be fair and competent, but the supervisee must follow the supervisor's directives and respect his or her limits, boundaries, and guidelines. In a broad sense, the supervisor is a guru, often held in awe by the supervisee. Although the relationship may eventually be characterized by friendship, the essential ingredient is professionalism. No friendship, no matter how well established or fostered can interfere with the professional objectivity so essential to the supervision relationship.

The supervisor-supervisee association is a close professional relationship with serious ethical overtones that affect all the individuals involved.

As a general rule, the supervisor-supervisee association is a close professional relationship with serious ethical overtones that affect all the individuals involved. These individuals include the supervisor, the supervisee, and the client or, in the event of family therapy, the clients. The state licensing boards and the national organizations for the mental health disciplines have clearly stated principles for supervision. These guidelines are constantly being amended, revised, and republished. Should a problem arise requiring immediate attention, therapists should consult the appropriate organization and obtain the most current published rules and regulations.

National Guidelines for Supervision

NASW Code of Ethics

3.01 Supervision and Consultation

(a) Social workers who provide supervision or consultation should have the necessary knowledge and skill to supervise or consult appropriately and should do so only within their areas of knowledge and competence.

(b) Social workers who provide supervision or consultation are responsible for setting clear, appropriate, and culturally sensitive boundaries.

(c) Social workers should not engage in any dual or multiple relationships with supervisees in which there is risk of exploitation of or potential harm to the supervisee.

(d) Social workers who provide supervision should evaluate supervisees' performance in a manner that is fair and respectful.

ACA *Code of Ethics and Standards of Practice*

Section D: Relationships with Other Professionals

k. Exploitive Relationships

Counselors do not engage in exploitive relationships with individuals over whom they have supervisory, evaluative, or instructional control or authority.

Section F: Teaching, Training, and Supervision

b. Relationship Boundaries with Students and Supervisees.

Counselors clearly define and maintain ethical, professional, and social relationship boundaries with their students and supervises. They are aware of the differential in power that exists and the students' or supervisees' possible incomprehension of that power differential. Counselors explain to students and supervisees the potential for the relationship to become exploitive.

c. Sexual Relationships.

Counselors do not engage in sexual relationships with students or supervisees and do not subject them to sexual harassment. (See A.6. and C.5.b.)

e. Close Relatives.

Counselors do not accept close relatives as students or supervisees.

f. Supervision Preparation.

Counselors who offer clinical supervision services are adequately prepared in supervision methods and techniques. Counselors who are doctoral students serving as practicum or internship supervisors to master's level students are adequately prepared and supervised by the training program.

g. Responsibility for Services to Clients.

Counselors who supervise the counseling services of others take reasonable measures to ensure that counseling services provided to clients are professional.

AAMFT *Code of Ethics*

4.   Responsibility to Students, Employees, and Supervisees

Marriage and family therapists do not exploit the trust and dependency of students, employees, and supervisees.

4.1 Marriage and family therapists are aware of their influential position with respect to students, employees, and supervisees, and they avoid exploiting the trust and dependency of such persons. Therapists, therefore, make every effort to avoid dual relationships that could impair professional judgment or increase the risk of exploitation. When a dual relationship cannot be avoided, therapists take appropriate professional precautions to ensure judgment is not impaired and no exploitation occurs. Examples of such dual relationships include, but are not limited to, business or close personal relationships with students, employees, or supervisees. Provision of therapy to students, employees, or supervisees is prohibited. Sexual intimacy with students or supervisees is prohibited.

4.2 Marriage and family therapists do not permit students, employees, or supervisees to perform or to hold themselves out as competent to perform professional services beyond their training, level of experience, and competence.

4.3 Marriage and family therapists do not disclose supervisee confidences except: (a) as mandated by law, (b) to prevent a clear and immediate danger to a person or persons; (c) where the therapist is a defendant in a civil, criminal, or disciplinary action arising from the supervision (in which case supervisee confidences may be disclosed only in the course of that action); (d) in educational or training settings where there are multiple supervisors, and then only to other professional colleagues who share responsibility for the training of the supervisee; or (e) if there is a waiver previously obtained in writing, and then such information may be revealed only in accordance with the terms of the waiver.

APA *Ethical Principles of Psychologists and Code of Conduct*

6.   Teaching, Training, Supervision, Research, and Publishing

6.03 (b) When engaged in teaching or training, psychologists recognize the power they hold over students or supervisees and therefore make reasonable efforts to avoid engaging in conduct that is personally demeaning to students or supervisees. (See also Standards 1.09, Respecting Others, and 1.12, Other Harassment.)

6.05   Assessing Student and Supervisee Performance.

(a) In academic and supervisory relationships, psychologists establish an appropriate process for providing feedback to students and supervisees.

(b) Psychologists evaluate students and supervisees on the basis of their actual performance on relevant and established program requirements.

General Rules for Supervision

Although the published guidelines differ in nature and scope of detail, certain principles may be extrapolated to form the following 16 general rules. Some are ethical in that they refer only to published guidelines, whereas others refer to legal principles that bind the supervisor-supervisee relationship and create controlling standards:

1. The supervisee's actions are the supervisor's actions when the supervisee is acting in the course and scope of the supervision.

2. Supervisees' negligent, malpractice, or perhaps criminal activities will be shifted to the supervisor if the supervisor knew, or, with reasonable diligence should have known of the negligent, malpractice, or criminal acts. "Don't ask, don't tell" does not apply to the supervisory relationship. For example, a supervisor could be held responsible if a supervisee has sex with a client or breaches confidentiality.

3. Supervision requires a periodic review of the file, a consultation concerning each case subject to supervision and notations made in the supervisor's and supervisee's files indicating the effect supervision had on the diagnosis, prognosis, or treatment plan of each case. The days when the supervisor could ask "How is John doing?" and get the answer "Fine" are over.

4. All supervision must be documented.

5. Where supervision is conducted, a review of the supervisor's malpractice policy is essential to ensure that the supervisee's actions are covered by both the individual supervisor's policy and the agency's or university's if that is the structure being utilized.

6. Just as a therapist cannot treat a good friend, relation, or business associate, neither can the therapist's supervisee. Another supervisor must be located to serve when a therapist's relative, friend, or associate requires treatment.

The supervisee's actions are the supervisor's actions when the supervisee is acting in the course and scope of the supervision.

All supervision must be documented.

7. When a potential supervisee feels a supervisor might have compromised or might have a tendency to compromise clinical or supervision objectivity, another supervisor must be obtained before supervision is commenced and a record created.

8. Clinical judgment and objectivity might be compromised in any "worst case scenario" if a supervisor asks a supervisee for a date. This can place all future supervision in jeopardy and has the appearance of a dual relationship, which is prohibited. The supervisor cannot ask a supervisee for a date, go on a date with a supervisee, or have any social or sexual relationship with a person under supervision. It is unclear whether supervisors may ethically date their supervisees following the supervisee's graduation.

Dual relationships are clearly prohibited.

9. Dual relationships are clearly prohibited. A student or a supervisee cannot become a client.

10. Supervisors must use self-discipline when conducting supervision in specialty areas. Each supervisor must be cognizant of his or her own professional limitations. For example, if a client presents with an alcohol problem and the supervisor is inexperienced in this area, he or she should consult a more learned professional. One never wants to be accused of exceeding one's level of competence or of expertise.

11. Supervisors must establish boundaries with their supervisees. Going out for a business lunch might be appropriate, whereas a postclinical drink at a local bar or the supervisor's apartment or home might blur the boundaries. Although supervisors should use common sense when establishing boundaries, common sense is hardly a national standard and can vary with each individual. The appearance of a boundary violation or dual relationship is often as harmful as the violation itself.

12. Any business relationship (e.g., buying a car from a supervisee or selling one) has a potential for exploitation. Anything that might affect objectivity must be avoided.

Supervisors should avoid informality with their supervisees.

13. Supervisors should avoid informality with their supervisees. The power differential between supervisors and supervisees must have clearly defined boundaries. Sharing a cup of coffee occasionally after a session to discuss a case might be acceptable, whereas meeting for coffee after or before each consultation has a tendency to shift the relationship from clinical to social, at least in the mind of the supervisee and is to be avoided.

14. Supervision may be, but is not always, reactive. The supervisor must prepare for the supervisory session by reviewing clinical notes, appraising each specific situation, and noting that the diagnosis, treatment plan utilized, and possible prognosis is appropriate. Misdiagnosis is a common ground for malpractice suits as well as a common ethical complaint. The supervisor is responsible for the efficacy of the treatment.

15. Supervisors should respect supervisees' confidentiality. The concept of danger to self or others presents a constant problem, and the duty-to-warn scenario is always in flux. Supervisors should take every available precaution when forced to breach a confidence. For self-protection, therapists should consult the licensing rules, the state boards, the malpractice carrier, and an attorney in their jurisdiction.

Ethical Flash Points

- Supervisees are not friends or professional colleagues, they are interns learning their profession.
- The supervisor is the teacher.
- The supervisee is the student.
- Clinical objectivity should never be compromised by dual relationships, blurring of boundaries, or kinship.
- The supervisor has the duty and obligation to establish clear and enforceable boundaries. The supervisee must respect those boundaries.
- Many of the prohibited relationships between therapist and client are likewise prohibited between supervisor and supervisee.
- The supervisor has the ultimate responsibility to the client. If the supervisee acts inappropriately, the supervisor is likely to be held responsible.
- Even if not set out specifically in the national or state standards, the compromising situations described in this chapter would likely be considered unprofessional conduct subject to sanctions.
- Exploitation in any disguise is still exploitation. Beware of free tickets, dinner invitations, gifts, and offers of preferential treatment by influential spouses.
- A malpractice policy might cover therapists in their capacity as clinician or provider. If they act as supervisors, however, they should review their policies to ensure that they are covered if a supervisee is negligent and the supervisor is ultimately held responsible.

Note. The authors receive more inquiries concerning duty to warn than any other subject. Each fact situation is slightly different. The authors advise practitioners to keep current with their state's law as well as national and state standards regarding duty to warn. When a question arises, there is usually little time for thorough inquiry and research.

16. Supervisees are entitled to fair and respectful feedback on a regular basis. Supervisors should systematically review all case files subject to supervision.

Summary

Most graduate programs provide for an internship, practicum, or supervised clinical contact with clients. Although the supervisee has the major client contact, supervisors accept responsibility for the supervisee's actions through their primary role by making suggestions, offering examples, and tinkering with the supervisee's treatment plan, diagnosis, and methodology. Therefore, the supervisor must take the job seriously, relate to the client and the supervisee within professional guidelines, and ensure that the supervisee's treatment is in the client's long- and short-term best interest.

PART FIVE

SPECIAL THERAPY CONSIDERATIONS

26

Forensic Evaluation

Sharon, a licensed social worker, evaluated a 3-year-old girl for several weeks after her mother, a former client, suspected the child was being sexually abused. The child went into hysterics each time her mother attempted to bathe her and was having nightmares. A pediatric examination was inconclusive. After 10 play therapy sessions, the child indicated her father hurt her. Her parents were in the middle of contested divorce and custody litigation. When asked to testify by the mother at a court hearing, Sharon testified that in her opinion the child's father had sexually abused her. The father lost custody and was awarded only very limited and supervised visitation. Four months later, the parties learned that the girl's 13-year-old cousin on the mother's side of the family actually was committing the sexual abuse when his mother caught him in the act. The girl's father immediately filed a complaint with Sharon's licensing board and a malpractice suit. The facts showed that Sharon had very limited training and experience in sexual abuse cases. She was eventually sanctioned by the board and placed on probation and supervision. Her malpractice insurance settled for an undisclosed sum.

~

After practicing 20 years as a psychologist and testifying in over 100 forensic cases for the state on the question of a criminal defendant's competency to stand trial, Mark learned that a complaint had been filed against him with the state licensing board. The attorney for a mentally retarded defendant charged with sexual assault learned that not once in over 100 cases had Mark ever rendered an opinion that a defendant was mentally incompetent. In each case, the district attorney prosecuting the case had hired and paid Mark. In the current case, the appellate court ultimately determined that the defendant was not competent to stand trial and reversed the conviction. Mark was accused of bias, unprofessionalism, and incompetence. After the licensing board began investigating the case, they moved to revoke Mark's license, which he surrendered voluntarily in lieu of a formal revocation hearing.

~

*Jacob, a licensed professional counselor, was experienced working with sex of-
fenders. He was court ordered to evaluate and treat a 19-year-old youth accused of having a sexual relationship with his 14-year-old sister. After six
months of therapy, the boy revealed that he had entered his sister's home sur-
reptitiously, gotten into bed with her, and fondled her. Jacob immediately notified the court, child protective services, and the police, who took the boy into
custody. Jacob's later testimony helped send the client to the penitentiary for
five years. While in prison, the client filed a complaint with the state licensing
board accusing Jacob of a breach of confidentiality, conflict of interest, and failure to warn him regarding the therapeutic limits to confidentiality. Although he
was not severely sanctioned by the licensing board, Jacob was privately repri-
manded for not securing informed consent from the client, documenting his relationship to the court, and disclosing to the client his duty to report sexual
offenses prior to beginning therapy.*

What Is Forensic Evaluation?

*Forensic work
involves an expert
witness
evaluating,
reporting, and
often testifying in
legal proceedings.*

Forensic work involves an expert witness evaluating, reporting, and
often testifying in legal proceedings. An expert witness is a person who
by education, learning, training, and experience is allowed to give testimony and render an opinion on facts or issues in a lawsuit. The court determines whether the individual is competent to testify as an expert in
the case. If the court decides that the individual has sufficient education,
training, or experience to advise the court on the disputed issue or fact,
then the court will find the witness competent and allow the testimony
or report into evidence. The testimony will be admissible even over the
objection of the other party. It will be heard by the judge, the jury or
both. Whether it will be believed is another question. Credibility is always a separate issue that depends on many factors, including presentation method, courtroom demeanor, individual preparation or lack
thereof, or, sometimes, a judge or jury's general feeling that the witness is
too glib to be believable. The weight to be assigned to admissible evidence is always personal to a judge or jury and neither has to justify their
personal reaction to anyone else.

Who Should Offer Forensic Services?

Many therapists actively seek forensic assignments from courts, litigants,
and attorneys as part of their practice activities and in a few cases as the

sum of their professional endeavors. Other mental health professionals get drawn into forensic work because of their prior work with a client who becomes involved in the legal system. Being asked to evaluate a client or render an opinion regarding a client or legal issue or both requires caution and consideration.

Therapists offering expert testimony in court can usually assume that one of the parties is not going to like their opinion or testimony. The disagreeing party is usually the opposing counsel or the person against whom the expert testifies. Even in situations where therapists testify that they cannot reach an opinion, a client or party who expected a favorable opinion may become incensed. Because the mental health professional's recommendations or opinions can significantly impact the legal proceeding and a client's well-being, forensic work should be approached with heightened professionalism, incredible sensitivity, and absolute competence.

As Sharon learned, exceeding one's level of competence can be embarrassing and expensive. Rendering an expert opinion in a legal proceeding when one is not sufficiently experienced is unethical; moreover, it magnifies one's competency, or lack thereof. Numerous parties, including the judge, jury, and attorneys for both sides will closely scrutinize the mental health professional's competency to testify. Every word said under oath from the witness stand (even after swearing on a bible) can be microscopically cross-examined by opposing counsel; and misstatements, exaggerations, allegations, or assumptions stated as truths can be revealed to the therapist's ultimate embarrassment and chagrin. Thus, therapists must be completely confident of their expertise in this area. Therapists must recognize their limits and resist being drawn beyond their professional competency levels by a pushy attorney or a needy client. It is unethical for a therapist to perform an evaluation or render an opinion if they do not have the requisite training, experience, or education.

Because the mental health professional's recommendations or opinions can significantly impact the legal proceeding and a client's well-being, forensic work should be approached with heightened professionalism, incredible sensitivity, and absolute competence.

National Guidelines Regarding Competency to Testify as an Expert Witness

AAMFT Code of Ethics

Section 3.8 Marriage and family therapists, because of their ability to influence and alter the lives of others, exercise special care when making public their professional recommendations and opinions through testimony or other public statements.

NASW Code of Ethics

1.04 Competence

I. Social Workers should provide services and represent themselves as competent only within the boundaries of their education, training, license, certification, consultation received, supervised experience, or other relevant professional experience.

II. Social workers should provide services in substantive areas or use intervention techniques or approaches that are new to them only after engaging in appropriate study, training, consultation, and supervision from people who are competent in those interventions or techniques . . .

APA Ethical Principles of Psychologists and Code of Ethics

7.01 Professionalism.

Psychologists . . . In addition, psychologists base their forensic work on appropriate knowledge of and competence in the areas underlying such work, including specialized knowledge concerning special populations . . .

ACA Code of Ethics and Standards of Practice

C.2 Professional Competence

a. Boundaries of Competence. Counselors practice only within the boundaries of their competence, based on their education, training, supervised experience, state and national professional credentials, and appropriate professional experience . . .

c. Qualified for Employment. Counselors accept employment only for positions for which they are qualified by education, training, supervised experience, state and national professional credentials, and appropriate professional experience . . .

Appropriate information gathering and proper testing and therapy techniques must be conducted and utilized to substantiate opinions and recommendations.

Conducting a Forensic Assessment

Assuming one has the competency to provide the forensic services requested, the mental health professional must then adequately perform the services, whether they involve courtroom testimony or treatment. Appropriate information gathering and proper testing and therapy techniques must be conducted and utilized to substantiate opinions and recommendations. Examining and interviewing the individuals involved in the case is almost always a necessity.

The authors have been involved in several cases where a mental health professional has rendered an opinion concerning a custody or abuse issue without ever having interviewed one of the parties in the case, or the accused perpetrator. It would be a very rare child custody case in which a therapist could give an opinion concerning which parent should be awarded custody without first clinically and thoroughly evaluating both parents. If a therapist interviewed at least one of the parents, he or she could offer an opinion on the mental health condition or the observed parenting abilities of that parent but ethically could not offer expert testimony concerning the child's best interest without evaluating *both* parents. Likewise, in child abuse cases involving very young children in which there is an absence of conclusive physical evidence or other corroboration, the failure to include the alleged perpetrator in the evaluation process could preclude a therapist from rendering an opinion of the accused's culpability. The accuracy of any testimony offered would be so subject to question as to be meaningless. If a court order or other document or entity demands that a mental health professional render an opinion for which adequate information, techniques, or testing have not been obtained or utilized, then the therapist should fully disclose the limitations of the opinion and lack of substantiation in testimony and in every written report.

National Guidelines for Conducting Forensic Assessments

APA Ethical Principles of Psychologists and Code of Ethics

7.02 Forensic Assessments.

(a) Psychologists' forensic assessments, recommendations, and reports are based on information and techniques (including personal interviews of the individual, when appropriate) sufficient to provide substantiation for their findings . . .

(b) Except as noted in (c), below, psychologists provide written or oral forensic reports or testimony of the psychological characteristics of an individual only after they have conducted an examination of the individual adequate to support their statements or conclusions.

(c) When, despite reasonable efforts, such an examination is not feasible, psychologists clarify the impact of their limited information on the reliability and validity of their reports and testimony, and they appropriately limit the nature and extent of their conclusions or recommendations . . .

Documenting Forensic Evaluations

It is critical for mental health professionals to thoroughly document all information gathering, therapy techniques, and testing results obtained and relied on during the evaluation and on which they base their opinions. This documentation is necessary during the legal proceeding itself when presenting the case in chief and also when cross-examining lawyers scrutinize and challenge the therapist's competence, work, professionalism, and opinions. Documentation is critical when defending a therapist's actions or alleged inaction if a licensing board complaint or malpractice suit is later filed.

Documentation is critical when defending a therapist's actions or alleged inaction if a licensing board complaint or malpractice suit is later filed.

Avoiding Conflicts of Interest

Therapists should avoid conflicts of interest when providing any professional services to a client, including forensic services. When mental health professionals are hired for forensic evaluations and treatment, as is often the case with court appointments involving sex offenders, obvious potential conflicts of interest may arise. Therapists have an obligation to report honestly and objectively to the court and to assist the court in its duty to protect society. At the same time, therapists have an obligation to protect the client's rights and interests. Reporting recidivism to the court that results in clients being sent to the penitentiary dramatically highlights the conflict of interest.

At best, therapists in this situation should clearly document that they disclosed the potential conflict of interest to the client as well as the limits of confidentiality and possible consequences of those limits. Therapists should make such disclosures in writing and document their receipt with the client's signature and consent allowing the therapist to proceed with treatment in the dual role. In the earlier example, Jacob's licensing board sanctioned him for failing to thoroughly document these disclosures and his client's consent. Written documentation is important because trials can be delayed for years after an action or event occurs.

Oral discussions may be forgotten, distorted, and molded to fit the circumstance of the moment. A signed document speaks for itself. The written documentation should be preserved in the permanent case folder and maintained and secured according to ethical standards.

National Guidelines for Conflicts of Interest in Forensic Evaluations

NASW Code of Ethics

1.6 Conflicts of Interest

1.06 Conflicts of Interest

(a) Social workers should be alert to and avoid conflicts of interest that interfere with the exercise of professional discretion and impartial judgment. Social workers should inform clients when a real or potential conflict of interest arises and take reasonable steps to resolve the issue in a manner that makes the clients' interests primary and protects clients' interests to the greatest extent possible. In some cases, protecting clients' interests may require termination of the professional relationship with proper referral of the client . . .

The Importance of Honest and Unbiased Opinions

Clients hiring a mental health professional as an expert witness are hoping for, if not actually expecting, reporting and testimony favorable to their case. Clients are allowed to shop around for experts, particularly ones who are able to testify favorably in court. This smug "hired gun" theory permeates many facets of the lawyer/client/expert/therapist relationship. Can it be avoided? That is another question!

Mental health professionals serving as expert witnesses should advise their clients in writing that ethical obligations require absolute honesty and accuracy and that clients may not be happy with their findings. Therapists should advise clients as early as possible regarding negative findings or opinions to allow them an opportunity to engage another expert.

If a therapist is hired and paid by one party to a lawsuit in any contested litigation and provides testimony favorable to that party, the

Mental health professionals serving as expert witnesses should advise their clients in writing that ethical obligations require absolute honesty and accuracy and that clients may not be happy with their findings.

A therapist who gives the opinion a paying client requested, regardless of whether that opinion was warranted, is at risk of being sanctioned for ethical violations.

opposing party will certainly challenge the report or testimony on bias and competency grounds. Paying an independent mental health professional a large fee for an evaluation and courtroom testimony should not guarantee favorable testimony. A therapist who gives the opinion a paying client requested, regardless of whether that opinion was warranted, is at risk of being sanctioned for ethical violations. In the second vignette, Mark testified over one hundred times in favor of the state. Mark's bias and lack of candor and accuracy seem at first glance to be blatant. On the other hand, any entity accusing Mark of bias or prejudice would still have to examine individual cases and prove that Mark was biased. Could it be that in each case Mark was clinically correct? Could it be that the district attorney only referred cases to Mark in which the defendant *was* competent?

Ethical Flash Points

- Forensic work should be approached with extreme caution and care.
- Competency is critical both ethically and professionally in tackling any forensic assignment.
- Courts, attorneys, clients, and other interested parties will scrutinize the mental health professional's forensic work as well as the professional's overall competency.
- The mental health professional can expect to displease at least one party involved in a legal proceeding, and a licensing board complaint filed after the trial should come as no surprise.
- Thorough documentation of all forensic activities is crucial in view of the third-party review of the mental health professional's work and the defense against the inevitable licensing board complaint.
- Conflicts of interest should be avoided, but if unavoidable, the therapist should disclose them and obtain consent given with written documentation.
- Mental health professionals must render unbiased, honest, and accurate reports and testimony.
- There is no substitute for complete and total preparation with an attorney prior to a court appearance.
- Being cross-examined concerning one's competence, background, personal history, diagnosis, treatment plan, and changing prognosis is uncomfortable, to put it mildly.

National Guidelines Regarding Honest and Unbiased Opinions in Forensic Evaluations

ACA Code of Ethics and Standards of Practice

C.5. Public Responsibility . . .

c. Reports to Third Parties. Counselor are accurate, honest, unbiased in reporting their professional activities and judgments to appropriate third parties including courts, health insurance companies, those who are recipients of evaluation reports, and others . . .

Summary

Forensic work for many mental health professionals is both financially and professionally rewarding. However, it should not be pursued by anyone who is not unequivocally competent, thoroughly honest, and completely unbiased. Expert witnesses should also possess a controlled temper and a skin thick enough for them to accept being questioned about every facet of any given case.

Most mental health services are provided in a relatively quiet office vacuum of client and therapist. There is a total contrast when compared with forensic services where numerous third parties examine and challenge the services performed and the person performing them. Therefore, awareness and understanding of ethical canons are even more important for therapists interested in or drawn into providing forensic services.

A therapist who thinks the courtroom is like a therapist's office is in for a rude awakening. The therapist controls what occurs in the clinical office setting but has no control over what happens in the courtroom. In a trial situation, the judge reigns supreme.

A therapist who thinks the courtroom is like a therapist's office is in for a rude awakening.

27

Group Therapy

Tracy, a group therapy participant, waited several months before opening up and discussing her problems and experiences in front of the group. She then consumed most of the session sharing with her fellow members and therapist many intimate details about herself and the problems she was having with co-workers. The next week one of her co-workers confronted her concerning some remarks she made in the group therapy session. At first dumbfounded, Tracy collected herself long enough to find out the co-worker was dating one of the other group members. Tracy then called the therapist and reminded him of a conversation they had before she joined the group. He had assured her that she did not have to worry about confidentiality because he carefully screened each potential new member before asking the person to participate in the group. Tracy felt betrayed and complained to the agency that the group's therapist had failed to adequately disclose to her the potential for breaches of confidentiality. The participants in Tracy's group never signed any acknowledgments pertaining to the limits of confidentiality and the risks of disclosure in group therapy.

~

While working with a couple in marital therapy utilizing both joint and individual sessions, Robert, a licensed marriage and family therapist, learned from the husband that he was bisexual and occasionally had sex with men. His wife did not know about his extramarital sexual activity or his bisexuality. When Robert insisted that the husband either reveal this information to his wife or allow Robert to tell her, the husband refused on both accounts. Robert struggled with his options and finally decided to refer them to another therapist. The wife later called Robert to tell him how upset she was because she felt they had been making wonderful progress. She pressed him for a reason for the termination beyond his stated position that he was having trouble working with them and that he felt another therapist might be able to do a better job. Robert did not disclose his real reason for terminating therapy, and she hung up far less than satisfied with the conversation. She realized there was a hidden agenda but did not know what it was. The mystery was disconcerting.

~

Prior to a group therapy session, one of the participants, Joe, approached Dr. Kindheart, the therapist conducting the group, and complained about threatening remarks Jake, another group member had made to him. Joe indicated that the altercations with Jake had occurred after several sessions when the participants were walking toward their cars in the parking lot. Dr. Kindheart promised to discuss the matter with Jake. After first confirming with several other participants that the altercations had indeed occurred, Dr. Kindheart decided to bring the matter up in group, hoping the peer pressure of the group would help Jake see the inappropriateness of his behavior. Rather than acknowledging his mistake, Jake became incensed and attacked Joe, breaking his jaw before the other group members could wrestle him down. Dr. Kindheart called the police who arrested Jake and charged him with assault. Joe filed a civil suit against Jake for the damages he sustained as a result of the assault and against Dr. Kindheart for negligence. During the legal proceedings, Joe's attorney took depositions from each group member and Dr. Kindheart. Jake, out of jail on bond, filed a complaint against Dr. Kindheart's licensing board alleging breaches of confidentiality for calling the police and providing them with information about him and for the information shared by each group participant in their depositions.

Ethical Risks for Conjoint Therapy: Confidentiality

The national guidelines for conducting conjoint therapy indicate that confidentiality should be of the utmost concern for therapists and their clients. Therapists must thoroughly discuss confidentiality issues with each group participant and secure written commitments from them to preserve confidentiality with respect to all information disclosed during group sessions. Therapists could also ask group participants to sign a lawyer drafted "hold harmless" agreement in which the participant agrees that if the facilitator is sued for breach of confidentiality, the participant who breached the confidentiality will hold the therapist harmless for any damages incurred, including attorney's fees. Moreover, each participant is personally responsible to the other group participants for

Therapists must thoroughly discuss confidentiality issues with each group participant.

breaches of confidentiality. This type of written instrument will have a sobering effect on the talkative or gossipy group member.

Some agencies and individual practitioners have used the same standard consent forms for decades, without challenge or litigation. Nevertheless, these forms often do not reflect the developing needs of managed care, licensing board requirements, or the legal requirements that reflect emerging case law and statutory amendments. When a complaint is filed or a suit is put before the judicial system, obsolete forms do the therapist little good. The therapist and lawyer should jointly prepare all forms and review them regularly. Proper forms will ensure effective therapy as well as a consumer-oriented climate. Proper documentation and orientation will automatically protect the client. Every therapist and mental health agency should review all internal and external forms with an attorney at least annually.

In addition to asking clients to sign confidentiality agreements, therapists should clearly establish the consequences for a breach of confidentiality, which at a minimum should include expulsion from the group.

In addition to asking clients to sign confidentiality agreements, therapists should clearly establish the consequences for a breach of confidentiality, which at a minimum should include expulsion from the group. Therapists should go one step further and advise each participant that although everyone involved in the group has made a confidentiality commitment, they cannot guarantee that breaches of confidentiality will not occur.

In the first example, Tracy complained that her therapist did not adequately explain the limits to confidentiality before she participated in the group therapy. Without any written and signed documents the therapist could not easily refute Tracy's allegations. Just as informed consent should be documented for individual therapy, so should it be for group or multiple client therapy. The informed consent should include the additional information that applies to multiple clients and disclosures ethically required by the ethics codes. Therapists should hold each participant personally and financially responsible for any inappropriate disclosure of information that comes out of the group (i.e., have them sign a "hold harmless" agreement). What is said in the group setting should remain there and cannot be disclosed to anyone, absent a legal exception to confidentiality.

A therapist is required to disclose whatever policy exists with respect to disclosure of confidential information. In the second case study, Robert struggled with the husband's confidential confession that he was bisexual and sexually active outside his marriage. The husband's right to confidentiality precluded Robert sharing that information with the wife or anyone else. A good practice for a therapist offering family or marital therapy is to establish a policy that any and all information the therapist deems relevant and material to achieving the goals and purposes of the therapy will be disclosed to other participants. Couples and families then would acknowledge in writing their understanding of and consent to the disclosure policy and its consequences prior to the commencement of therapy, which will allow the therapist to avoid being handcuffed by conflicting ethical interests. Robert was restricted by not receiving such consent in advance.

National Guidelines for Confidentiality in Conjoint Therapy

ACA Code of Ethics and Standards of Practice

B.2   Groups and Families

a. Group Work. In group work, counselors clearly define confidentiality and the parameters for the specific group being entered, explain its importance, and discuss the difficulties related to confidentiality involved in group work. The fact that confidentiality cannot be guaranteed is clearly communicated to group members.

b. Family Counseling. In family counseling, information about one family member cannot be disclosed to another family member. Counselors protect the privacy rights of each family member.

NASW Code of Ethics

1.7   Privacy and Confidentiality . . .

(f) When social workers provide counseling services to families, couples, or groups, social workers should seek agreement among the parties involved concerning each individual's right to confidentiality and obligation to preserve the confidentiality of all information shared by others. Social workers should inform participants in family, couples, or group counseling that social workers cannot guarantee that all participants will honor such agreements.

(g) Social workers should inform clients involved in family, couples, marital, or group counseling of the social worker's, employer's, and agency's policy concerning the social worker's disclosure of confidential information among the parties involved in the counseling.

APA Ethical Principles of Psychologists and Code of Conduct

4.03   Couple and Family Relationships.

(a) When a psychologist agrees to provide services to several persons who have a relationship (such as husband and wife or parents and children), the psychologist attempts to clarify at the outset (1) which of the individuals are patients or clients and (2) the relationship the psychologist will have with each person. This clarification includes the role of the psychologist and the probable uses of the services provided or the information obtained.

Ethical Risks for Conjoint Therapy: Client Access to Therapy Records

Another problem facing a therapist with multiple clients is client access to records. The authors get numerous calls from therapists asking for legal advice after an individual involved in family or marital therapy requests a copy of his or her record when the therapists have not received authorization from the spouse or other family members to disclose the information.

If therapists do not maintain separate files for each group member, they are faced with the problem of extracting confidential information pertaining to another family member or spouse.

If therapists do not maintain separate files for each group member, they are faced with the problem of extracting ("whiting out") confidential information pertaining to another family member or spouse. The simplest way for mental health professionals to deal with this problem is to secure consent from each client that separate client files will be maintained for all individual sessions and one file will be maintained for joint sessions. Each participant then further consents that each participant has the right to access the joint file and the information in it.

National Guidelines Regarding Client Access to Records in Conjoint Therapy

ACA Code of Ethics and Standards of Practice

Section B.4 d.   In situations involving multiple clients access to records is limited to those parts of records that do not include confidential information related to another client.

Ethical Risks in Conjoint Therapy: Conflicting Goals

It is not uncommon in multiple-client therapy for participants to come into conflict with one another and have different goals and objectives. Participants' therapeutic objectives may vary as the therapy progresses, sometimes without the therapist's or other participants' knowledge. This is often true in marital therapy where one or both spouses may decide that the marriage is irreconcilable and pursue a divorce.

Under these circumstances, it is not uncommon for therapists to provide individual therapy to one or more participants; however, their susceptibility to accusations of breaches of confidentiality by the other member(s) is great. The separate and confidential knowledge the therapist has about each participant makes continuing with one client problematic under these circumstances. The better practice would be to discontinue therapy with each participant and refer each participant to a different provider.

If it is apparent that the mental health professional will be asked to testify in any legal proceedings among group participants, immediate termination and referral is usually the best practice. The potential that the therapist's testimony may harm one client dictates this action.

It is not uncommon in multiple-client therapy for participants to come into conflict with one another and have different goals and objectives.

The separate and confidential knowledge the therapist has about each participant makes continuing with one client problematic.

National Guidelines for Conflict of Interest in Conjoint Therapy

APA Ethical Principles of Psychologists and Code of Conduct

Section 4.03(b) As soon as it becomes apparent that the psychologist may be called on to perform potentially conflicting roles (such as marital counselor to husband and wife, and then witness for one party in a divorce proceeding), the psychologist attempts to clarify and adjust, or withdraw from roles appropriately.

NASW Code of Ethics

1.06 Conflicts of Interest . . .

(d) . . . Social workers who anticipate having to perform in potentially conflicting roles (e.g., a social worker is asked to testify in a child custody dispute or divorce proceedings involving clients) should clarify their role with the parties involved and take appropriate action to minimize any conflict of interest.

Note. Although this section does not specifically instruct a social worker to terminate a therapeutic relationship it is probably a rare case where any other action would best minimize conflict. Giving testimony in a lawsuit adverse to a client is not going to have a positive impact on therapy.

Ethical Risks of Conjoint Therapy: Group Member Safety

The therapist conducting the group is responsible for the safety and well-being of each participant.

The therapist conducting the group is responsible for the safety and well-being of each participant. It is the therapist who admits participants; thus he or she is responsible for screening each person carefully before asking them to join the group. Failure to carefully study a person's background, characteristics, and suitability for the particular group can be a strong basis for liability if a participant is harmed by the inadequately screened member.

In the third case example, Joe argued that Dr. Kindheart did not properly screen Jake, failing to learn of his violent tendencies, before admitting him to the group. He also argued that Dr. Kindheart failed to protect Joe from Jake and in fact placed Joe in a potentially harmful situation by confronting Jake during a group session about his previous threats to Joe. Dr. Kindheart clearly failed to fulfill his ethical obligations to Joe and the other group participants.

National Guidelines Regarding Group Member Safety in Conjoint Therapy

ACA Code of Ethics and Standards of Practice

Standard of Practice Five (SP-5): Protecting Client During Group Work. Counselors must take steps to protect clients from physical or psychological trauma resulting from interactions during group work.

A.9. Group Work

a. Screening. Counselors screen prospective group counseling/therapy participants. To the extent possible, counselors select members whose needs and goals are compatible with goals of the group, who will not impede the group process, and whose well-being will not be jeopardized by the group experience.

b. Protecting Client. In a group setting, counselors take reasonable precautions to protect clients from physical or psychological trauma.

Ethical Flash Points

- Informed consent for group and other multiple client therapy should include all additional disclosures required by ethics codes and should be documented with a written and signed lawyer-approved consent form.

- Confidentiality must be thoroughly and completely discussed with each group participant.

- A written commitment to preserve the confidentiality of all information disclosed to the group should be secured from each participant.

- Consequences for breaches of confidentiality should be established and an understanding of them should be acknowledged in writing by each participant.

- The inability to *guarantee* confidentiality should be disclosed to each participant.

- Separate records should be kept for all individual sessions held with each participant and a common file for all joint sessions.

- Secure written consent from each participant that all participants shall have access to the information in the file and information pertaining to joint sessions.

- Policies regarding revealing information to other participants must be disclosed, as well as all the legal, statutory, and common-law exceptions to confidentiality. A lawyer approved handout pamphlet would be advisable.

- Securing written client consent in advance to share confidential information with other participants when deemed relevant and material to goals and purposes of the therapy can ward off a potential ethical quandary for the therapist.

- When conflicts between participants in marital and family therapy become apparent and cannot be reconciled, the therapist must consider terminating with each participant and offering appropriate referrals.

- If family or marital therapists learn that they may be asked to testify by one client in a lawsuit between two or more clients, they should consider terminating therapy with each family member or spouse.

- The therapist is responsible for adequately screening each group participant prior to admission.

- The therapist is responsible for the safety of each participant and must take reasonable precautions to prevent physical or psychological trauma.

- The reward of saving attorney's fees by failing to have a lawyer review the consent document is not worth the risk of utilizing a faulty, obsolete, and legally unenforceable form.

Summary

Individual therapy is risky enough but multiple-client therapy compounds the risk to the therapist. One could say that the risks and responsibilities increase proportionately with each additional person who participates in the conjoint therapy. The desire of managed care companies to decrease costs has led to an increase in group therapy. The stresses on the family are legion and the need for marital and family therapy is also increasing. Multiple client therapy, therefore, is here to stay. Careful screening and selective composition of the group are critical to a healthy and successful group therapy practice. By understanding the ethical requirements and risks unique to multiple-client therapy, mental health professionals can safely treat these clients and enjoy more profitability in their practices. More forms will have to be drafted and reviewed by lawyers to protect confidentiality, but in the long run, such creative and defensive tactics are worth the effort.

Careful screening and selective composition of the group are critical to a healthy and successful group therapy practice.

Epilogue: Ethics in the Twenty-First Century

Karen is the unhappy consumer of mental health services. She wants to file an ethics complaint. She has not really been damaged, and several competent attorneys have already indicated to her that she does not have a viable case for a malpractice action. All lawyers accept malpractice cases on a contingent fee basis, (i.e., for a percentage of the recovery should recovery occur). Therefore, after considering her complaint without charge, these attorneys refused her case and offered her no enthusiasm or encouragement for continuing with her suit. Her therapist may have committed an ethical wrong, but it was not a financially worthwhile lawsuit or an item for litigation. "File an ethics complaint" they said. "You will be vindicated."

To file an ethical complaint, Karen first had to locate the provider's state licensing boards and the national organizations. That meant she had to determine just which license had been issued to her provider. Was it a PC, LPC, SW, LMSW, LMSW-ACPLMFT, ACSW, AAMFT, LCDC, and so forth, or was the therapist a licensed psychologist? The therapist's business card and the letterhead on the bill contained more initials than Karen had ever thought about, and this even included some affiliations and registrations, such as RPT (Registered play therapist). Finally, Karen discovered four sympathetic disciplinary groups: (1) the complaints committee of one of the state licensing boards, (2) the complaints committee of another of the state licensing boards (this particular provider had two licenses: an LPC—Licensed Professional Counselor and an LMFT—Licensed Marriage and Family Therapist), and also (3) the disciplinary committee of AAMFT and (4) APA. The first two had in-state offices, and the second two maintained national offices out of state.

After researching these organizations on her computer and making several calls to their offices, she determined that each had a separate complaint procedure and a separate complaint form that needed to be completed, signed, and forwarded to the appropriate committee. That was just the beginning. After Karen filed her complaint, the therapist would have an opportunity to respond to each entity for each complaint, and Karen could be required to furnish additional details, perhaps answer questions and, in some cases, appear before these organizations and testify as if she were a prime witness in a litigated, hotly contested, lawsuit.

Karen already feels wounded by the provider. Nevertheless to complete the complaint process, and bring an alleged ethical wrong to conclusion, she must investigate the method used to discipline unethical providers, spend hours processing a claim or claims, and deal with multiple entities, each with its own turf to protect. Is there a better way?

~

Donald is a 35-year-old PhD, a psychologist and licensed marriage and family therapist in his state. He has chosen to apply for and receive two licenses as it is good for business. He also belongs to two national organizations and has clarified with his malpractice insurance carrier that should a complaint arise, he would be covered for any injury to a client regardless of whether it is classified as the practice of marriage and family therapy or psychology. Now, after 7 years in practice, he faces a choice: either rent another office for storage or get rid of old files. He decides to begin culling or shredding his files but worries about his ethical responsibilities.

Each licensing board and perhaps both national organizations have different "retention of files" mandates. Some are definite in terms of years: 5-7-10, while others are more difficult to determine with any degree of certainty. If a client is a minor, the rules change even more. The problem: licenses conflict and national organizations are inconsistent. Both ignore the commonsense solution of keeping files forever in case some client in play therapy "remembers" something 30 years later and wants to make Donald's life "interesting." Remember that discovery statutes may extend malpractice statutes of limitations.

Another preservation of records problem exists with rapidly changing technology. What happens if records are preserved on a disk and the disk self-destructs? Or if the problem occurs at a time when the new technology has made the current retrieval system obsolete. After all, Donald is only 35 and he might not retire for 30 years. By then the whole system of record keeping and preservation could be entirely different. Certainly the technology used today won't be around in 30 years. It will be in the Smithsonian.

The proposal is to create a national Ethical Canons or Codes, unanimously adapted, suitable for all the nonmedical mental health professions.

A National Ethics Code

The proposal is to create a national *Ethical Canons or Codes,* unanimously adapted, suitable for all the nonmedical mental health professions. Certain footnotes or clarifications might have to be added to serve particular constituencies (e.g., addictions counselors or play therapists), but the general ethics code would be universal.

Establishing a common ethics code would bring immediate clarity to the mental health professions and to consumers of mental health services. A careful review of ethics codes for the various mental health disciplines reveals that their concerns are essentially the same. All the ethical problems outlined in Chapter 23 and listed in the index of this book have been considered and processed by all the mental health professions. The spirit of these codes are the same, only the wording differs. No matter how it is said, mental health professionals must protect their clients' confidentiality; and dual relationships, boundary violations, and sex with clients are unethical for all clinicians. Discrimination is discrimination no matter how it is described, and the professional vulnerabilities remain essentially the same. So why are dozens of similar yet distinct national and state ethics codes necessary? The very thought creates a nightmare when one imagines conscientious students and professionals seeking ethical guidance as they pursue their professional goals and advanced degrees.

Establishing a common ethics code would bring immediate clarity to the mental health professions and to consumers of mental health services.

Creating a National Ethics Code

We propose that the various mental health professional associations and licensing boards elect representatives to a national ethics congress that would convene to develop a mutually acceptable standard of ethics. Once the standard is drafted and approved by the congress, each association and licensing board would need to vote to approve the new code. The result would be a unified declaration of all the mental health professions that would be adopted and adhered to by all mental health professionals, whatever their particular affiliation.

The ethical canons and codes, once consolidated into a single understandable and enforceable form, would be subject to amendment or additions as experience dictates. When unethical acts develop, perhaps due to advancing technology, cyberspace therapy, new theoretical approaches, or the creativity of providers, certain acts that are not currently specified ethical prohibitions should be added to the disallowed or proscribed list. The congress could meet periodically to determine whether modifications or amendments are needed to the national code, which would be subject to the same approval process as the original code.

The ethical canons and codes, once consolidated into a single understandable and enforceable form, would be subject to amendment or additions as experience dictates.

Faye is a play therapist. Sometimes her children need reinforcement in the form of an occasional hug, a pat, even a squeeze. She has been patting, squeezing, and hugging for years. No parent or child has ever complained. Yet the question arises: should a counselor hug a child? Would she be vulnerable?

Her licensing regulations prohibit hugging, although this was probably drafted with adults in mind. But children are not excluded.

The statute does not say: "Do not hug adults, but children, well, that is different. It is okay."

Note. The authors have offered their conservative, "Don't ever allow yourself to be vulnerable . . . don't ever touch a client beyond a handshake" philosophy to countless groups in seminars. During one question-and-answer period, an experienced, caring, and dedicated, near-retirement school counselor raised her hand. "Mr. Hartsell and Mr. Bernstein," she said, "You lawyers just don't get it. My children need affection, caring, nurturing and, yes, touching. They don't get enough at home and they will get it here in school, and by me as long as I am part of a nurturing school system." "And," she added, "If you think we are going to do away with such an effective supportive method, you're nuts." We backed down, but we are concerned, because we know the rule: "No touching."

And so the best of all possible worlds might be a universally accepted national mental health ethics code, taught in every college and university. It would be clearly understood and establish precedents that could be footnoted, clarified, or particularized to accommodate the specific variations of specific disciplines, specialties or subspecialties.

Reporting Ethics Violations

Names could be included in reporting ethics violations, as is now the case in state and national organizations, or they could be omitted. But wouldn't it be helpful if unethical activities were reported and published on a national level? Statistical compilations from such data would be helpful to insurance companies for risk analysis and managed care entities for credentialing purposes. They would also be useful to ethics professors who would know exactly what to emphasize in their classes. If students learned that certain activities were prohibited, perhaps they would refrain from acting on impulse when later faced with a potentially threatening practice situation or issue. Often the ethical infraction is not an intentional unethical act, but rather a thoughtless or naive act of commission or omission. The therapist may have been unaware of its importance at the time, but after a complaint is filed and client records are scrutinized, the therapist realizes the act was a major ethical violation.

Reported ethics infractions should be recorded and clarified, and then precedents established that denote the ethics violation, an explanation, the penalty, and the rationale. Over the years, these annotated precedents would explain and interpret the written codes and give uniform guidance to professors, students, practitioners, supervisors, and the consuming public.

Reported ethics infractions should be recorded and clarified, and then precedents established that denote the ethics violation, an explanation, the penalty, and the rationale.

Many consumers of mental health services, along with the majority of the general public, are not sophisticated in the area of mental health ethics. Published universal codes with annotations to clarify what might be obscure would be helpful. An informed public able to gather easily available information would assist in policing the profession.

Enforcement

One hesitates to suggest another national governmental bureaucracy to enforce mental health ethics. The possibility of a national mental health

---

Ethical Flash Points

- The ethical canons of all the nonmedical mental health professions are remarkably similar.
- The problem is that they are not identical, and so individuals affiliated with different disciplines or who maintain multiple licenses could, and probably do, easily get confused. The consumers of mental health services would, if they were to examine the various codes, get even more confused.
- Enforcement of the ethical canons is divided between national and state organizations and the disciplinary committees of licensing boards. Each has its own rules, processes, and procedures, and the application of these rules changes as personnel changes occur. Thus enforcement, though more than whimsical, is not uniform.
- The consumer of mental health services usually acts instinctively.
- Lawyers, proficient in ethics as it concerns lawyers, and malpractice as it concerns professions, have little training in mental health ethics. Many have no contact at all with the enforcing bodies of the various enforcement agencies.
- Representing clients (therapists of any discipline) before a disciplinary board is not familiar to most lawyers.
- Consumers and providers would both benefit from a national system.

policing agency established by the national organizations might be difficult to organize, laborious to augment, and impossible to implement due to turf problems, lack of volunteers and professional staff, and the geographic complexity of our country.

A possible solution or approach would be for the state licensing boards to enforce nationally adopted ethical canons. States that do not now provide for complaints to be processed by licensing boards, could use the complaint committees of state chapters of the national organizations. All the legal safeguards, such as procedural due process, would have to be put into place to protect the provider as well as the consuming public.

This solution might not be flawless, but once established, it could be refined by experience and made as perfect as it could be in our society. It would eliminate the multiple complaint systems a consumer now faces when a therapist has acted unethically.

A possible solution or approach would be for the state licensing boards to enforce nationally adopted ethical canons. States that do not now provide for complaints to be processed by licensing boards could use the complaint committees of state chapters of the national organizations.

Summary

The ethical canons or codes of the non-medical mental health professions are remarkably similar. The differences are usually semantic, and these semantic differences could be clarified in footnotes, or perhaps in an attachment to a uniform ethical code with a bill of rights to protect such individual differences as exist between the professions, disciplines or sub specialties within a discipline.

If this were accomplished in the twenty-first century, the practitioner or the consumer with a computer, or with a friend with a computer, could easily obtain the canons of ethics of the mental health profession, the annotations or the situations which have been decided under the cannons, the interpretation of the cannons, and the statistical data concerning disciplinary actions. In addition, the necessary procedures for filing a complaint could be readily accessible.

The twenty-first century should streamline the complaint procedure, make useful information quickly available and speed up the complaint process from initial alleged ethical infraction to ultimate conclusion. National rules and enforcement procedures would be helpful to both the practitioner and the consuming public.

WELCOME TO THE TWENTY-FIRST CENTURY

References and
Reading Materials

I. Current Information

FMS (FALSE MEMORY) FOUNDATION
   3401 Market Street, Suite 130, Philadelphia, PA 19104-3318; 215-387-1865

MENTAL HEALTH LAW REPORTER
   Bonnie Becker, editor, 951 Pershing Drive, Silver Spring, MD 20910-4464; 301-587-6300

PRACTICE STRATEGIES
   A Business Guide for Behavioral Health Care Providers, 442½ East Main Street, Suite 2, Clayton, NC 27520; 919-553-0637

PSYCHOTHERAPY FINANCE
   Managing Your Practice and Your Money, P.O. Box 8979, Jupiter, FL 33468; 800-869-8450

II. Reference Books

Bernstein, B., and Hartsell, T. *The Portable Lawyer for Mental Health Professionals* (John Wiley & Sons, Inc., 1998).

Corey, G., Corey, M.S., and Callanan, P. *Issues and Ethics in the Helping Professions,* 5th ed. (Brooks/Cole, 1998).

Davis, Kenneth C. *Administrative Law* (West Publishing Co., 1977).

Lawless, Linda L. *Therapy, Inc.—A Hands-On Guide to Developing, Positioning, and Marketing Your Mental Health Practice in the 1990s* (John Wiley & Sons, Inc., 1997).

Psychotherapy Finance. *Managed Care Handbook—The Practitioner's Guide to Behavioral Managed Care* (Ridgewood Financial Institute, Inc., 1995).

Roach, William H., Jr., and The Aspen Health Law Center. *Medical Records and the Law* (Aspen Publishing, Inc., 1994).

Simon, Robert I. *Clinical Psychiatry and the Law* (American Psychiatric Press, Inc., 1987).

Stout, Chris E., Editor-in-Chief. *The Complete Guide to Managed Behavioral Healthcare* (John Wiley & Sons, Inc., 1996).

Tuttle, G., and Woods, D. *The Managed Care Answer Book* (Brunner/Mazel, 1997).

Wiger, Donald E. *The Clinical Documentation Sourcebook—A Comprehensive Collection of Mental Health Practice Forms, Handouts, and Records* (John Wiley & Sons, 1997).

III. Organizations with Periodic Publications on Law and Mental Health

American Association of Marriage and Family Therapists.

American Association of Pastoral Counselors.

American Bar Association (especially mental health or hospital law sections).

American Counseling Association.

American Medical Association.

American Mental Health Counselors Association.

American Psychiatric Association.

American Psychological Association.

National Association of Social Workers.

Note: All state licensing boards publish lists of licensed practitioners who have been disciplined by the boards. Usually, the names of the individuals who have been disciplined are given, together with the rule allegedly violated.

IV. Library List for Background

Banton, Ragnhild, *The Politics of Mental Health* (1985).

Beis, Edward B., *Mental Health and the Law* (1984).

Corey, G., Corey M., and Callanan, P., *Issues and Ethics in the Helping Professions* (5th edition) (1998).

Dutton, Mary Ann, *Empowering and Healing the Battered Woman* (1992).

Hunter, Edna J., Editor, *Professional Ethics and Law in the Health Sciences* (1990).

Kermani, Ebrahim J., *Handbook of Psychiatry and Law* (1989).

Lidz, Charles W., *Informed Consent, A Study of Decision Making in Psychiatry* (1984).

Nadelson, Carol C., Editor, *Marriage and Divorce* (1984).

National Institute of Mental Health, *Handbook of Mental Health Consultation* (1986).

Pederson, Paul, *Handbook of Cross-Cultural Counseling and Therapy* (1985).

Rosner, Richard, MD, Editor, *Ethical Practice in Psychiatry and the Law* (1990).

Shuman, Daniel W., *Law and Mental Health Professionals* (1990).

Stout, Chris E., Editor, *The Complete Guide to Managed Behavioral Healthcare* (1996).

U.S. Department of Health and Human Services, *Legal Opinions on the Confidentiality of Alcohol and Drug Abuse Patient Records, 1975–1978* (1980).

V. Web Sites

American Association of Marriage and Family Therapists—www.aamft.org

American Counseling Association—www.counseling.org

American Psychological Association—www.apa.org

National Association of Social Workers—www.naswdc.org

Shrinks Online—www.shrinksonline.com

Appendix I

Addresses for Mental Health Professional Organizations

The professional associations update their ethical policies and standards regularly. You may obtain the most current version of your organization's ethics code by contacting the national headquarters or by visiting the organization's Web site. We have included contact information for several associations here for your convenience.

American Association for Marriage and Family Therapy
1133 15th St., NW, Suite 300
Washington, DC 20005-2710
(202) 452-0109
(202) 223-2329 (fax)
www.aamft.org

American Counseling Association
5999 Stevenson Ave.
Alexandria, VA 22304
(703) 823-9800
(703) 823-0252 (fax)
www.counseling.org

American Psychological Association
750 First Street, NE
Washington, DC 20002-4242
(202) 336-5500
www.apa.org

American School Counselor Association
801 North Fairfax Street, Suite 310
Alexandria, VA 22314
(703) 683-2722
(800) 306-4722
(703) 683-1619 (fax)
www.schoolcounselor.org

National Association of Social Workers
750 First Street, NE, Suite 700
Washington, DC 20002-4241
(202) 408-8600
(800) 638-8799
www.naswdc.org

Appendix II

Healthcare Professional and Supplemental Liability Insurance Policy—TIG Insurance

Table of Contents of Occurrence Form

NOTICE:

THIS IS OCCURRENCE COVERAGE. IT COVERS INCIDENTS THAT OCCUR DURING THE COVERAGE TERM. IT IS NOT CLAIMS-MADE COVERAGE.

PLEASE REVIEW THE POLICY CAREFULLY AND DISCUSS THE COVERAGE WITH YOUR AGENT OR BROKER.

Words that are in boldface (other than captions) have a special meaning and are defined in the policy.

The Insurance Company indicated in the Declarations (hereinafter, "Company") hereby agrees with the **Insured** named in the Declarations made a part hereof, in consideration for payment of the premium and the statements contained in the Declarations and application and subject to the limits of liability, exclusions, conditions, and other terms of this insurance as follows:

I. INSURING AGREEMENT

A. Coverage A—Professional Liability

1. Individual Coverage

The Company will pay on behalf of the **Insured** those sums the **Insured** becomes legally obligated to pay as **Damages** because of an **Incident** that occurs during the **Coverage Term** and results from the practice of the profession described in the Declarations by the **Insured,** or by a person for whose acts or omissions the **Insured** is legally liable. This includes service by the **Insured** as a member of a formal accreditation or similar professional board or committee of a hospital or professional society.

2. Association, Partnership or Corporation Coverage

The Company will pay on behalf of the **Insured** those sums the **Insured** becomes legally obligated to pay as **Damages** because of an **Incident** that occurs during the **Coverage Term** and results from the practice of the profession described in the Declarations by a person for whose acts or omissions the association, partnership, or corporation named in the Declaration is responsible, provided that a Limit of Liability for this coverage is stated in the Declarations.

B. Coverage B—Supplemental Liability

1. Bodily Injury and Property Damage Coverage

The Company will pay on behalf of the **Insured** those sums the **Insured** becomes legally obligated to pay as **Damages,** other than those for which coverage is provided under COVERAGE A, for **Bodily Injury** or **Property Damage** that occurs during the **Coverage Term,** caused by an **Occurrence** and that arises out of the profession described in the Declarations.

2. Personal Injury Coverage

The Company will pay on behalf of the **Insured** those sums the **Insured** becomes legally obligated to pay as **Damages,** other than those for which coverage is provided under COVERAGE A, for **Personal Injury** that occurs during the **Coverage Term** and that arises out of the profession described in the Declarations.

II. DEFENSE, SETTLEMENT, AND SUPPLEMENTARY PAYMENTS

In addition to the applicable Limit of Liability, the Company will:

A. Defend any **Claim** or **Suit** that seeks covered **Damages** against the **Insured** even if such **Claim** or **Suit** is groundless, false, or fraudulent.

B. The Company has the right to make such investigation, negotiation, or with the consent of the **Insured,** settlement of any **Claim** or **Suit** as may be deemed expedient by the Company. The Company will not commit the **Insured** to any settlement without his or her written consent. If however, the **Insured** refuses to consent to any settlement recommended by the Company and elects to contest the **Claim** or continue any legal proceedings in connection with such **Claim,** then the Company's liability for the **Claim** will not exceed the amount for which the **Claim** could have been settled. The Company's duty to defend the **Insured** will end on the date of such refusal.

The Company's duty to defend any **Claim** or **Suit** will end at the time the applicable Limits of Liability are exhausted by payment of settlements or judgments.

C. Pay:

1. All premium on bonds to release attachments for an amount not in excess of the applicable Limit of Liability.

2. All premium on appeal bonds required in any such defended **Claim** or **Suit,** but not for any uncovered portion of a **Claim** or **Suit** or for any portion in excess of the Limits of Liability. The Company will not have any obligation to apply for or furnish such bonds.

3. All costs taxed against the **Insured** in any such **Claim** or **Suit.**

4. All expenses incurred by the Company.

5. All interest accruing after entry of judgment until the Company has paid, tendered, or deposited in court the covered part of such judgment as does not exceed the applicable limit of the Company's liability thereon.

6. First-aid expenses incurred by the **Insured,** in the event that immediate medical and/or surgical relief to others is imperative at the time of injury.

D. Reimburse the **Insured,** subject to a limitation of up to $500 per day and $7,500 per **Claim** or **Suit** for actual loss of earnings incurred at the Company's request.

E. Pay for reasonable **Fees, Costs, and Expenses** of defending a state **Regulatory Authority** investigation of or proceeding against the **Insured** for an **Incident** otherwise covered under this policy. This is subject to a limitation of $5,000 per **Insured,** but no **Insured** will be reimbursed more than $5,000 per **Incident.** The Company will have no duty to defend this action.

F. Pay for reasonable **Fees, Costs, and Expenses** of representing an **Insured** for appearance at a deposition, to which the **Insured** is required to submit and that involves their professional occupation listed in the Declarations. This is subject to a limitation of $2,500 per **Insured,** but no **Insured** will be reimbursed more than $2,500 per **Incident** unless the deposition results from an **Incident** otherwise covered under this Policy.

III. PERSONS INSURED

Each of the following is an **Insured** under this Policy to the extent set forth below:

A. Under COVERAGE A.1. PROFESSIONAL LIABILITY, INDIVIDUAL COVERAGE, each individual named in the Declarations is an **Insured.**

B. Under COVERAGE A.2. ASSOCIATION, PARTNERSHIP, OR CORPORATION COVERAGE, the association, partnership, or corporation named in the Declarations is an **Insured.** In addition, any employee, member, partner, officer, director, or shareholder thereof is an **Insured** but only while acting within the course and scope of his or her duties as such.

C. Under COVERAGE B. SUPPLEMENTAL LIABILITY, each person or entity who qualifies as an **Insured** under COVERAGE A. PROFESSIONAL LIABILITY is an **Insured.**

D. Under COVERAGES A and B, the heirs, executors, legal representative or assigns of a **Insured** who is dead, incompetent or bankrupt is an **Insured,** but only in his or her representative capacity for the **Insured.**

E. Under COVERAGES A and B, no person or entity is an **Insured** for injury to an employee of any **Insured** arising out of or in the course of employment by an **Insured.**

IV. LIMITS OF LIABILITY

No insurance is afforded unless a monetary limit is shown in the "Limits of Liability" portion of the Declaration for that specific type of coverage.

A. Coverage A—Professional Liability Coverage

1. Individual Coverage

   Regardless of the number of **Claims** made or **Suits** brought, or persons or organizations making **Claims** or **Suits:**

   a. The total liability of the Company for all **Damages** arising out of any one **Incident** will not exceed the Limit of Liability stated in the Declarations as applicable to "Each Incident." The Limits of Liability described in this section will apply separately to each **Insured.**

   b. The total liability of the Company for all **Damages** because of all **Incidents** during the **Coverage Term** to which this insurance applies, regardless of the number of **Insureds,** will not exceed the Limit of Liability stated in the Declarations as "Aggregate."

2. Association, Partnership or Corporation Coverage

   Regardless of the number of **Insureds** under this coverage, **Claims** made or **Suits** brought, or persons or organizations making **Claims** or **Suits;**

   a. The total liability of the Company for all **Damages** caused by any one **Incident** will not exceed the Limit of Liability stated in the Declarations as applicable to "Each Incident."

   b. The total liability of the Company for all **Damages** because of all **Incidents** during the **Coverage Term** to which this insurance applies will not exceed the Limit of Liability stated in the Declarations as "Aggregate."

B. Coverage B—Supplemental Liability

The total liability of the Company for all **Damages** because of all **Bodily Injury, Property Damage,** or **Personal Injury** during the **Coverage Term** to which this insurance applies will not exceed the Limit of Liability stated in the Declarations for COVERAGE B.

C. Coverage A and Coverage B

If both COVERAGES A and B apply to the same **Claim,** the Company's liability is limited as follows:

1. In no event will the Limits of Liability of COVERAGES A and B be added together, combined, or stacked to determine the applicable Limit of Liability.

2. The total Limits of Liability under both COVERAGES A and B will not exceed the highest applicable limit of COVERAGE A or of COVERAGE B.

3. The Company, in it's sole discretion, will conclusively determine which coverage applies and in what proportion.

Only the "Limit of Liability" for the **Coverage Term** in which the first negligent act, error, or omission involved in the **Incident** occurs will apply, regardless of the number of **Coverage Terms** in which **Damages** occur or are manifested or over which a **Claim** arises.

V. EXCLUSIONS

This insurance does not apply to any **Claim, Incident,** or **Suit** arising out of:

A. Any occupation, business, profession, or personal activity other than the profession specified in the Declarations.

B. Any intentionally wrongful or dishonest, fraudulent, criminal, oppressive, or malicious act. However, this exclusion does not apply to the Company's duty to provide a defense for the **Insured** against a **Claim** or **Suit** otherwise covered under COVERAGE B.2. PERSONAL INJURY.

C. **Bodily injury** that arises solely out of humiliation or other emotional distress and that does not arise out of a physical intrusion or other physical event that first causes a physical injury or physical sickness to the person suffering the emotional distress or illness.

D. The **Insured's** rendering of or failure to render professional services while his or her license is suspended, restricted, revoked or terminated, or arising out of an **Incident** occurring while the **Insured** is on probation.

E. Any services rendered while the **Insured** is under the influence of any alcoholic beverages or any drugs, chemicals, or other substance, the possession or use of which is prohibited by law.

F. Ownership or operation of any healthcare facility or any other business undertaking other than the professional occupation designated in the Declarations.

G. Physical abuse, threatened abuse, sexual abuse or licentious, immoral or sexual behavior whether or not intended to lead to, or culminating in any sexual act, whether caused by, or at the instigation of, or at the direction of, or omission by any **Insured.** However, the Company will defend any civil **Suit** against an **Insured** seeking amounts that would be covered if this exclusion did not apply. In such case, the company will only pay **Fees, Costs and Expenses** of such defense up to per $25,000 per **Incident.**

H. Discrimination or harassment of any kind by an **Insured** including discrimination and harassment on the basis of race, creed, age, religion, sex, nationality, marital status, disability or sexual preference.

I. **Property Damage** to property lent, leased, or rented from or owned, sold, rented, leased or occupied or abandoned by, used by, or in the care, custody, or control of any **Insured** or as to which any **Insured** is for any purpose exercising physical control at any time the **Property Damage** is caused, occurs or manifests.

J. Ownership, maintenance, use, or entrustment to others of any aircraft, **Motor Vehicle,** or watercraft owned or operated by or leased, rented or loaned to or from any **Insured,** including loading or unloading thereof.

K. Ownership, maintenance, or use of any equipment or device either sold, lent, leased or rented to others by or on behalf of the **Insured.** This exclusion does not apply to injury or damage other than **Property Damage** while any equipment or device is being used by the **Insured** during treatment in the course and scope of the **Insured's** professional occupation designated in the Declarations.

L. The interviewing, hiring, compensation, evaluation, advancement, training, termination, recommendation or other treatment of a potential, current or former employee of any **Insured** or other employment-related practice or act.

M. Liability to any employee of any **Insured** arising out of or during the course of employment, or to any obligation that any **Insured** may be held liable for under any employer's liability, workers compensation, disability benefits, or unemployment compensation law, or any similar law.

N. Any contact or agreement unless such liability would have attached in the absence of such agreement. This exclusion does not apply to liability that is assumed by the **Insured** in a written contract executed prior to the **Incident, Bodily Injury, Property Damage** or **Personal Injury** with a Managed Care Organization (MCO) for the tort liability of such organization or association to pay for **Damages** to a third party that results from the negligence of the **Insured.**

O. For injuries, **Damages,** cost, or other obligation arising out of:

1. The actual, alleged or threatened seepage, discharge, dispersal, release, migration, escape or disposal of **Pollutants** at any time;

2. Any order, demand or request that the **Insured** test for, monitor, clean up, remove, contain, treat, detoxify or neutralize, or in any way respond to, or assess the effects of **Pollutants,** or any voluntary decision to do so; or

3. Any **Claim** or **Suit** by or on behalf of a governmental authority for **Damages** or costs because of testing for, monitoring, cleaning up, removing, containing, treating, detoxifying, or neutralizing, or in any way responding to, or assessing the effects of **Pollutants;**

   This exclusion does not apply to **Bodily Injury** to a patient that arises directly, suddenly, immediately, and accidentally out of the rendering of or failure to render professional services otherwise covered under COVERAGE A.

P. Radioactive, toxic, explosive, hazardous, or other properties (known and unknown) of any nuclear material, including source, processed, or by-product material, fuel, or waste, without limitation, if it was or was at any time possessed, handled, used, stored, transported, or disposed of by or on behalf of any **Insured.**

This exclusion does not apply to **Bodily Injury** to a patient which arises directly, suddenly, immediately, and accidentally out of the rendering of or failure to render professional services otherwise covered under COVERAGE A.

Q. War, whether or not declared, civil war, riot, insurrection, rebellion, or revolution or to any act or condition incident to any of the foregoing.

VI. CONDITIONS

A. Cancellation

1. The **Insured** may cancel this Policy by mailing or delivering advance written notice of cancellation to the Company.

2. The Company may cancel this Policy by mailing or delivering to the **Insured** written notice of cancellation at least:

   a. 10 days before the effective date of cancellation if the Company cancels for nonpayment of premium.

   b. 60 days before the effective date of cancellation if the Company cancels for any other reason.

3. The Company will mail or deliver the cancellation notice to the **Insured's** last mailing address known to the Company.

4. Notice of cancellation will state the effective date of cancellation. The **Coverage Term** will end on that date.

5. If this Policy is canceled, the Company will send the **Insured** any premium refund due. If the Company cancels, the refund will be pro rata. If the **Insured** cancels, the refund may be less than pro rata. The cancellation will be effective even if the Company has not made or offered a refund.

6. If notice is mailed, proof of mailing will be sufficient proof of notice.

B. Insured's Duties

1. The **Insured** must notify the Company as soon as is practicable of every event which may result in a **Claim.** The notice will identify the **Insured** and will include the circumstances, the place and time of events, and the names and addresses of any witnesses and injured persons.

2. If a **Claim** is made or **Suit** is brought against the **Insured,** the **Insured** will give the Company written notice of the **Claim** or **Suit** as soon as is practicable.

3. The **Insured** will:

   a. Immediately send the Company copies of any complaints, demands, notices, summonses, or legal papers received in connection with the **Claim** or **Suit;**

   b. Authorize the Company to obtain records and other information;

   c. Cooperate with the Company, and upon request, assist in the preparation of the defense, attend hearings, other proceedings, depositions, arbitrations, and trials, and assist in effecting settlements, securing and giving evidence and obtaining the attendance of witnesses in the conduct and investigation of a **Claim** or **Suit;**

   d. Assist the Company, at the Company's request, in the enforcement of any right of recovery against any person or organization that may be liable to the **Insured** because of an event giving rise to a **Claim** or **Suit;**

   e. Not, except at the **Insured's** own cost, voluntarily make a payment, assume any obligation, admit any liability, or incur any expense, other than for first aid, without the Company's consent.

C. Changes in Insured's Practice or Privileges

If the licensing agency or if any other governmental agency in the state in which the **Insured** practices, restricts, suspends, revokes, or otherwise terminates the **Insured's** license to practice, the **Insured** must inform the Company immediately in writing.

If the **Insured's** privileges to practice at a hospital, surgi-center or other healthcare facility are revoked, suspended or otherwise restricted, the **Insured** must inform the Company immediately in writing.

If the **Insured** enters a diversionary or rehabilitation program for alcohol, drug, or other substance abuse, the **Insured** must inform the Company immediately in writing. If the **Insured** leaves such a diversionary or rehabilitation program, the **Insured** must inform the Company immediately in writing.

D. Bankruptcy or Insolvency

Bankruptcy, insolvency or other financial impairment of the **Insured** or of the **Insured's** estate will neither relieve nor increase the obligations of the Company under this Policy.

E. Other Insurance

If all or part of any covered **Claim** or **Suit** is covered by other insurance, whether on a primary, excess, umbrella, contingent, or any other basis, then this Policy;

1. Will be excess with respect to COVERAGE A.

2. Will not apply and no coverage will be afforded under this Policy with respect to COVERAGE B. However, when the limits of this Policy are greater than the limits of all other insurance, then this Policy will provide excess insurance up to an amount sufficient to give the **Insured,** as respects the amount afforded under COVERAGE B, a total limit of insurance equal to the limit of insurance provided by this Policy.

This will apply even as to fully or partially self-insured programs, and policies in which the **Insured** has a deductible or has retained a self-insured portion of the risk. In no event will this Policy be construed to contribute more than on an excess basis. This will not apply to coverage under an excess Policy that is specifically written to be excess of this Policy and that specifically refers to this Policy as an underlying Policy.

F. Subrogation

In the event of any payment under this Policy, the Company will have all of the **Insured's** rights of recovery. The **Insured** will execute all papers required and will do everything that may be necessary to assist the Company in enforcing such rights.

G. Changes

Notice to any agent, broker or representative, or knowledge possessed by any agent, broker, representative or any other person, will not effect a waiver or a change in any part of this Policy or stop the Company from asserting any right under the terms of this Policy. The terms of this Policy will not be waived or changed, except by written endorsement issued to form a part hereof, signed by an officer of the Company or its authorized representative.

H. Assignment

Assignment of any interest under this Policy will not bind the Company unless and until the Company consents in writing.

I. Action Against the Company

No action will lie against the Company unless, as a condition precedent thereto, the **Insured** will have fully complied with all of the terms of this Policy, nor until the amount of the **Insured's** obligation to pay will have been finally determined either by judgment against the **Insured** or by written agreement of the **Insured,** the Claimant, and the Company. Any person or his legal representative who has secured such judgment or written agreement will thereafter be entitled to recover under and subject to the terms of this Policy. Nothing contained in this Policy will give any person or organization any right to join the Company as a codefendant or party in any action against the **Insured** to determine the **Insured's** liability.

J. Territory

This Policy applies anywhere in the world, provided that **Claim** is made or **Suit** is brought in the United States of America, its territories, or its possessions.

K. Integration of Entire Agreement

This agreement, including all attachments hereto, contains all the terms and conditions agreed upon by the parties regarding the subject matter of this agreement. Any prior agreements, promises, negotiations, or representations of or between the Company and the **Insured,** either oral or written, and whether express or implied, relating to the subject matter of this agreement that are not expressly set forth in this agreement, are null and void and of no further force and effect.

L. Conformity to Statute

The terms of this Policy that are in conflict with the statutes of the state wherein this Policy is issued are hereby amended to conform to any such statute.

M. Liberalization

If the Company receives approval to issue a revised version of this form that would broaden the coverage under this Policy during the **Coverage Term,** the broadened coverage will apply to this Policy on the date of such approval, without additional premium.

VII. DEFINITIONS

A. **"Bodily Injury"** means physical injury, sickness or disease sustained by any person, that occurs during the **Coverage Term,** including humiliation or other emotional distress or death resulting from these at any time.

B. **"Claims"** means a written demand for money or services, including the institution of **Suit** or a demand for arbitration, to which this insurance applies.

C. **"Coverage Term"** means the time period from the effective date to the expiration date indicated in the Declarations, or earlier termination of this insurance, if canceled mid-term.

D. **"Damages"** mean only actual damages for which the **Insured** is legally liable. **Damages** will not include:

1. Punitive/exemplary damages, formula damages based upon and in addition to

actual damages, or any other enhanced damages;

2. Fees, fines or penalties imposed by law;

3. Restitution, including the return, withdrawal or reduction of professional fees; or

4. Non-pecuniary, injunctive or equitable relief.

E. **"Fees, Costs and Expenses"** mean reasonable fees and expenses of legal counsel and expert consultants for investigation and travel, transcripts, filings fees and other reasonable costs and expenses incurred in the defense of a proceeding. This does not include:

1. Any salary, wages, overhead or benefit expenses or other payments to the **Insured** or to an employee of an **Insured;** or

2. Any amounts incurred in defense of any proceeding that any other insurer has a duty to defend, regardless of whether such other insurer undertakes such duty.

F. **"Incident"** means any negligent act, error, or omission in the rendering of or failure to render professional services that results in **Damages.** Any such negligent act, error, or omission together with all related acts, errors, or omissions in the rendering of professional services to any one person will be considered one **Incident.**

G. **"Insured"** means the individual or the association, partnership, or corporation named in the Declarations or qualifying as an **Insured** under the "Persons Insured" provision of this form.

H. **"Insured's Products"** means goods or products manufactured, sold, handled, repaired, or distributed by the **Insured** named in the Declarations or by another person under that **Insured's** direction, supervision, or control.

I. **"Motor Vehicle"** means an automobile, truck, motorcycle, moped, tractor, farm equipment, all-terrain vehicle, or other land **Motor Vehicle,** trailer, or semi-trailer that is in whole or in part propelled by an engine or motor that utilizes gasoline, diesel fuel, electricity, or other fuel.

J. **"Occurrence"** means an accident, including continuous or repeated exposure to substantially the same conditions.

K. **"Personal Injury"** means injury arising out of one or more of the following offenses committed in the conduct of the professional occupation designated in the Declarations:

1. False arrest, detention, imprisonment, or malicious prosecution;

2. Publication or utterance of a libel or slander, or a publication or utterance in violation of an individual's right of privacy, except publications or utterances in the course of or related to advertising, broadcasting, or telecasting activities conducted by or on behalf of the **Insured** named in the Declarations; or

3. The wrongful eviction from, wrongful entry into, or invasion of the right of private occupancy of a room, dwelling or premises that a person or entity occupies where the occupation was authorized by or on behalf of its owner, landlord or lesser.

L. **"Pollutants"** mean:

1. Any substance having or alleged to have hazardous characteristics as defined by or identified on a list of hazardous substances issued by the United States Environmental Protection Agency or any other federal, state, county, municipal or local government or agency;

2. Contaminants or irritants of any kind whether or not now known to be a contaminant or irritant that includes, without limitation, solid, liquid, gaseous, radioactive, radiant, electromagnetic or sonic matter or characteristic. By way of example, "contaminants and irritants" include, but are not limited to, lead, asbestos, silica, formaldehyde, benzene, carbon monoxide, and PCB's; or

3. Waste, that includes without limitation, material to be disposed of, recycled, reconditioned or reclaimed.

M. **"Property Damage"** means:

1. Physical injury to or destruction of tangible property, including the loss of use thereof; or

2. Loss of use of tangible property that has not been physically injured or destroyed, provided such loss of use is caused by an **Incident** or **Occurrence** during the **Coverage Term.**

N. **"Regulatory Authority"** means a licensing board, a peer review board, or any other proceeding to which the **Insured** is required to submit testimony, as pertains to their professional occupation listed in the Declarations.

O. **"Suit"** means a civil lawsuit or proceeding as well as arbitration proceedings to which the **Insured** is required to submit or to which the **Insured** has submitted with the Company's consent.

Appendix III

Social Service Agency Professional Liability Occurrence Policy Form—American Home Assurance Company (NASW Insurance Trust)

AMERICAN HOME ASSURANCE COMPANY
70 PINE STREET
NEW YORK, NEW YORK 10270
A CAPITAL STOCK COMPANY FOUNDED 1853

NOTICE: A $25,000 SUB-LIMIT OF LIABILITY AP-PLIES TO JUDGMENTS OR SETTLEMENTS WHEN THERE ARE ALLEGATIONS OF SEXUAL MISCON-DUCT. (SEE THE SPECIAL PROVISION "SEXUAL MISCONDUCT" IN THE POLICY). THIS LIMIT IS PART OF AND NOT IN ADDITION TO THE LIMITS OF LIABILITY SHOWN IN THE DECLARATIONS.

Various provisions in this Policy restrict coverage. Read the entire Policy carefully to determine rights, duties and what is and is not covered.

Throughout this Policy the words **you** and **your** refer to the Named Insured(s) shown in the Decla-rations and any other person(s) or organization(s) qualifying as an **insured** under this Policy. The words **we, us** and **our** refer to the Company provid-ing this insurance. The word **insured** means any person or organization qualifying as such under SECTION II. WHO IS AN INSURED. Other words and phrases that appear in boldface have special meaning. Refer to SECTION VI. DEFINITIONS.

SECTION I. COVERAGE

We shall pay **your loss** arising from a **claim** for any actual or alleged **wrongful act**. The **wrongful act** must take place during the **policy period** and solely in the conduct of **your** business as a social service agency.

SECTION II. WHO IS AN INSURED

A. Individual

If **you** are shown in the Declarations as an individual, **you** and **your** spouse are **in-sureds** only for the conduct of a business as a social service agency of which **you** are the sole owner.

B. Corporation

If **you** are shown in the Declarations as a corporation or organization other than partnership or joint venture, **you** are an **in-sured. Your** stockholders are also **insureds** but only with respect to their liability as stockholders.

C. Partnership or Joint Venture

If **you** are shown in the Declarations as a partnership or joint venture, **you** are an **in-sured. Your** partners or co-ventures and their spouses are also **insureds** but only for the conduct of **your** business as a social service agency.

D. Employee

Your employees, executive officers, direc-tors, trustees, volunteers and student in-terns are **insureds** within the scope of their employment by **you** or while performing duties related to the conduct of **your** business as a social service agency. **Your employee,** executive officer, director, trustee, volunteer or student intern will be an **insured** if he/she was **your employee,** executive officer, director, trustee, volunteer or student intern on the date of the actions complained of which constitute the basis for a **wrongful act,** even if he/she is no longer **your employee** at the time a **claim** for such **wrongful acts** is made.

E. Acquisitions

Any organization that **you** acquire or form during the **policy period** is an **insured** provided that:

1. if the organization is a corporation, **you** own 51% or more of the issued and outstanding shares entitled to vote in the election of directors; or

2. if the organization is not a corporation, **you** own directly or indirectly, a 51% or greater interest in either the profits or losses of the organization.

   However, no organization that **you** acquire or form during the **policy period** will be insured for more than ninety (90) days from the date that **you** acquire or form it or the remainder of the **policy period,** whichever is less. This Policy will not provide coverage for any such organization for any **wrongful act** that happened or commenced before **you** acquired or formed it, or for which other insurance is available. An organization ceases to be an **insured** under this Policy when the Named Insured ceases to own more than a 51% interest in such organization.

SECTION III. LIMITS OF LIABILITY

A. The Limits of Liability shown in the Declarations to this Policy and the information contained in this section fix the most **we** shall pay regardless of the number of:

1. Persons or organizations covered by this Policy; or

2. Claimants or **claims.**

B. The **wrongful act** Limit of Liability is the most **we** shall pay for all **claims** that result from a single **wrongful act.**

C. The Aggregate Limit is the most **we** shall pay for all **claims** covered under this Policy, including all **claims** covered under the Sexual Misconduct Provision.

D. All **claims** arising from continuous, repeated, or related **wrongful acts** shall be treated as one **claim.** Such **wrongful acts** shall be considered to have taken place when the earliest **wrongful act** took place.

E. The Limits of Liability of this Policy apply separately to each consecutive annual period and to any remaining period of less than 12 months, starting with the beginning of the **policy period** shown in the Declarations, unless the **policy period** is extended after issuance for an additional period of less than 12 months, at no additional premium charge. No extension of the **policy period** shall be deemed to reinstate the Limits of Liability.

SECTION IV. SEXUAL MISCONDUCT PROVISION

A. **Our** Limit of Liability shall not exceed $25,000 in the aggregate for all damages with respect to the total of all **claims** made against **you** involving any actual or alleged erotic physical contact, or attempt thereat or proposal thereof:

1. By **you** or any other person for whom **you** may be legally liable; and

2. With or to any former or current client of **yours,** or with or to any relative or member of the same household as any said client, or with or to any person with whom said client or relative has an affectionate personal relationship.

B. In the event that any of the foregoing are alleged at any time, either in a complaint, during discovery, at trial or otherwise, any and all causes of action alleged and arising out of the same or related courses of professional treatment and/or relationships shall be subject to the aforesaid $25,000 aggregate Limit of Liability and shall be part of, and not in addition to the Limits of Liability otherwise afforded by this Policy.

C. The $25,000 aggregate Limit of Liability for sexual misconduct afforded by this section shall be part of, and not in addition to, the Limit of Liability shown in the Declarations. **We** shall not be obligated to undertake nor to continue to defend any **claim** or proceeding subject to the $25,000 aggregate Limit of Liability after the $25,000 aggregate Limit of Liability has been exhausted by payment of judgments, settlements and/or other items included within the Limit of Liability.

SECTION V. DEFENSE COSTS, CHARGES AND EXPENSES

We shall pay the cost related to the following, which are in addition to the Limits of Liability:

A. **We** have the right and duty, at **our** expense to defend and to appoint counsel for any **claim** brought against **you** for a covered **wrongful act,** even if the **claim** is groundless or fraudulent. **Our** duty to defend any **claim** ends after the applicable Limit of Liability has been exhausted by payment of judgments, awards, or interest accruing thereon prior to entry of judgment or issuance of an award and settlements.

B. **We** have the right to investigate and settle any **claim** that **we** believe is proper.

1. **We** shall pay all reasonable costs **we** ask **you** to incur other than loss of earnings while defending a **claim.**

2. **We** shall pay premiums for appeal bonds, or bonds to release property used to secure legal obligation, if required in a **claim we** defend. **We** shall only pay, however, for bonds valued up to the applicable Limits of Liability. **We**

have no obligation to appeal or to obtain these bonds.

C. **We** shall pay all interest on that amount of any judgment up to the Limits of Liability:

1. Which accrues after entry of judgment; and

2. Before **we** pay, offer to pay, or deposit in court that part of the judgment within the applicable Limits of Liability.

D. **We** shall not be obligated to make any payment nor undertake or continue defense of any **claim** or proceeding after **our** applicable Limits of Liability has been exhausted by payment of judgments and awards.

SECTION VI. DEFINITIONS

A. **Automobile** means a land vehicle whether or not self-propelled, or a trailer or semitrailer, including any machinery or apparatus attached thereto, whether or not designed for use principally on public roads.

B. **Bodily Injury** means physical harm, sickness, or disease, including death resulting therefrom.

C. **Claim(s)** means:

1. a written demand for money;

2. a written demand to toll or waive a statute of limitations;

3. a civil proceeding or arbitration proceeding for monetary relief which is commenced by:

   a. service of a complaint; or

   b. notice of an arbitration, mediation or alternative dispute resolution proceeding.

D. **Defense Costs** mean:

1. Fees charged by an attorney designated by **us;**

2. Premiums for any appeal bond, attachment bond or similar bond, but the Company shall have no obligation to apply for or furnish such bond; and

3. All other fees, costs and expenses resulting solely from the investigation, adjustment, defense and appeal of a **claim,** if incurred by **us.** However, **defense costs** do not include salary charges of **our** regular employees or officials, **your** salary, or the salary of **your** regular **employees** or officials.

E. **Discrimination** means a violation of any law, whether statutory or common law, which prohibits disparate treatment based on race, color, religion, national origin, age, sex, marital status, sexual orientation, disability, veteran status or any other legally protected status.

F. **Employee** means an individual whose labor or service is engaged by and directed by the **insured** for remuneration. This includes parttime, seasonal, and temporary **employees** as well as any individual whether employed in a supervisory, co-worker, subordinate position or otherwise. Independent contractors are not **employees.**

G. **Household Member** means any person who regularly resides with **you.**

H. **Loss** means damages, judgments, settlements and **defense costs. Loss** does not include fines, penalties, sanctions, taxes, or punitive or exemplary damages, the multiplied portion of multiplied damages, or reimbursements of legal fees, costs, or expenses.

I. **Policy Period** means the period commencing on the effective date shown in the Declarations. This period ends on the earlier of the expiration date or the effective date of cancellation of this Policy. If **you** became an **insured** under this Policy after the effective date, the **policy period** begins on the date that **you** became an **insured** and ends on the earlier of the expiration date or the effective date of cancellation of this Policy.

J. **Pollutant** means any solid, liquid, gaseous, or thermal irritant or contaminant, including: smoke, vapor, soot,

fumes, acids, alkalis, chemicals and waste. Waste includes, but is not limited to, material to be recycled, reconditioned or reclaimed, as well as medical waste.

K. **Property Damage** means:
1. Physical injury to, or destruction of, tangible property including the loss of use of it; or
2. Loss of use of tangible property, which has not been physically injured or destroyed.

L. **Wrongful Act** means any actual or alleged negligent act, error, misstatement, misleading statement, or omission in performing or failing to perform professional services for others.

SECTION VII. EXCLUSIONS
This Policy shall not apply to:

A. Any liability of **yours** as a proprietor or owner of any medical clinic with bed and board facilities, hospital, sanitarium, nursing home or laboratory;

B. Any medical, surgical, dental, x-ray or radiological service or treatment or the furnishing or dispensing of drugs or medical, dental or surgical supplies or appliances. This exclusion shall not apply to:
1. Medical services or treatment performed by **you** at the direction of a physician, or the furnishing or use of biofeedback equipment as is customary in **your** practice as a social service agency; or
2. **Your** social service agency employed psychiatrists; if a premium charge is indicated for them in Item 6 of the Declarations;

C. Any disputes involving **your** cost estimates, fees, or charges;

D. Any **wrongful act** of a managerial or administrative nature that is not directly related to services rendered to a patient or client;

E. Any **wrongful act** arising out of **your** activities as a member of a formal accreditation or professional review board of a hospital or professional society, or professional licensing board;

F. Any liability arising out of the ownership, maintenance, operation, use, loading or unloading of any **automobile,** aircraft or watercraft;

G. Any **bodily injury** or **property damage** to any **employee** or independent contractor working for **you,** or to any obligation **you** may have to indemnify another because of damages arising out of any **bodily injury** or **property damage;**

H. Any actual or alleged violation of antitrust, price fixing or restraint of trade law or infringement of copyright, patent, trademark, service mark or trade name;

I. **Property damage** to:

1. Property owned or occupied by or rented to **you;**

2. Property used by **you;**

3. Property in **your** care, custody or control, or property over which **you** are exercising physical control for any purpose; or

4. Premises sold, given away or abandoned by **you,** if the **property damage** arises out of any part of those premises;

J. Any liability arising out of any business relationship or venture with any prior or current client of **yours;**

K. Any employment practice including, but not limited to, application for employment, refusal to employ, termination of employment, coercion, demotion, evaluation, reeassignment, discipline, harassment including sexual harassment, humiliation, or violation of civil rights;

L. Any **discrimination** on any basis whatsoever;

M. Any liability arising out of any **wrongful act** if **you** were found to be legally intoxicated or under the influence of any illegal substance or drug;

N. Any fines or penalties or punitive, exemplary or multiplied damages; if permitted by law **we** shall, however, pay up to $25,000 in the aggregate for all punitive, exemplary or multiplied damages with respect to all **claims** against **you.** This $25,000 sub-limit for punitive, exemplary or multiplied damages shall be part of and not in addition to the applicable Limits of Liability;

O. Any dishonest, fraudulent, criminal or malicious act, error, or omission or material misrepresentation of **your** professional capacity; but this exclusion shall not apply if **you** did not personally participate in or direct such act, error, or omission;

P. Any liability in which **you** expected or intended injury or damage, regardless of whether **you** intended the specific injury or damage sustained. This exclusion shall not apply to **bodily injury** resulting from the use of reasonable force to protect persons or property;

Q. Any **claim** brought by any person or organization covered under this Policy, or for injury or damage sustained by **your** spouse or any **household member.**

R. Any obligation which **you** may have under any workers' compensation, unemployment compensation, social security or disability benefits law, or under any similar law;

S. Any liability **you** assume under any contract or agreement. This exclusion shall not apply to liability:

1. **You** assume under a contract or agreement, which arises solely from **your** **wrongful act,** or

2. Which would arise against **you** in the absence of the contract or agreement;

T. Any **claim** arising from:

1. The actual, alleged, or threatened, discharge, dispersal, seepage, migration, release, or escape of **pollutants;** or

2. Any direction or request, to test for, monitor, cleanup, remove, contain,

treat, detoxify, or neutralize **pollutants** or in any way respond to or assess the effects of **pollutants;**

U. Any liability because of **wrongful acts** due to war, whether or not declared, or any act or condition incident to war. War includes civil war, insurrection, rebellion or revolution or terrorism;

V. Any **claim** arising from nuclear fission, nuclear fusion or radioactive contamination;

W. Any liability arising from that part of any **claim** seeking non-monetary relief including, but not limited to, injunctive relief, declaratory relief, disgorgement, or other equitable remedies;

X. Any breach of a fiduciary duty, responsibility or obligation;

Y. Any thefts, burglary, robbery, mysterious disappearance, inventory shortage or inventory shrinkage. Further, no coverage shall be provided for any direct or consequential damage resulting from or contributed to by any of the foregoing;

Z. Any goods or products, other than real property, manufactured, sold, handled or disposed of by:

1. **You;**
2. Others trading under **your** name; or
3. A person or organization whose business or assets **you** have acquired.

AA. Any **claim** arising from divorce mediation counseling unless:

1. Prior to providing divorce mediation services, the **insured,** if he or she is an attorney, shall provide a written statement to all parties, explaining his or her role as a neutral intermediary and stating that he or she may not act as an advocate for either party.
2. In cases where **you** assist in preparing a written statement agreement in connection with the provision of divorce mediation services, **you** shall advise each participant in writing to have the settlement agreement independently reviewed

by counsel of their own choosing before executing the agreement;

BB. Any **claim** brought by or on behalf of an **insured** against another **insured.**

SECTION VIII. CONDITIONS

A. COVERAGE TERRITORY

We cover **wrongful acts** anywhere in the world, but only if a **claim** is made and brought for such **wrongful act** in the United States of America, its territories and possessions, Puerto Rico, or Canada.

B. YOUR ASSISTANCE AND COOPERATION

1. **You** agree to cooperate with and help **us:**
   a. Make settlements;
   b. Enforce any legal rights **you** or **we** may have against anyone who may be liable to **you;**
   c. Attend depositions, hearings and trials; and
   d. Secure and give evidence, and obtain the attendance of witnesses.
2. **You** shall not admit any liability, assume any financial obligation, or pay out any money without **our** prior consent. If **you** do, it shall be at **your** own expense.

C. LAWSUITS AGAINST US

1. No one can sue **us** to recover under this Policy unless all of the terms have been honored.
2. A person or organization may sue **us** to recover up to the Limits of Liability under this Policy only after **your** liability has been decided by:
   a. Trial, after which a final judgement has been entered; or
   b. Written settlement agreement signed by **you, us,** and the party making the **claim.**

D. BANKRUPTCY

You, or **your** estate's, bankruptcy or insolvency does not relieve **us** of **our** obligations under this Policy.

E. INSPECTIONS AND SURVEYS

We have the right but are not obligated to:

1. Make inspections and surveys at any time;

2. Give the first Named Insured reports on the conditions **we** find; and

3. Recommend changes.

   Any inspections, surveys, reports or recommendations relate only to insurability and the premiums to be charged. **We** do not make safety inspections. **We** do not undertake to perform the duty of any person or organization to provide for the health or safety of workers or the public. In addition, **we** do not warrant that conditions:

1. Are safe or healthful; or

2. Comply with laws, regulations, codes or standards.

   This condition applies not only to **us,** but also to any rating, advisory, rate service or similar organization, which makes insurance inspections, surveys, reports or recommendations on **our** behalf.

F. PREMIUMS

The first Named Insured shown in the Declarations:

1. Is responsible for the payment of all premiums; and

2. Shall be the payee for any return premiums **we** pay.

G. TRANSFER OF YOUR RIGHTS AND DUTIES UNDER THIS POLICY

Your rights and duties under this Policy may not be transferred without **our** written consent except in the case of death of an individual **insured.**

If **you** die, or are declared legally bankrupt **your** rights and duties shall be transferred to **your** legal representative, but only while acting within the scope of duties as **your** legal representative. Until **your** legal representative is appointed, anyone having proper temporary custody of **your** property shall have **your** rights and duties but only with respect to that property.

H. CHANGES

The first Named Insured in the Declarations is authorized to request changes in this Policy. This Policy can only be changed by a written endorsement **we** issue and make part of this Policy.

I. CONFORMANCE TO STATUTE

To the extent terms of this Policy conflict with a statute of the State within which this Policy is issued, the term shall be deemed amended to conform to minimum requirements of the statute.

J. DUTIES IN THE EVENT OF WRONGFUL ACT, CLAIM OR SUIT

1. **You** must see to it that **we** are notified as soon as practicable of a **wrongful act** that may result in a **claim.** To the extent possible, notice should include:

   a. How, when, and where the **wrongful act** took place;

   b. The names and addresses of any injured persons and witnesses; and

   c. The nature and location of any injury or damage arising out of the **wrongful act.**

2. If a **claim** is made against any **insured,** the first Named Insured must:

   a. Immediately record the specifics of the **claim** and the date received;

   b. Notify **us** as soon as practicable; and

   c. The first Named Insured must see to it that **we** received written notice of the **claim** as soon as practicable.

3. The first Named Insured and any other involved **insured** must:

   a. Immediately send **us** copies of any demands, notices, summonses or legal papers received in connection with the **claim;**

   b. Authorize **us** to obtain records and other information;

c. Cooperate with **us** in the investigation or settlement of the **claim;** and

d. Assist **us,** upon **our** request, in the enforcement of any right against any person or organization that may be liable to **you** because of injury or damage to which this insurance may also apply.

4. **You** will not, except at **your** own cost, voluntarily make a payment, assume any obligation, or incur any expense, other than for first aid, without **our** consent.

K. OTHER INSURANCE

We shall be excess over any other insurance including, but not limited to, any self-insurance. If there is other insurance that applies to the **loss** resulting from a **wrongful act,** the other insurance shall pay first. This Policy applies to the amount of **loss** that is more than:

1. The Limits of Liability of the other insurance; and

2. The total of all deductibles and self-insured amounts under all such other insurance.

   We shall not pay more than **our** applicable Limits of Liability.

L. OTHER MEMBER COMPANIES OF THE AMERICAN INTERNATIONAL GROUP, INC. POLICIES

1. **We** or other member companies of American International Group, Inc., may issue two or more insurance policies. These policies may provide coverage for:

   a. **claims** arising from the same, continuous, repeated or related **wrongful act;** and

   b. Persons or organizations covered in those policies that are jointly and severally liable.

2. In such a case, **we** shall not be liable under this Policy for an amount greater than the proportion of the **loss** that this Policy's applicable Limit of Liability bears to the total applicable limits of insurance under all such policies.

3. In addition, the total amount payable under all such policies is the highest, single applicable Limit of Liability among all such policies.

M. REPRESENTATIONS

1. By accepting this Policy, the first Named Insured agrees that the statements made in the Application and Declarations are true;

2. The first Named Insured agrees that this Policy is issued in reliance upon the truth of those representations; and

3. All relevant provisions may be void by **us** in any case of fraud, intentional concealment, or misrepresentation of material fact by the first Named Insured.

N. TRANSFER OF RIGHTS OF RECOVERY AGAINST OTHERS TO US

In the event of any payment under this Policy, **we** shall be subrogated to the extent of such payment of **your** rights of recovery therefor, and **you** shall execute all papers required and shall do everything that may be necessary to secure such rights, including the execution of such documents necessary to enable **us** effectively to bring suit in **your** name. **You** shall do nothing after a **loss** to prejudice such rights.

O. ARBITRATION

1. Any controversy arising out of or relating to this Policy or its breach shall be settled by arbitration in accordance with the rules of the American Arbitration Association. The arbitration panel shall consist of three (3) arbitrators. The first Named Insured shall choose one of the arbitrators and **we** shall choose one arbitrator. Those two arbitrators shall then choose a third arbitrator. Unless the parties otherwise agree, the arbi-

tration shall be held in the first Named Insured's state of domicile.

2. Unless the parties otherwise agree, within thirty (30) days of the parties submitting their case and related documentation, the arbitration panel shall issue a written decision resolving the controversy and stating the facts reviewed, conclusions reached, and the reasons for reaching those conclusions. The arbitration panel may make an award of compensatory damages, but shall not award punitive or exemplary damages. The findings of the arbitration panel, however, shall be finding.

3. The first Named Insured shall bear the expense of the arbitrator which it chooses. **We** shall bear the expense of the arbitrator chosen by **us.** The first Named Insured and **we** shall share equally the expense of the other arbitrator. The arbitration panel shall allocate any remaining costs of the arbitration proceeding.

P. TITLES OF PARAGRAPHS

Titles of paragraphs are inserted solely for convenience of reference and shall not be deemed to limit, expand or otherwise affect the provisions to which they relate.

Q. WHEN WE DO NOT RENEW

If **we** decide not to renew this Policy, **we** shall mail or deliver to the first Named Insured shown in the Declarations written notice of the nonrenewal not less than thirty (30) days before the expiration date. If this notice is mailed, proof of mailing shall be sufficient proof of notice.

R. CANCELLATION/NONRENEWAL

1. The first Named Insured shown in the Declarations may cancel this Policy by mailing or delivering to **us** advanced written notice of cancellation.

2. **We** may cancel this Policy by mailing or delivering to the first Named Insured written notice of cancellation at least:

   a. Ten (10) days before the effective date of cancellation if **we** cancel for non-payment of premium; or

   b. Thirty (30) days before the effective date of cancellation if **we** cancel for any other reason.

3. **We** shall mail or deliver **our** notice to the first Named Insured's last mailing address known to **us.**

4. Notice of cancellation shall state the effective date of cancellation. This **policy period** shall end on that date.

5. If this Policy is canceled, **we** shall send the first Named Insured any premium refund due. If **we** cancel, the refund shall be pro rate. If the first Named Insured cancels, the refund may be less than pro rata. The cancellation shall be effective even if **we** have not made or offered a refund.

6. If notice is mailed, proof of mailing shall be sufficient proof of notice.

7. If the first Named Insured cancels, the first Named Insured shall return the Policy or a properly executed Lost Policy Release by mail or delivery to **us** or **our** authorized representative within seven (7) days of the effective date of cancellation.

IN WITNESS WHEREOF, we have caused this Policy to be signed by our President and Secretary and countersigned where required by law on the Declarations page by our duly authorized representative.

_____   _____

Secretary   President

Index